James D. Ladd served with the Royal Marines during the Second World War, and has since made the history of amphibious warfare his speciality. He is the author of several books on the subject, including *Royal Marines 1919–1980: An Authorized History, Assault from the Sea* and *Commandos and Rangers of World War II.*

SBS

The Invisible Raiders

The History of the Special Boat Squadron
from World War Two to the Present

James D. Ladd

With a Foreword by
Lieutenant-Colonel P. G. Davis
DSC, RM

Fontana/Collins

First published by Arms and Armour Press,
Lionel Leventhal Ltd 1983
First issued in Fontana Paperbacks 1984

Set in 10 on 11pt Linotron Baskerville
Made and printed in Great Britain by
William Collins Sons & Co. Ltd, Glasgow

Grateful acknowledgment for permission to reproduce photographs
is made to the Imperial War Museum (1, 2 and 5), the Royal Marines
Museum (3, 4, 7, 8, 9, 10, 12, 14 and 15) and the US Navy (7).
Photographs 6, 11, 13 and 16 are Crown copyright.

Contents

Appendices

List of Maps and Drawings

Foreword

I was honoured when James Ladd asked me to write the foreword to his book – because the forewords of books that I have read have been written by known authorities or by officers of high rank.

I was fortunate to serve with Special Units in the Adriatic in 1944, and from then until I left the Royal Marines in December 1971 my name was associated, and I was involved, with most aspects of SBS work. It is a fact that each of the Second World War Special Units was formed around the personality of its own 'founding father', whether the unit specialized in beach reconnaissance, swimming, parachuting, raiding or underwater work. These founding fathers are the legendary names, and their units are part of the story that James Ladd now tells.

The transition from wartime to peacetime service was difficult because we had lost the original personalities and had to mould the expertise of many varieties of men and units into one branch of one Corps. The Royal Marines of the Special Boat Squadron today are justly proud of their forebears of the Royal Navy, Army and Royal Marines, whose epic stories are unfolded in this book.

In the 'post-Falkland' era, all thinking men and women understand that to prevent techniques, experience and lives being lost in the future we cannot expect to be told *all* the stories and *all* the methods of operation of the Special Boat Sections of today.

We are all grateful for the work, training, hardship and valour exercised by the men of the Special Boat Sections from the early 1940s to the present day. Our gratitude extends to their wives, mothers and families who have had to put up with much separation, both in the peacetime training and during operations on active service. This must be the continuing burden of the families of the anonymous professionals of the 1980s as it was to the dashing heroes of the 1940s.

Lieutenant-Colonel Peter G. Davis, DSC, Royal Marines,
Bournemouth, April 1983

ORIGINS OF THE SPECIAL BOAT SQUADRON
A SIMPLIFIED OUTLINE

Swimmer-canoeists included surface swimmers, paddlers and shallow-water divers in the Second World War. All could carry out two or more of these roles, and on occasions served with units other than their parent units for particular operations; SBS swimmers, for example, accompanied COPPs on certain operations. Since 1946, all swimmer-canoeists have been Royal Marines, and since the early 1950s all of them have been both parachutists and divers. Many individual swimmer-canoeists have, and do, carry out part of their SC recce and other roles in general commando operations while serving outside the Squadron itself.

	ARMY COMMANDO	ROYAL NAVY	ROYAL MARINES	OTHER
1940	Commando Special Boat Sections			
1941	'Z' Group (Mediterranean)	Kabrit canoe teams		
	101 Troop			
1942	Jellicoe's SB Sections in SAS / Dis-banded		RMBPD	SSRF
	New SB Sections in UK	COPPs		
1943	Special Boat Squadron	Dis-banded		SRU / Disbanded
1944			Detachment '385'	
1945	Disbanded / Disbanded			Disbanded
1946		Disbanded but one party joins RMBPD	Becomes SCOBBS	
1947			Small Raids Wing	
1957			Special Boat Coy of SB Sections	
1975			Renamed Special Boat Squadron of SB Sections	

© Arms and Armour Press, 1988.

Preface

The history of the Special Boat Squadron and its predecessors has long been a closed book. Indeed, there are still passages on which doors cannot be opened without putting men's lives at risk. Other aspects of the history are politically delicate and for reasons of state security cannot be revealed in their full detail. Nevertheless, within these parameters the story unfolds to reveal high drama and raw courage, not only in action but also in developing those tricky techniques that enabled the unseen swimmer-canoeist to steal ashore for a reconnaissance or a raid.

Much of the information on which this story is based has been gathered over the years from various sources, but the opinions expressed in this book (whether attributed or not) are not those of Her Majesty's Government nor in any way official views. The author has a list of the sources which, for reasons of length, have not been included in the appendices. These show details of SBS and related units' organization until recent times, with technical details of some Second World War and other equipment used by the swimmer-canoeists.

In conclusion, this book is a small tribute to the many brave Royal Marine commandos who over the years have served in the Special Boat Squadron, and to their predecessors in the Army commandos. Their courage, in flimsy canoes pitted against powerful enemy forces and the constant dangers of the sea, has made a lasting contribution to our national safety, so that men may be free.

J. D. Ladd, Southsea, 1983

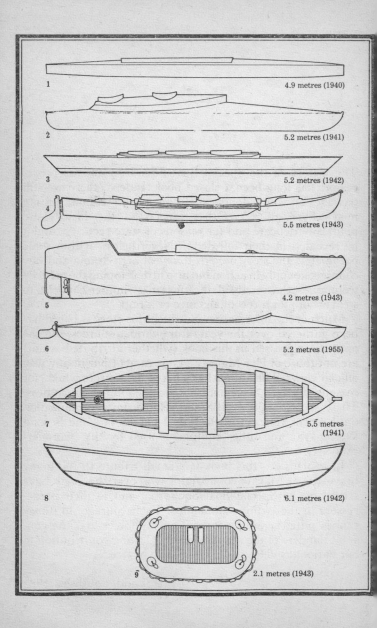

1   4.9 metres (1940)

2   5.2 metres (1941)

3   5.2 metres (1942)

4   5.5 metres (1943)

5   4.2 metres (1943)

6   5.2 metres (1955)

7   5.5 metres (1941)

8   6.1 metres (1942)

9   2.1 metres (1943)

Left: Collapsible canoes, from the Mark I Folbot of 1940 (1) through the sturdier Mark I** (2), and the differently designed Mark II** (3) to the Klepper canoe (6) of the 1950s to the present day, were and are the work-horses of the SBS. Other designs, including the powered Mark VI (4), were built in the Second World War. These have been superseded by helicopters for infiltrating swimmer-canoeists over long distances. The Motor Submersible Canoe ('Sleeping Beauty', 5) was used to place limpet-mines while submerged alongside a target ship. The pilot brought his submerged MSC near the surface and then pushed the joystick backward/forward to porpoise through the surface to gain a half-second glimpse of his target during his approach to it, and as necessary during the hour his breathing set allowed him to stay submerged. (6) Klepper canoe. Dories like the 18-foot craft (7) were used to land on rocky coasts and the 20-foot Surf Boat (8) could land through large waves breaking on a beach. Inflatables from the simple 1943 Y-type with two CO_2 gas bottles (9) to the outboard-powered Gemini of today are general purpose craft used by all three services. The SBS use them in particular to land four men or more where weather and other conditions are unsuitable for canoes.

Acknowledgments

I am most grateful to Lieutenant-Colonel P. G. Davis, DSC, RM, for his foreword to this book. I would also like to thank the retired members of the Special Boat Squadron and its predecessors for their help in the writing of this book. Their suggestions and improvements have been gratefully received, but any errors remain entirely my own. Even in retirement, many of these ex-servicemen prefer to remain anonymous; therefore, none has been named.

My thanks go also to Major A. J. Hawley, RM, and Mr F. W. ('Taff') Evans, BEM, who kindly read the typescript; to Mr T. Charman for his help with the research; and to Mrs Tina Baines for preparing the typescript.

In addition, I am indebted to the authors of earlier histories of the SBS and the SAS, in particular to John Lodwick, whose narrative of the SBS in the Mediterranean (*The Filibusters*, published by Methuen & Co. Ltd, London, 1947) contains a wealth of studies on these operations; to A. Cecil Hampshire, whose books (including *The Secret Navies*, published by William Kimber & Co. Ltd, London, 1978) provide detailed information on various SB-type units; and to the many contributors to *Globe and Laurel* over the years, whose first-hand observations on SBS activities have provided lines of enquiry for other research.

PART ONE

The Legendary Heroes

1 The Concept
The Mediterranean, 1941–2

With a convulsive thrash of its horny, scaled tail and the snapping of fanged jaws, a crocodile suddenly sent waves of muddy water across the placid surface of the Nile. The 'crack' of Roger Courtney's hunting rifle had barely echoed away across the waters before he was paddling towards his dead quarry with deft strokes which belied his size in a small canoe. Yet this big-game hunter from East Africa was as steady in the flimsy craft as most other men standing on two feet. He had once paddled his canoe from Lake Victoria down the Nile into Egypt and, like the duck hunters in their small punts, he could fire his hunting rifle over the canoe bow without being capsized in the dangerous waters of the Nile. He came to England at the outbreak of the Second World War and by 1940 was serving in Scotland. A big man in every sense of the word, with a bellow of a laugh, he could 'drink any two men under a mess table'. He was also a gifted persuader of men, but his proposals for the use of canoes, flimsy canvas-covered wooden frames of the sporting Folbot type, were considered ridiculously foolhardy even by the adventurous Staff of Combined Operations.

Courtney, undaunted by the seniority of generals, had the guile to establish his point by practical demonstration at a conference of senior officers of Combined Operations, the organization that controlled the commando units at that time. This meeting in an hotel on the banks of the Clyde had been under way for some hours one June evening in 1940, discussing the programme for landing exercises from HMS *Glengyle* lying out in the bay, when Courtney appeared. He carried a dripping canvas gun cover and laid it quietly beside the senior officer. Earlier that evening he and another canoeist had paddled out quietly to *Glengyle*, making no noise as they stole up to her anchor chain. Risking the chance that an alert deck sentry might shoot them before challenging (for that summer all Britain was alive to the threat of fifth columnists, even if these existed more in the propaganda of Dr Goebbels than in the towns and cities of Scotland), Courtney heaved himself up the chain, over the guard rail and went aft to remove the gun cover that was to prove his point more forcefully than any words.

That was the initial venture, but more prosaically, Courtney undertook a second 'raid' as a prearranged exercise, reaching the ship undetected in the dark. He made several chalk marks on the hull to show where he would have placed limpet-mines, before he saw a tempting rope dangling from the deck. He did not realize that this was a trap set by the ship's officers, and as he climbed up it to an open porthole he was caught. Nevertheless, his chalk marks had proved the potential value of canoes in anti-shipping raids.

He was given permission to train Folbot sections, with the idea of attaching one such 30-man section to each Commando. By the end of the summer, ten volunteers were training off Arran in Folbot canoes. This simple collapsible canoe was the forerunner of the principal short-distance delivery craft used by the SBS over the years for with training two men could (and can) often cover the distance at which coastal radar scans picked up their parent ship. But the light-framed Folbot was not robust enough for hauling across a beach when loaded with 70 kg of combat stores, yet it carried a great deal.

The Folbot Company had gone out of business by 1940, but their name lives on, many histories tending to speak of 'Folbots' as an all-embracing name for the canoes of the Second World War. 'Cockle' was the official term. The Folbot, a sports canoe, lacked a number of refinements essential when men are risking their lives with nothing more than the craft's canvas skin between them and a beach's defences. Built-in buoyancy is a quality that today is accepted as part of any small boat; but in 1940 it was featured only in a few high-performance racing dinghies designed by Uffa Fox. Although this feature would not give the canoeist any protection from the enemy, it was a lifesaver if the craft became waterlogged.

The Rhodes Recce

In January 1941, General Wavell was planning to exploit his successes of December 1940 in the Western Desert. The first phase of this new plan was to advance further westward, seizing all the coast of Cyrenaica (modern Libya). The second stage was to seize Rhodes. This island, four times the size of the Isle of Wight, lies 10 km from the Turkish coast. It will appear a number of times in the SBS saga for it lies strategically at the southeast of those Greek islands, the Dodecanese, which run north-south just off the coast of Turkey. In 1941, when Turkey was neutral, the island was held by an Italian garrison and the Axis powers were putting pressure on the Turkish government to remain out of the war. The British meanwhile, if they could secure the Dodecanese, might persuade the Turks to join the Allies.

At the planning stage of the proposed capture of islands like Rhodes, Wavell's staff asked for commandos, and 'Layforce', Lieutenant-Colonel (later General Sir) Robert Laycock's 7, 8 and 11 Commandos, sailed for the Middle East, arriving on 11 March 1941. With them went Roger Courtney and fifteen canoeists. On the planning staff, as senior navigator for the ships being assembled to land the Rhodes force, was Lieutenant-Commander (N) (later Captain) Nigel Clogstoun-Willmott, RN, a tall good-looking man aged thirty. He had seen action off Narvik and well knew the difficulties of inshore navigation, for more than half the British ships lost off Norway had foundered on shoals or rocks. He determined therefore to make a thorough survey of the intended landing points, making first a

periscope recce from a minelaying submarine. She spent
three days off the island, often edging her way inshore at
1½ knots, for, as in many places, the charts showed little
detail of beaches beyond the low-water mark. A submarine's crew nevertheless could learn much of the inshore
currents and something of the ever-changing contours of a
coastal seabed. What neither they nor Clogstoun-Willmott
could tell from periscope studies was whether the copse
near the water's edge hid anti-tank guns, or if the line of a
hedge held beach defence trenches. Was the rough grass
behind the beach firm going? Or marsh? Aerial photographs could be interpreted with uncanny accuracy, if not
in 1941 certainly by 1943, yet they would leave many such
questions unanswered. Even the techniques for measuring
wave heights off a beach, in order to tell the depth of water
scanned in a photograph, had its pitfalls. Clogstoun-Willmott therefore determined to go ashore himself and make
an 'eyeball recce'.

The commander's uncle had landed with the Australians
at Gallipoli, when the battleships whose support fire should
have covered the assault were deterred from entering the
Narrows after HMS *Irresistible* and HMS *Ocean* had been
mined in March 1915. Knowing the problems of the
Gallipoli landings made him even more certain that a beach
recce was essential.

This would require a submarine or possibly an MTB to
put him ashore by dinghy, ploys which posed too many
risks in the view of the planning staff: such vessels were
scarce in 1941 and the risks of loss heightened when man-
oeuvring inshore, where they could easily be spotted by
enemy aircraft or coast guns' crews in daylight, and the
hazards of night navigation might strand them on the very
shoals they had come to chart. Secondly, should the enemy
discover that someone had been ashore, the defenders
would be warned and the beaches that more heavily
guarded, making a main assault landing all the more
difficult.

Clogstoun-Willmott nevertheless persuaded the staff that

a reconnaissance ashore was vital. He was also aware of the grave limitations of the navigators on landing craft: a few were yachtsmen and bank clerks; others were amateur cricketers and lawyers; and most had no greater experience of the exacting science of navigation than could be imparted in a four-week course on coastal pilotage. They would need help to bring their craft into the right landing points on a dark night. So he proposed landing a small beach party to set up shaded marker lights that would pinpoint the exact spots – some few tens of metres wide – where the leading three craft forming the first wave of an assault might safely beach. Forty years later the SBS would be employing the very same tactics at San Carlos Bay in the Falkland Islands.

Permission to make a recce was one thing; executing it was quite another. With single-minded determination the commander began that February a routine of swimming, each morning, 40, then 100, and later even more lengths of an hotel swimming pool in Cairo. And he hardened his muscles – a contradiction for swimmers – by runs and a daily routine of exercises, which made him, despite the languid heat of the Nile delta, one of the fittest naval officers in the Mediterranean Fleet. He also worked out with his usual forethought (a trait he has imparted to canoeists of the 1980s) what he would need for a long swim in relatively cold waters: 'Long John' underwear, and a seaman's jersey heavily coated in periscope grease, as would be the hand-held prismatic compass he had drawn from naval stores. His torch, sheathed in issue contraceptives, was watertight, but the waterproof case for his revolver was to prove less than adequate.

He had been practising secretly with this improvised kit when late in March Colonel Laycock introduced him to Roger Courtney. The army lieutenant, soon to be a captain, had established his Folbot section at Kabrit, that sand-blown stone-frigate (camp) HMS *Saunders*, where Rear-Admiral Maund had established a Combined Operations training base on the shores of the Great Bitter Lake. Laycock, who was in close touch with Maund, introduced

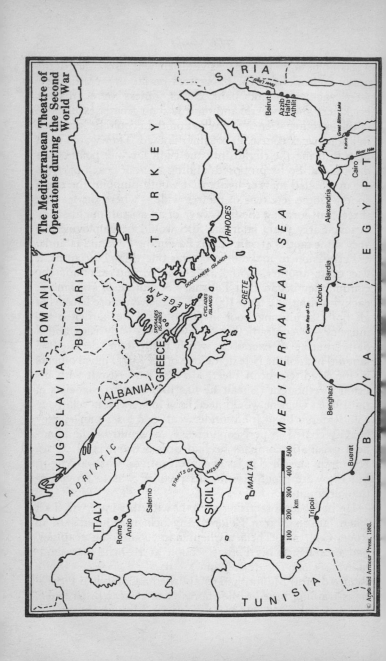

The Mediterranean Theatre of Operations during the Second World War

© Arms and Armour Press, 1983.

Clogstoun-Willmott to Courtney, whose canoes would prove ideal for beach reconnaissance. The two canoeists (or rather, the skilled Folbot canoeist and his keen student) rehearsed for the recce to Rhodes. A carelessly raised arm as the commander swam to a beach brought the sharp splash of a stone from his instructor. At other times, on moonless nights, as they practised passing each other in silence, the crunch of foot on gravel would again bring a stone of retribution, in warning of a more lethal missile if the offender were caught making such a noise on the real raid.

They were ready after a couple of weeks and sailed in the submarine *Triumph* during March to Rhodes. There, at times during the day, she had to dive to 30 m or more to avoid being seen by aircraft flying over the clear waters, as she made periscope recces of the coast. At night she needed several precious hours of moonless dark to recharge her batteries before taking her canoeists inshore. Their Folbot was brought up from below while the submarine trimmed down till her saddle-tanks were just awash. The canoe being steadied on one of the hydroplanes as small waves washed around it, the final checks were made. Already aboard were a Thompson sub-machine gun, a 'gangster' tommy gun, in the jargon of the time, grenades and the infra-red RG signalling equipment with its beam of invisible light. Clogstoun-Willmott had also put aboard a thermos of coffee laced with brandy.

The two canoeists swallowed their benzedrine tablets, and in their heavily greased clothing came up from the fug of the submarine the moment she surfaced, in order that their eyes could become accustomed to the dark, for even the dim and shaded conning tower lights left a man relatively blind in the pitch black. With the canoe now in the water, Courtney jumped – remarkably lightly for his size – into the aft position, for the paddler sat behind the swimmer in a two-man canoe. Clogstoun-Willmott steadied himself on the gently rising casing before jumping cat-like to the canoe, his knees flexing to reduce any shock.

They cast off and began a sweat-raising rhythmic paddle, which in thirty minutes took them 2.5 km on a
compass course to within 100 m of the beach. There
Courtney steadied the craft, keeping her bows on to the
beach – and therefore barely visible. On this first recce
the commander was to be the swimmer. He leant back,
legs outstretched athwart the cockpit before he made a
quick flip with one hand on the floorboards, a single
motion to bring him lying face downwards across the
canoe. This was a trick he had carefully practised, for
despite Courtney's skill in keeping the canoe balanced,
had the swimmer bungled this piece of gymnastics, then
both men would be thrown in the water.

In a second, Clogstoun-Willmott went over the side.
The sharp cold of the water after the sweat of paddling
took his breath away, and he hung on to the stern of the
canoe while he recovered. Then he set out for the beach
with a strong, smooth breaststroke that covered the distance at a steady speed. His feet touched the sandy
bottom opposite a rocky promontory, not the place to
land armoured vehicles, as he could now clearly see in
the star-glow. He moved back, cautious not to stir up too
much phosphorescence that might attract a sentry's
attention. Then he was swimming again, several hundred
metres parallel to the shore before turning back towards
the beach. Dog-paddling, he tested the depth and felt
firm sand under his feet before moving into shallow
water, where he lay with his chin on the pebbles at the
water's edge. He could hear sentries talking and could
just make out their two figures behind a wall. With each
surge of the waves breaking on the beach, he edged
forward, gritting his teeth to stop them chattering with
cold as he lay stock-still, for as he later remarked, 'beach
reconnaissance needs the patience of an animal'. Had the
sentries seen him? He felt that they must be looking
straight at him, but if they did, then they must have
taken his dark shape for some beach rock. Presently, they
moved off.

Now was the opportunity for the commander to slip stealthily ashore to find the road behind the beach, gathering shingle samples as he went; on later recces he would bring a bag for these, but for now he could only stuff them into his jersey. He made another three landings along the beach, noting depths in chinagraph crayon on a piece of slate. He heard a sentry yawn by the command post, and after three hours' swimming and creeping around the beach defences, Clogstoun-Willmott too found that the liveliness induced by his benzedrine tablets was wearing off. It was time to make his rendezvous with Courtney in the canoe. He swam out from the beach before freeing his numbed fingers to flash the letter 'R' on his hooded torch. There was no response. Numbed with a cold fatigue, the commander had his first doubts as to whether he would be recovered. But Courtney suddenly loomed out of the darkness, the canoe surging alongside Clogstoun-Willmott, who was quickly hauled inboard, gulps from the flask of coffee bringing the first faint warmth back into his body. Then they paddled back out through thickening mist on their compass course, which Courtney could follow from the P8 aircraft compass secured to the floorboards between his knees. When they were about the spot where the rendezvous was to be made, they flashed their RG lamp, which sent out an infra-red beam to be picked up by a lookout aboard the submarine who scanned the sea with a camera-like receiver. As the beam from the canoeists fell on the receiver-lens, the lookout saw a green spot through the eyepiece, against a speckle of green pin-prick reflections from the stars' infra-red light.

The first beach recce in the Mediterranean had been successful, and four more recces were made on subsequent nights. The last nearly brought disaster when fierce cramps immobilized Courtney on the tide line. He was the swimmer that night, and only Clogstoun-Willmott's quick thinking and Courtney's determination enabled them to get off the beach as the commander brought the canoe up to the shore. Had they been caught, they might have compromised more than the Rhodes landing, for their RG equipment included a component that was highly secret and one which would indicate the British potential development of a night-sight. (For this reason the War Office had been very reluctant to allow RG equipment to be taken on raids.) Among the intelligence they had gathered on this mission was information regarding a false beach some 13 m off one intended landing point whose immediate area was free of coast batteries. From the shingle, scientists calculated whether beach-roadways of timber slats or metal strips were needed for wheeled vehicles to cross the beach. In the event, however, this information was not used in 1941, for German bombers reached Greece before the summer, making any major use of shipping too hazardous.

1 SBS in the Mediterranean

The commander's navigation skills were put to good use in the service of the Long Range Desert Group (of which more later), while Courtney's Folbot teams trained in demolition work. Now in 1941, the Mediterranean provided scope for the first SBS sabotage raids, the confusion of controls governing raiding from the United Kingdom having prevented all but a few such operations. The reasons for this stemmed in part from the Secret Service's wish to keep commando raids at a level where they would not stir up German coast garrisons and thus would not make the landing of agents any more difficult than was necessary. In Cairo these problems were less acute, and in April, Layforce, now 7, 8 and 11 Commandos joined by 50 and 52 Commandos raised in the Middle East, were to raid Bardia. This port lay 400 km west of Alexandria, beyond the range of British fighter aircraft, and over 300 km behind the Axis lines after their spring advance to Egypt. 7 Commando were embarked in the LSI *Glengyle*, and she with her escorts was off Bardia on the night of 19/20 April. Courtney was to have placed a navigation light beacon on an islet near the port, but the submarine bringing him and his canoe was forced to dive and delayed by British aircraft activity. A further mishap occurred when the canvas skin of his Folbot was slit as the crew tried to launch it. Despite this, the Commando got ashore, although late in landing, and came off before daylight after killing 45 Italians and destroying 25 vehicles.

Courtney's second in command was Lieutenant 'Tug' Wilson, Royal Artillery, a canoe fanatic who, with Marine Hughes, made the first SBS demolition raid. Hughes had joined the Royal Marines in about 1939, and as one of that corps' first swimmer-canoeists became a legend in his own lifetime, all too sadly cut short in a motorcycle accident after the war. On the night of 22 June, he and Lieutenant Wilson brought their canoe up from the bowels of the submarine that had brought them to this point, over 6 km off the west coast of Sicily, and now lay on the surface of a calm sea. It was a moonless night and a slight mist hung over the sea. After twenty minutes of accustoming their eyes to the dark, they climbed into the canoe, which was loaded mainly with explosives and a pick. Landing techniques had improved since Courtney's canoe was damaged off Bardia. The two raiders now sat in their canoe on the submarine's casing as she eased inshore to a position just over a kilometre from the beach, where there was still sufficient water for her to gently flood down further and float off the canoe. Once free of the submarine, they floated gently on the sea, free of that ever-present vibration of the vessel's machinery which you only seem to notice once you have left her.

As they paddled inshore, careful not to make too obvious splashes with their paddles, they could hear voices and dimly make out fishing boats. These would prove in many ways a curse to SBS operations in the Mediterranean, for throughout the Second World War fishermen continued to gather their harvests from the seas, often under the supervision of armed German guards in the boats. 'Tug' Wilson had no specific point for landing – unlike Clogstoun-Willmott in the Rhodes recces – as their target railway ran parallel to the coast for several kilometres. However, a study of the chart for the area had shown a large rock rising some 100 m out of the sea. After checking the course on the compass, Wilson headed for the shadow of this rock. They came in to a narrow shingle beach and hid the canoe among the rocks, where it would not only be safe from prying eyes but also, in the virtually tideless Mediterranean, be unlikely to get damaged by some unexpectedly heavy sea.

Clear of the beach, they could make out telegraph poles halfway up the steep incline of the spur of hills running out to the high rock. These poles, as Wilson knew from the map, led to the point where the railway line entered a tunnel. They moved cautiously towards this entrance, but there were no guards, and only a distant signal light up the line showed that a train might be expected. Laying charges under railway lines was to become something of an exact science, but on this early raid Hughes and Wilson had to improvise. To have used the pick would have been far too noisy, so they scooped out the stone chippings between two sleepers and placed the charges in the gap. The fuse with its raised studs was laid flush beneath the underside of the rail, where it should go off as the engine's wheels pressed the track down a few millimetres. Wilson was putting the finishing touches to this charge, making sure no doubt that the fuse was set to ignite the detonator embedded in the sticks of plastic explosive of the main charge, when Hughes tapped his shoulder. The light down the track had turned to green: a train was due. Easing the safety-pin gingerly from the fuse, Wilson nodded towards the beach. Hughes picked up the unused pick and set off. The cactus bushes on the slope seemed sharper now, for the adrenalin of their initial excitement had worn off. On this first raid they were perhaps more cautious than in later years, and when they heard voices as they neared the beach, the two men hid by the canoe.

Lying in the midge and mosquito torment of a warm Italian night, they could smell the tang of the sea close by and hear the ripple of waves on shingle. In the bay to their left, two boats with their oil lanterns lit bobbed on the gentle swell; the fishermen were still at work. The moon was due to rise in half an hour, two hours after they had landed, and the submarine must not wait inshore in the moonlight. So if the canoeists were to get off that night, they must make a move. They each took one end of the canoe, stooping low near the water's edge to avoid any sentry's eye as they slid the boat into the water.

Although the canoe floated in 10 cm of water, on the steeply shelving shingle banks, Hughes at the bow was waist deep before 'Tug' Wilson could slide aboard. Movement was minimized as each man – still bent low in the boat – used a single blade for the dozen, strong paddle strokes that would take the canoe clear of the headland. The fishing boat lights were now well behind them and they paddled on, pausing only to refit their double paddles when they were 300 m from the shore. They saw the hooded torch (why they did not have RG is not clear) flashed by the submarine as they neared her 800 m out. There had been no sound of the train they had expected, and, as they clambered on to the gun platform of the submarine, they must have wondered if the green light had been an illusion. They had not been aboard very long as the submarine ran silently out towards deep water, when her skipper called Wilson to the conning tower. The whistle of a train could be heard entering the tunnel. A minute later the vivid flash of exploding PE lit the sky.

There would be other raids and beach recces in the Mediterranean, but during the traumas of the May battle for Crete after their defeat in Greece, the Allied Command had all they could cope with in defending Cairo. The only recce made that summer was on 7/8 June by Sub-Lieutenant F. N. Colenut, RNVR, a former Palestine Policeman with knowledge of the Lebanon coast. He swam ashore in the estuary of the River Litani, where frequently there was heavy surf, to find a suitable landing point for LCAs which were to put 11 Commando ashore the following night to outflank the Vichy French defences.

Courtney's men continued training at Kabrit where as 1 SBS in the summer of 1941 he organized closer links with the Royal Navy and his canoe teams were taken aboard the depot ship of the 1st Submarine Flotilla, HMS *Medway*, for Admiral Maund, directing Combined Operations for the General Headquarters in Cairo, appreciated that the potential use of raiders in this theatre was dependent on submarines. There were few boats in the 1st Flotilla, and even including those operating from Gibraltar, the Royal Navy had relatively few submarines to cover the whole length (3600 km) and breadth (750 km) of the Mediterranean from the Ligurian Sea in northern Italy to the coast of Africa. Not surprisingly, therefore, when the Allies were reeling back from the loss of Greece, Crete and much of the Western Desert, submarines were not to be diverted from attacks on Axis convoys to Africa. Nevertheless, one canoe team successfully attacked ships in Benghazi on the North African coast, but were captured as they paddled back to rendezvous with a submarine.

By September 1941 the opportunities for disrupting road and rail communications on the mainland of Italy were again considered, as aircraft bombing had limitations with only a few Middle East squadrons not directly involved in round-the-clock attacks on Axis transport on the roads of North Africa and their ship convoys approaching its coast. SB Section raids could be precise, putting a minimum of explosive – compared with bombs – to the most effective use, as Wilson and Hughes had proved the previous June. They were to repeat the exercise, but this time in a series of raids on the southwest coast of Italy and Sicily.

They embarked with 190 kg of explosive in HMS *Utmost*, their canoe stowed below decks, probably slung over a mess-deck table. By this date the practice of dismantling the wooden frame to stow a canoe into its canvas pack (1.4 m × 30 cm × 30 cm, weighing 22 kg) had long been discontinued. Instead, a canoe was kept permanently assembled with the joints of the rods socketed to make its 5-m length. The points where these fitted into the six or so marine-plywood cross-section timbers were all heavily taped with strong black adhesive strips, thus keeping the frame intact whatever battering it might receive in choppy water. Bulldog clips held a canvas screen around the canoeists to prevent water entering the cockpit, while mae wests or other buoyancy bags were firmly fixed in bow and stern. Everything that might float away in the event of a capsize was also tied by lengths of cod line to the frame, including the tea mugs (used as bailers) hooked under the coaming, and the map case (with attached parallel rule) behind the forward backrest. Many paddlers kept a loose loop of line around one wrist and secured it to their paddle.

Preparations for this operation were also planned in more detail, for, unlike the raid in Sicily the previous June, this time there was a specific target. The first objective of Wilson and Hughes was to block a tunnel on the Italian coast, and on the night of 22/23 September the two men were launched from HMS *Utmost*. The overloaded Folbot reached the shore with over 50 kg of explosive and propaganda leaflets, which required seven trips to transfer from the beach to the tunnel entrance. They laid the main charge under the track – no doubt linking it to secondary charges in the tunnel walls – before scattering the leaflets on the railway banks to leave a clear indication of who had made the raid and thus direct suspicion away from local secret service activities. There were no sentries to disturb the canoeists nor any signs of civilians from the nearby houses. But the raiders had barely begun setting up the fuses to the charge when an Italian patrol could be heard clumping down the track in the tunnel. Wilson and Hughes immediately slipped away into the scrub bushes on the embankment. With luck they might continue their sabotage when the patrol had passed, but as the Italians reached the entrance, one man's torch fell right on to the neatly laid charge strapped to the track. The game was up – but not lost. Wilson quickly jumped down from behind a bush and ordered the patrol to put their hands up, whereupon the Italians fled back to the safety of the tunnel, followed by a burst of fire from the lieutenant's tommy gun. Lights came on in the houses as the inhabitants awoke to the commotion outside, and the Italian soldiers could be heard coming back along the tunnel so, with a final burst from his Thompson, the lieutenant abandoned the raid. He and Hughes got off the beach without further incident and were successfully recovered by *Utmost*.

The next target was further south, a three-span bridge over the River Oliva in northern Sicily. The canoeists got ashore there the following night (23/24 September) to find sentries and workmen, several with lanterns, near the bridge. To the challenge of one, Wilson answered 'Amico', but the man cocked his rifle and Wilson shot him. This brought a hail of fire from a Breda machine gun somewhere to Wilson's left forcing them to make a hurried retreat. They had more luck five weeks later when, coming ashore after a long paddle over shallows from HMS *Truant*, they successfully derailed the engine and some of the fourteen sleeping-cars of a passenger train on the Milan-Brindisi line. This piece of sabotage took the Italians several days to clear up, but most derailments were only temporary setbacks. More important was the effect of these raids in diverting Axis forces from the main battle areas: that Breda's crew in Sicily, for example, meant one less Italian machine gun facing the Eighth Army.

Roger Courtney was embarked that autumn in the submarine *Osiris* bound for Albania, where he was to search for the first SOE agent to land in that inhospitable country, and who seemed to have disappeared without trace. At Scutari, they saw workmen building coast defences, but there would remain many thousands of kilometres of unprotected coast. Others of Courtney's SB Section were helping to land agents and partisans. Sergeant (later Lieutenant) James Sherwood, Royal Army Service Corps, with Corporal Bill Booth landed eight agents in a series of trips from HMS *Thunderbolt*, only to find that the first ones landed had disappeared before they ferried the rest ashore 'on that exasperating island' of Crete.

In November, thinking that they were to attack Rommel's headquarters at Beda Littoria, 200 km from the coast, some 40 commandos were landed on a barren stretch of coast where Captain J. E. Haselden, a British intelligence officer, signalled for the men to come ashore, their inflatables guided by canoeists. These 1 SBS canoeists returned to HMS *Torbay* and *Talisman*, which were due back eight days later on 20 November. The raiders made their attack on 17 November, but found that Beda Littoria was a transport headquarters which it is doubtful if Rommel had even visited. Their commander, Lieutenant-Colonel Geoffrey Keyes, son of Admiral Keyes, was killed and Captain Robin Campbell badly wounded. The commandos returned to the beach ready for their rendezvous with the two submarines. But on the night of the 20th, *Torbay* signalled that it was too rough for the pick-up and she would make another attempt the following night. (Indeed, when the initial attempt was made, Lieutenant Ingles and Corporal Severn had been unable to leap into their inflatable before it was washed clear of *Torbay*'s casing.) On the submarine's return the following night, Lieutenant Tom Langton and Corporal Feeberry were launched in a canoe, but a heavy surf was still running up the beach and this capsized them. Admittedly, the canoe was low in the water before this, for together the canoeists weighed nearly 180 kg. Once they had righted the boat, however, they found a number of mysteries. First, no one was on the beach. Launching the canoe and paddling out beyond the breakers, they saw a light of the expected colour but it was flashing an incorrect code letter. Nearby, they could see the glow of several cigarettes. Wisely, they headed back to the submarine, their canoe needing all its buoyancy bags to prevent it sinking as seas half-filled the cockpit. Langton later learnt from Colonel Robert Laycock that first Arab levies and then Germans had attacked the men on the beach. The colonel and Sergeant Jack Terry managed to escape and completed a remarkable 41-day trek to reach the British lines.

On *Torbay*'s next cruise in mid-December, she launched the formidable team of Wilson and Hughes off Navarino, Greece, where enemy destroyers had been seen during an aerial reconnaissance. Despite paddling 20 km one night, they found no sign of the ships. Five days later, still lurking off the port, *Torbay* made a periscope recce and spotted a destroyer near Navarino pier. After positioning their canoe to within 150 m of their target, the lieutenant went over the side. A mae west kept him afloat as he swam towards the destroyer while Hughes paid out the light line attached to a floating 'buffet' (buoy) on which were several limpet-mines. Each mine had 2 lb of plastic explosive in a metal case that could be held to a ship's side or a bridge pier by six strong magnets, and was capable of blowing a two-metre-diameter hole in the hull of a merchant ship or destroyer. It was fired by a time 'pencil' fuse, its glass ampoule of acid when broken eating through the small retaining plate that held back the spring to fire the detonator of the charge. Depending on the thickness of the retaining plate, pencil fuses gave varying times of delay from fifteen minutes to several days.

Wilson moved with great caution as he pushed the mines before him, careful not to disturb the waters. Hughes, expecting the lieutenant to return in about fifteen minutes, at least, realized that no one without a wet suit or even its 1940s predecessor could survive in the cold. Gently pulling the swimmer's line, he brought Wilson back to the canoe. This was their last raid together, for Wilson returned to England. He was later captured in a canoe while paddling in an Italian harbour, after testing new weapons.

SAS Command

Although the chain of command was not at first formalized, by the winter of 1941, a number of SB canoeist volunteers from Allied forces in the Middle East were being trained at Kabrit along with some canoeist troopers of the Special Air

Service, and several teams from 1 SBS. All these canoeists then came directly or indirectly under Major (later Colonel) David Stirling of the Scots Guards, whose original raids against Axis aerodromes were made by volunteers parachuting behind the enemy lines. As 'L' Detachment, these forerunners of the Special Air Service had made the first intentional parachute drops (as opposed to pilots bailing out) in the Middle East. Among those making these early experiments was Corporal D'Arcy of 8 Commando's SBS who made some of the first drops near Kabrit in the late summer of 1941. Thereafter, SBS canoeists began to consider a parachute as an alternative means to canoes for reaching their target. But parachuting has its snags, as Stirling's men discovered when they were scattered by high winds on an early raid.

By December 1941, Roger Courtney was too ill to continue the rigorous training needed to keep fit for raids. Not that he made a fetish of training (few early SBS hands did), but the cramp he suffered in Rhodes, long hours in the confined cockpit of a Folbot, with legs stretched out and no space to flex the muscles, took their toll. He was nevertheless able to continue advising on policies for the training of SBS canoeists in the United Kingdom. In the Mediterranean, he was succeeded by Captain Mike Kealy, but GHQ Cairo, always suspicious of private armies, virtually passed control of SBS operations to Stirling, as the staff of the Combined Operations Directorate became more involved in training troops for amphibious landings.

David Stirling had gathered around him (if that does not sound too homely) some remarkable men as founders of the SAS. Captain 'Jock' Lewes, an Australian by birth with boundless energy, could march 50 km in a night and survive in the heat of a desert day on one water-bottle. He originated the SAS motto 'Who Dares Wins', but paradoxically he was killed in December 1941 when his jeep convoy was strafed by a Messerschmitt 110. Major Blair ('Paddy') Mayne was an air ace in the sense that he destroyed more aircraft – albeit on the ground – than any Allied airman, destroying

23 of his 130 aircraft on Tamet airfield in the first major success of November 1941. Captain Maclean had been sent to Baghdad in November 1942 to recruit an SAS squadron to be ski-trained for operations in the Armenian passes of the Caucasus should the Germans advance into Persia. This would add an additional squadron to the SAS's 'A', 'B' and 'C' Squadrons with jeeps for overland operations and 'D' Squadron of canoeists. These seaborne raiders were at first under the command of Tommy Langton, and, with George Jellicoe and his SAS canoeists in the squadron, it had absorbed all the commando canoe sections in the eastern Mediterranean.

Several SAS desert raids were accompanied by canoeists. Folbots, if packed in their large carrier bags, might have made the long journeys across the desert, but carried on the roof of a jeep, the assembled canoe proved too fragile. Nevertheless, Captain George Duncan and Corporal Barr on foot passed a sleeping sentry to destroy 23 trucks, 8 fuel dumps and part of a radio station near Buerat, with limpet-mines and other explosives intended for the harbour's shipping. George Duncan, who believed that riding breeches were more suitable attire for raiders than battledress trousers or shorts, spoke passable German but his Italian could be faulted. On a second SAS raid, this time to Benghazi, Captain (later Brigadier) Fitzroy Maclean tried a couple of inflatables for attacks on ships lying off the quay, but both rubber boats were holed; and only the captain's fluent Italian persuaded curious Axis soldiers – before he escaped – that they should keep better guard of the harbour approach roads. Captain Ken Allott, known as 'Tramp' because of his indifference to uniform, took a Folbot on the Benghazi raid and confirmed that fragile canoes could not be taken safely across the great sand seas.

The following May, Allott with Lieutenant Duncan Ritchie (a naval canoeist from teams at Kabrit) made a recce of 240 km (150 miles) of enemy coastline, landing at Cape Ras-el-Tin and paddling this distance apparently in little over a week. The start of the voyage on 22 May was not without some excitement, for the sandy beach of the Cape was to be used that day by large bathing parties of Germans. Their beach games took them in among the scrub and bushes where Allott and Ritchie were hiding, but neither they nor their canoe were found. They had with them the first wireless set used by SBS. Having contacted Cairo after dark, they began to paddle eastwards, but the seas became rough, and their radio with its heavy 'wet' batteries (accumulators) had to be ditched. After this the voyage was uneventful. So too were recces of Syrian beaches made by SBS teams in anticipation of a possible German attack on this French colony, when Axis forces advanced into Russia and their desert victories forced the British back to the El Alamein line.

In June, Mike Kealy took three Sections to Crete. He personally led the raid to Maleme airfield in the northwest of the island, but found it heavily guarded with dog patrols and electrified wire around the perimeter. No SB raid ever succeeded in penetrating these defences; but at Kastelli field, George Duncan and teams from 'M' Section, guided by a British intelligence officer, got through the wire and their charges destroyed targets that included four bomb dumps. The exploding dumps reportedly killed 70 Germans and Italians. 'S' Section found Timbaki field deserted, but 'Dinky' Sutherland put their few days on the island to good use, for he would visit the island again. David Stirling also sent some of his SAS canoeists under Captain the Earl Jellicoe to help with a Free French raid on Heraklion airfield at the same time.

Jellicoe, in his mid-twenties, was a thick-set young man with curly hair who had been studying at Cambridge University when the war started. In the desert he had been one of Stirling's best officers, and would prove a leader of ingenuity as well as dash when he later commanded the Special Boat Squadron. Landing near Heraklion that June, he came ashore from HMS *Triton* in captured German inflatable dinghies, which his team sank offshore once they had been unloaded. They then made their way to a cave above the port, where George Jellicoe's four French commandos and their Greek guide, Lieutenant Costi, lay up for a day. This was truly a raid by Allies. Next evening the senior French officer and the Greek made a recce of Heraklion, counting 66 aircraft, which the raiders thereupon set out to attack. They had made their way with wire-cutters through the outer barbed strands of the perimeter defences when an Italian patrol passed along the inside wire. With the skill of a professional, one Frenchman feigned a drunken snore – which answered the patrol's curiosity over bodies lying among the wire. But when the soldiers returned, there was an obvious gap in the wire where Jellicoe's men had entered the airfield, and the alarm was raised. The raiders seemed bound to be caught on the perimeter road; then, out of the night sky came a perfectly timed, if accidental, diversion – three Stukas landed, followed closely by an RAF Blenheim light bomber 'in their shadow'. As the British aircraft bombed the runway, the airfield erupted in confusion, giving the raiders the brief chance they needed to place their explosives. Ninety minutes later the first of these charges went off while Jellicoe's team were still *inside* the perimeter wire. He boldly led his men out through the main gate by tagging along behind a German patrol in the half light before dawn – a step requiring cool nerves and a good sense of timing. Once clear of the airfield on a road leading out of the area, Jellicoe's men had to melt away into the cover of bushes by the road and give the Germans time to get well clear of the hiding place, before climbing back to their cave.

Unfortunately, although this daring move succeeded, the story had a bitter ending, for the French were betrayed three days later when invited to a Greek's home for a meal. But Jellicoe and Costi escaped, crossing hills and a mountain range to reach their rendezvous 190 km from Heraklion, and were safely picked up.

The raids in June coincided with an unsuccessful attempt to sail convoys to the relief of Malta. A second attempt was to be made in August, and Stirling's special forces were again to attack airfields to help protect the ships. 'M' Section moved forward to Malta as a jumping-off point for Sicily. They and the other two SB Sections had been for further training with the SAS near Kabrit, where they were taught how a small charge on the propeller of an aircraft could be as damaging as a larger charge on its fuselage, a practical point for men who could carry a good number of small charges in a canoe. Their instructor in this and other equally devastating devices was Captain Bill Cumper, Stirling's senior Royal Engineer officer, who as a ranker in the 1930s had served in Egypt and who spoke of Mersa Matruh as 'an 'ole I remembers from 1935'.

There was little time for 'M' Section to make any special rehearsals in Malta, however, before they sailed for the raid against Sicily (11 August 1942). There they got ashore with the bulky thermite bombs fired by PE and were just about to disperse around the parked aircraft when a squad of Italians came up. Unconvinced by Duncan's 'Camerati Tedeschi', nor by his breeches, they became decidedly aggressive when one of the SBS fired at them. All the floodlights of the airfield came on, and in the confusion Eric Newby, the author, nearly shot Duncan, mistaking him for a German as he bellowed in that language at some Italians. A hurried whisper of orders as 'M' Section took cover behind a building ended abruptly as, in plain English, an NCO told Duncan it was 'time we "effed" off'. The parked Junkers 88s had to be left in their many ranks as the raiders made their escape. Their route passed between Italian trenches, set in places a mere 50 m apart behind the beach, and here one sergeant fell into captivity when he stepped on the blanket covering sleeping guards in a trench. About 2245 hours – this was to have been a quick 'in-and-out' raid – six men reached the canoes partially buried by the beach. One was damaged, a second sank and the third was picked up next morning by Italian fishermen. Although waterlogged, the surviving canoe kept four exhausted swimmers afloat through the night. They went into captivity, as did the others.

About this time, 'S' Section went to Beirut for raids on Rhodes, while six canoes were sent under Captain Montgomerie to destroy an Axis ammunition dump at Daba. This was so close to the German front line that once ashore the canoeists found themselves among the tents of a forward airstrip. Nevertheless, Montgomerie reached the dump 2.5 km from the beach and set it alight. Others set charges in a cookhouse, among the tents and on piles of stores before coming safely off the beach. But Lieutenant Mike Alexander stayed behind with Corporal Gurney, who had been wounded, and both were captured.

Tommy Langton's 'L' Section had an even more difficult time when they went on an ill-fated raid against Tobruk, with the task of signalling-in MTBs carrying 150 infantry and machine gunners, while 11 Battalion, Royal Marines, landed from two destroyers. The landing craft, built in Palestine, were not up to the job, and there is clear evidence that the Germans had been warned of the landing by a double agent. The result was that the landing forces were nearly all killed or captured. Langton boarded a beached MTB as dawn was breaking, and was soon joined by other canoeists, but they could not get the boat off. They fired her machine guns at Germans attacking an LRDG patrol on cliffs above, before moving to an abandoned landing craft, which they paddled clear of the carnage. Coming ashore further to the east, they joined up with others and 25 set out in small groups for the Allied lines. Only three survived the six-week march: Langton and Privates Hillman and Watler of the SBS. German patrols, dysentery and starvation took their toll of the others, but Arab villagers helped the three SBS survivors over the last part of their journey.

Meanwhile, Sutherland's Section had been given the job of raiding the two main airfields on Rhodes, Maritza in the north and Calato to the southeast. The raids were to be made on Saturday 12 September, and the teams were given ample time to study their final approach, and a Greek officer and two guides were to land with the British party. This comprised Sutherland, 'Tramp' Allott, the physically strong Sergeant Moss (who normally crewed with Sutherland in the captain's canoe), a corporal and three marines. They were landed from the Greek submarine *Papanikolis*, eight days before the raids were to be made, coming ashore fortunately in a flat calm for they used three Carley liferafts, not the driest of 'craft', and one Folbot. Supplies of their precious canoes were scarce by the autumn of 1942. Each man carried 23 kg of rations, explosives and ammunition, up the steep-sided valleys and over the mountains travelling by night and laying up by day. The guides lost their way – if they had ever known it – the party making only 5 km on the first night and 8 km on each of the next two, when eventually they reached a cave where Sutherland struck north for Maritza and Allott's party moved off towards Calato. The strongman Sergeant Moss went with Allott, and they reached a hill overlooking the aerodrome three days later. Below them in an open valley were runways surrounded by wire, a series of guard posts and German patrols. Nevertheless, Allott, with Sergeant Moss and Corporal McKenzie, infiltrated their way through the defences and planted the delayed-time charges, coming out before these went off. By next morning, they were well clear of the area. They were due to rejoin Sutherland on Wednesday 16 September, but he was having his own problems at that time. 'Dinky' Sutherland, as neatly turned out as ever, had gone north nine days earlier on Monday 7 September, and by Wednesday night was high in the mountains overlooking Maritza airfield. His guide, with local knowledge and apparently related to most of the inhabitants of a village in the valley, was able to provide the SBS teams with not only water – a rare commodity in this part of Rhodes – but also a good deal of intelligence, for his relatives had been employed in the building of many strongpoints, anti-aircraft gun-sites around the airfield and the beach defences where it edged the coast.

For three days the raiders lived comfortably on fruit, cheese and goats' milk, even sleeping at night despite the cold. Sutherland divided them into two teams, he and Marine Duggan being one and the Greek Lieutenant

Calambakidis with Marines Barrow and Harris forming the second. The Greek guide with a second Greek officer who had joined them, all the rations for their escape, a reserve of ammunition and spare clothing, stayed in the rendezvous high in the mountains. At dusk, the parties set out, winding their way down the mountain in driving rain, to what had been a dry river bed near the floor of the valley. The Greek and his two marines moved off towards their targets, all of which the teams had carefully studied in daylight from their mountain OP. The captain and Duggan meanwhile reached their first Savoia-Marchetti bomber to find a sentry sheltering under its wing. The two Britons waited patiently. About midnight the guard went off, no doubt looking for his relief, and Sutherland laid some small charges, probably in the aircraft's propellers. An isolated aircraft did not warrant a thermite charge. Quickly, he placed charges on two other aircraft at this dispersal point before setting off for the main runway. To reach it they crossed some wire and an anti-tank ditch and passed between buildings. Here a sentry challenged them but, before he could fire, Duggan had caught Sutherland's sleeve and drawn him around a building. Moving even more cautiously now, they found the petrol dump they were looking for, placed a charge or two on it and made their escape. The last of their charges they left on the three aircraft they had already attacked, making doubly sure of their destruction.

They had reached the river bed before their four sets of charges went up, followed shortly afterwards by those of the Greek and his marines. The exploding petrol dump caused other explosions, and within a few minutes the glow from fifteen separate fires added to the bright light from searchlights probing the bay beyond the airfield. The Italians, however, soon realized that no one had landed there, so they began searching the mountainside with more than lights. Sutherland and Duggan had safely made their way back to the guide at the rendezvous, but at 0300 hours they heard the chatter of machine-gun fire answered by the 'thud-thud-thud' of a Thompson. The Greek and his marines had been killed or captured.

The guide refused to take any further part and went off to rejoin his relatives, but the Greek officer, Captain Tsoucas and Sutherland made a recce at first light. They saw many burnt-out aircraft, damaged store dumps and signs of repair gangs at work. At that time there was no way of damaging a runway, however, and the first aircraft to land, at 0900 hours, probably brought senior officers to assess the damage. It was time to move off, and the two observers made their way back to the rendezvous to join Duggan. That night all three began to make their way to a hiding place above the little bay where a submarine would recover them on the following Wednesday night, 16 September. En route they lay up during Tuesday below the crest of a hill overlooking cliffs, but that afternoon, when Duggan was keeping watch, he saw 24 Italians with some civilians moving into the valley below. The three fugitives grabbed what kit they could and fled over the crest, across a shallow high valley and up the mountainside. They reached a sloping ledge, but had no time to conceal themselves before more search parties appeared. The raiders could only crouch low and 'freeze' motionless on the ledge.

Some Italians passed below them, one party only three or four metres away, before the searchers disappeared. After a couple of hours, Sutherland saw a motor boat come down the coast and disappear into a bay beyond the cliffs. It came back towing the Carley floats. That night, he and Duggan crept down to the cave near where the rafts had been hidden, finding two mae wests and a hooded torch. But their way back to the ledge, where Captain Tsoucas kept watch, was cut off by another patrol, 50 men obviously preparing to intercept anyone approaching the beach. By now, if not earlier, it was clear that someone had talked. Later, Sutherland was to learn that one of the guides had been tortured for information.

They had little option now but to lie cramped in a hide among the rocks, as they saw more search parties along the cliffs. The sun grew hotter, and the fugitives' thirst became almost unbearable by midday. About this time there was much to-ing and fro-ing, shouts and commands echoing from near one of the caves. The searchers had found Allott and his party. Perhaps the Italians thought that they had caught all the surviving raiders. . . . Sutherland did not know. But no doubt the searchers would be back in the hope of catching anyone landing from the submarine to look for the raiders. At dusk, therefore, he and Duggan went down to the shore. Tsoucas had not joined them and had been captured that day.

At 2130 hours they sent out their first set of signals from the torch. A reply flashed through the submarine's periscope was seen faintly by Duggan, but an hour and a half passed before a clear signal was seen. Where were the Italian soldiers? Had they seen it? The sea was glassy calm, but Sutherland decided they must chance someone seeing any splashes they might make. They waded into the water and began swimming. Not having eaten a proper meal for five days nor had water for two, they were weak, and swam with difficulty, Duggan occasionally forcing his arm as high as his mae west would float him to flash the recognition signal. After an hour, in which they covered some two and a half kilometres, they heard the soft purr of what they thought was the submarine's electric motors, but was probably an Italian MAS (an anti-submarine motor launch). Then the noise faded away. The swimmers thought all was lost, for they did not have any strength left to swim ashore. But five minutes later, the submarine loomed out of the night. They were saved.

2 Independent Units
Raids from the UK, 1940–3

Although the development of beach reconnaissance as understood in the 1980s has its origins in the Mediterranean recces, the reconnaissances for the first commando raid of the Second World War were made over a three-week period before the night of this four-part raid on 23/24 June 1940, when parties came ashore at points along a 30-km stretch of coast around Boulogne. These landing points had been checked by Lieutenant-Commander J. W. F. Milner-Gibson, RN, in five solo landings by dinghy, when he no doubt checked for false beaches with a weighted line and studied the beach gradients. On the night of the raid, his boat developed some trouble with her compass, highlighting the difficulties of pinpoint navigation. (Clogstoun-Willmott was unaware of these recces when he later made his surveys of Rhodes beaches.)

There had only been one other commando raid in 1940, when 100 men of that burgeoning force set out for Guernsey. The reconnaissance for this raid had been made by an officer who was a native of the island, landed at night by dinghy and later brought off the same way. Unfortunately, when the commandos got ashore, the great noise of their crash-boats being cloaked by Anson aircraft flying overhead, they found that the positions of the German troops defending the island had changed since the reconnaissance. Lieutenant-Colonel John Durnford-Slater, Royal Artillery, who led this raid, once described it as 'a pretty amateurish affair'. But, in the early months of 1941, a more professional approach to small-scale commando operations in all theatres was developed, as much from the necessity to bring back intelligence as to minimize the chances of the

raiders' death or captivity. There was no point in gathering
military intelligence unless it could be transmitted to those
planning an operation, which in 1941 meant at least some of
a reconnaissance party returning to an Allied base.

For commando canoeists and others we will meet in
similar roles, experiences under the Middle East Command
and the need for intelligence of activities on the French
Channel coast crystallized in three clear roles: beach reconnaissance, anti-shipping raids and sabotage raids; two
others would come later in the clandestine landing of agents
and the use of canoe raids to deceive an enemy of your true
intentions in making major amphibious landings. Volunteers for these roles would come initially from soldiers and
marines in Commando units through the usual routine
signing of your name to a call for volunteers for hazardous
service, pinned up on the unit notice board. Other volunteers were drawn into small boat units – a term sometimes
confused with SBS – through chance meetings at some
officers' mess bar or through a friend who knew that you
had the talents required for such work. The army majors
and naval commanders who raised these units were men
who believed in the value of one or more SBS-type role and
who had the respect of senior officers like Mountbatten to
give them that support essential to the formation of 'odd-
ball' units – for these are detested by staff officers with
enough on their desks in handling conventional forces without becoming involved in the convoluted work of special
forces. The unit majors and commanders were also the
arbiters of who might join, and had no hard and fast rules in
the early days when attitude and brains were more important than brawn in the selection of canoeists. Indeed, after
the initial flush of enthusiasm for 'muscle' men, all commandos tended to be recruited for their intelligence rather
than their ability to lift weights.

101 Troop

The canoe units within the Commandos had been known as Special Boat Sections since 1940, and the name 'SBS' became almost a generic term for canoeists. Although many units were involved (as well as the Special Boat Sections), they exist in the 1980s as Sections of the Special Boat Squadron, Royal Marines, drawing the threads of their history not only from the SB Sections of the Second World War but from a number of raiding units. Their beach reconnaissance roles come mainly from the Combined Operations Assault Pilotage Parties formed by Clogstoun-Willmott to develop the techniques he had tested on Rhodes. The sabotage roles link back to the work of SB Sections in what was an army SB Squadron commanded by Lord Jellicoe. The anti-shipping raids have a number of origins including, as we will see, the canoe work of RM units; the clandestine role in part stems from Major Gus March-Phillips's Small Scale Raiding Force, working for the Special Operations Executive; and the SBS's habits of aggressive raiding can be traced back to a number of small boat units in the Second World War.

To disentangle the niceties of War Establishments and chains of command for these units is largely a paper exercise, for in the very nature of their commanders was the push for action with a casual approach that puts paper straight *after* an event. For example, the canoists of 6 Commando's Special Boat Troop trained hard in Arran in the summer of 1941 as part of that Commando without any express purpose of forming 101 SB Troop when they were transferred to the command of the naval patrols in the English Channel and moved to Dover where they were introduced to regular work with the Royal Navy at the shore base HMS *Lynx*. Somewhat to the Navy's surprise, there emerged a relationship of confused ranks and titles. One corporal, a regular army reservist, succeeded in persuading the petty officers of *Lynx* that he should use their mess in this camp, although in the normal course of events corporals messed with leading seamen.

Courtney had chosen one of the more difficult waters in which his men had trained. The Island of Arran, with the 900-m Goat Fell falling in an almost sheer drop on its eastern coast, lies in the mouth of the broad Firth of Clyde, where a short, sharp sea can rise unexpectedly in the hour. During February 1941 one team had made the dangerous crossing of the waters of Loch Sunart and open sea to reach the Island of Mull. Their Folbot had none of the usual buoyancy additions (mae west life jackets, air bags or netting filled with table tennis balls, stuffed into the spaces at the bow and stern); they did not even have a spray cover around them over the cockpit. They landed on Mull, nevertheless, to find canoeists were not welcome. An exercise by commandos the previous week had ended in rather spectacular fashion when a supposedly 'mock' explosive charge placed at the end of the pier had proved violent enough to break several shop windows. Such a misappreciation of the power of explosives tells something of the early commandos' rugged, not to say 'gung-ho', approach to the use of their weapons.

The intention was to use these canoeists in anti-shipping raids, an idea which had already been tried in the Mediterranean. They would also be used for beach recces, the first of which took place on the night of 11 November as Operation 'Astrakhan'. The troop had barely been given its title of 101 Troop, the first SB Sections to have a title and badges independent of a Commando, as the Mediterranean canoeists were still part of another Commando formation at this time, albeit working independently. (The independent existence of SBS from major formations can therefore be traced from 101 Troop.)

'Astrakhan' proved to 101 Troop the difficulties of canoe work. Lieutenant Smith and his paddler, Corporal Woodhouse, had capsized in heavy seas when coming inshore near Calais, despite every effort to keep their canoe stern-on to the incoming waves. In the flurry of water, both men lost their paddles and found themselves with a waterlogged canoe, its skin ripped in several places. They had no choice but to sink it, hopefully where it would not be too obvious at low water, and set off inland. The lieutenant wore no badges of rank, while the corporal wore the three chevrons of a sergeant, a confusion of ranks that enabled Smith to survive four years in a prison camp (for this *nom de guerre* cloaked his Jewish origins). There were many others among the raiding parties whose identities and origins were similarly hidden behind completely fictitious records of service in British regiments. The use of badges of higher rank by corporals at least afforded them some possibilities of better treatment than their fellows in prisoner-of-war camps.

The MTB that had waited for Smith and Woodhouse reluctantly quit the rendezvous half an hour before daylight and returned to Dover to report their loss. Just over a fortnight later, two canoes of 101 Troop were again nosing their way into the French coast, this time near the German coast battery at Houlgate, which stood on a clifftop east of the River Dives. (Some 30 months later it would cover the invasion beaches on D-Day, 6 June 1944, by which time a number of aerial bombing and other raids would have been mounted against it.) On 23/24 November 1941, 9 Commando planned to make the first of a number of raids, landing west of the four-gun battery to encircle it. The question, unanswered from the available maps and aerial photographs, was whether the proposed landing point was suitable for LCAs. An MTB therefore launched two Folbots on the night of 22/23 November to recce the beach. Both canoes were safely brought ashore; and although they managed only to get 200 m up the beach and across a low cliff, they could confirm that there were suitable landing points for at least three LCAs to beach abreast, enabling 100 commandos to get ashore.

One canoe rendezvoused with the MTB and the intelligence gathered was passed to Combined Operations Headquarters in London. The second canoe missed the RV, but the two canoeists, undaunted, paddled back across the

Channel to be picked up by a British ship some 8 km from the English coast. The main force landed the next night, coming ashore over 400 m from the intended landing point. Without any lead lights to guide them in, there had been the inevitable difficulty in identifying the correct beach along a stretch of coast that had few visible distinguishing features at night. Raiders at that time worked to a strict time schedule, and on this occasion they were unable to reach the battery. German patrols arrived to attack the rearguard, which only got off the beach with difficulty.

The main Commando units were being reshaped that spring to provide a more manageable force, as the early ideas of independent raids by individual Commando units were clearly not practical. There were insufficient escort ships and planes to protect supply convoys let alone to protect any sizeable raiding force. Only two major landings were made in 1941: in March 500 men of 3 and 4 Commandos went ashore for half a day on the undefended Lofoten Islands off northern Norway; and in August Canadians destroyed mining equipment at Spitzbergen, 950 km north of the Arctic Circle. Both raids required strong naval and air support for the initial part of the voyages. Less powerful escorts sufficed for smaller-scale raids and although the complexities of command still limited these, three were made to the French coast in 1941: parties from 12 Commando raided Gravelines, west of Dunkirk in March and Ambleteuse (Operation 'Chess') in July, with a troop of 1 Commando spending a day ashore that September in the St Vaast-St Aubin area.

Operation 'Chess' was mounted on the night of 27/28 July and is typical of these small raids. The sixteen raiders, led by Second Lieutenant Philip Pinckney (later to join the SBS), crossed the Channel in an LCA accompanied by a second assault craft carrying Bren gunners who would cover the commandos' landing, west of Calais. The commandos were ashore only long enough to collect a few bits of the Germans' defence wiring and some inconsequential pieces of intelligence. The only casualty was a stoker en-

gineer, who was killed by enemy fire as the craft withdrew. Such small raids would become a part of the SBS
tradition, but in the Second World War there were a
number of adventurous units providing men for such
operations: for example, 12 Commando, known as the
Irish and Welsh Commando, and 14 Commando, formed
for raids against German airfields and torpedo stores in
northern Norway, one of the SBS's hunting grounds in
the 1980s. A number of SBS-type raids were carried out
in the Second World War by men in the general Commando raiding parties, a thread of the Squadron's history
that has thicker strands in the post-war actions of Royal
Marine Commandos, who by the 1950s had a number of
swimmer-canoeists, SBS trained, serving on general
duties away from the Squadron, as later chapters make
clear. 101 Troop made a limpet-mine attack on 11/12
April, Captain Gerald Montanaro (Royal Engineers),
who had commanded the Troop since Lieutenant Smith's
capture, and Trooper Freddie Preece putting limpet-
mines on an ore carrier, despite the rough passage they
had to make into Boulogne harbour. The ship with a
cargo of 5500 tonnes of copper had to be beached by
tugs, and unloading her became a salvage operation. In
the next few months, the Admiralty and Combined
Operations Headquarters decided that the idea of SBS
teams being deployed in submarines without specific
raids in view was a waste of resources, and therefore 101
Troop was disbanded. Some of the Sections remained in
the UK; other canoeists went to the Mediterranean, but
there continued to be a wide variety of interest in the SB
Sections, albeit somewhat disjointed. What they needed,
and would later have, was an overall command to
coordinate their various activities. By the end of 1941,
however, planning staffs were only beginning to understand the potential for beach reconnaissance and for deception raids, while SOE were mainly involved in sabotage raids with various forces in central Europe, France
and North Africa.

101 Troop became the nucleus for 2 SBS, formed in Scotland in the early months of 1942. 1 SBS continued in the eastern Mediterranean until the autumn of 1942, but its ranks were depleted after several raids and – as mentioned earlier – some of its canoeists joined the SAS. 2 SBS operated in Europe and the western Mediterranean, where its sub-division, known as 'Z' Group, served before going to the Far East early in 1944. From there, some officers and men went to work with the Australians, the others were joined by 'A', 'B' and 'C' Groups later that year for operations in the southeast Asia theatre.

SSRF and COPPs

Another force was formed by the jaunty Major Gus March-Phillips, who in September 1941 took a trawler out of Freetown, West Africa, to capture an Italian liner in a Portuguese colonial port. His Small Scale Raiding Force was formally created in February 1942, to work mainly for the British Special Operations Executive. But before then, in January 1942, March-Phillips led some dozen or so of his raiders – No. 5 Detachment of the Warsash School of Raiding – in a so-called exercise landing on the French coast at St Laurent. The SSRF also began in 1942 landing agents for their masters in the Special Operations Executive, but canoes proved unsuitable for this work: two German agents, landed in Scotland on a fine summer's day, were captured because 'they arrived at a wayside station, wet to above the knees' stirring the station master's curiosity! Dories were preferable for this work, and the 5.4-m CN1 dory with its moulded plywood frame had been developed in the summer of 1941 by Gus March-Phillips and the yacht builders Camper & Nicholsons of Hampshire. In full production by 1942, it was a craft capable of carrying a six-man raiding team. The tommy gunner and a man with a silenced Sten sub-machine gun sat in the bows; the signaller and any passengers were amidships; behind them sat a rifleman and, in later years, a man with a specially waterproofed mine-detector for checking shallow water. Aft was the engineer, coaxing the 7-hp Austin or some other type of marine engine from its temperamental ways, while opposite him the raid commander used the engine casing top as a chart table. In the stern the coxswain steered the boat by a tiller, he and the engineer staying with the boat when others landed, which they could often do without getting their feet wet – 'dry shod' in the raiders' jargon – as the finely pointed bow of the dory was driven hard into a beach. There were also larger dories that carried ten raiders as well as a two-man crew.

That spring, Commodore (later Admiral of the Fleet) Lord Louis Mountbatten became Chief of Combined Operations. Like Laycock, who now commanded the Special Service Brigade of Commandos, he understood the value of beach reconnaissance and coordinated small raids. He ordered that there should be one small-scale offensive raid every fortnight while preparations were made to survey the beaches for the invasion of Europe. The SSRF had made eight raids after their training raid as 'No. 5 Detachment' in January 1942, taking their dories inshore from MTBs or using canoes when agents had to be recovered from a lonely beach. On their ninth raid, Operation 'Aquatint', during the night of 12/13 September 1942, they intended to test the defences near the small harbour of Port-en-Bessin (later to be the junction of American and British beaches in the Normandy invasion of 1944). The nine officers and men taking part in the 'Aquatint' raid came ashore in a collapsible canvas Goatley boat at St Honoriné. They had by this time become confident but not careless, as they moved into ambush positions before a small German patrol crunched along the beach. The raiding party then attacked, but the noise of this action alerted a company of Germans from their bunkers behind the beach. The SSRF teams withdrew and managed to launch the canvas boat, but Gus March-Phillips and three others were killed. Sergeant-Major Tom Winter and another three raiders were immediately captured, but Captain Graham Hayes swam along the coast and escaped. He made his way to Spain, but there the police handed him over to the Germans who took him back to Paris and then shot him.

While Hayes was escaping, a raid of sad significance was made against the island of Sark by men of the SSRF, including the Dane Anders Lassen. A cadet in the Danish Merchant Navy, he had joined the British Army in 1940 and, as a lance-corporal, was the only non-commissioned officer in March-Phillips's raid on the Portuguese colonial port. He was commissioned shortly afterwards. Geoffrey Appleyard led the raid against Sark, his team – Lassen and three others – being joined by Philip Pinckney and four men of 12 Commando. They were ashore for five hours on the island. Such raids forced the Germans to maintain a large garrison in the Channel Islands to defend their heavy coast gun batteries from attack. All went well in the first hour ashore on 4 October, and the raiders took several prisoners who, for simplicity, they tied up. But after a while there were problems. To lie low and evade search parties on a small island was difficult enough, but to keep prisoners quiet at the same time (they did not stuff the Germans' mouths with grass, as some reports claim) proved impossible. The Germans at last made contact with the raiders as they tried to reach their hidden boats. One prisoner was killed in the ensuing fire-fight, but the raiders escaped. Hitler, on hearing that the prisoners' hands had been tied with pyjama cord, issued that month an order which, paradoxically, would ensure that no SBS canoeist would willingly surrender, for he was promised 'in uniform or not . . whether in battle or whilst escaping . . . [such raiders] will be destroyed to the last man'. Undoubtedly Appleyard's men had broken the Geneva Convention, but so too had the Germans only a few weeks earlier, when they manacled Canadian prisoners captured after their August raid on Dieppe.

We must backtrack to the beginning of the year to see how the development of SBS-type operations was progressing. The changes were not so much in matters of technique, for the intention was unchanged in its purpose of putting ashore small raiding parties initially undetected for whatever the purpose of the raid might be, including deception raids in most cases. What did change during 1942 and over later years was their equipment: they were to have better canoes, improved surface swimming suits and methods for waterproofing kit. Many of these improvements resulted from work by experimental sections of Combined Operations Headquarters and from meetings of its Canoe Committee. The minutes of one *ad hoc* meeting at this headquarters in February 1942 also make clear that steps were being taken to regularize the work and training of canoeists. There were 30 Folbots in the Commando Brigade, which at that time constituted some ten Commando units, some of which were not formed on the normal establishment, and the SBS (significantly, not detailed in this order of battle). No mention is made of the men training at Kabrit, but presumably 1 SBS's canoes in the Mediterranean are included in the 30.

The meeting outlined a course for training canoeists in three weeks, one of which was to be spent in practice landings from submarines, although the meeting concluded that coastal forces craft would be used for cross-Channel raids rather than submarines. Among those at the meeting were the Brigade Commander, Brigadier J. Haydon, Captain T. A. Hussey, RN, who headed the Headquarters experimental teams, Commander B. W. Taylor, RN, a senior officer in the submarine service, and Major Hasler, RM, who later that year formed the first RM canoe detachment. This meeting and minutes of later meetings of the Canoe Committee provide a scant record of the informal and close cooperation between all commanders of small boat units like the SBS and later COPPs. No mention was made in records of the February meeting of operations in the Mediterranean and Norway.

In the autumn of 1942 the major actions in the western hemisphere switched back to North Africa, where throughout the year SBS canoeists had been improving their skills in raids. They were joined that November by Commander Nigel Clogstoun-Willmott's newly formed COPPs for beach reconnaissance. Clogstoun-Willmott had spent much of the summer in the desert with the Long Range Desert Group, supposedly protecting British road traffic, but in fact raiding the exposed Axis lines of communication. His contribution to SBS techniques was destined to be far greater than the simple beginnings might suggest: just as Roger Courtney was the originator of military canoeing, Nigel Clogstoun-Willmott was the creator of modern beach reconnaissance. In April he had rowed ashore with a signaller in a skiff from the destroyer HMS *Kelvin* to recce a beach on Kupho Nisi, a small island off the southeast coast of Crete. He had found a gap through some reefs and a suitable beach for a company of marines to land, but the signaller's set had been damaged. Nevertheless, the Royal Marines had landed from the ship's boats, attacked the Italian defences and came off with radio codebooks. Clogstoun-Willmott was recalled to England soon afterwards, where plans were afoot to land an American army that November in North Africa, their first land force operation in Europe after coming into the war eleven months earlier. The commander did not, however, get formal authority to form his beach recce force until a mere eight weeks before this planned invasion (8 November), codenamed 'Torch'. He was joined by Roger Courtney's brother, Major (later Colonel) Godfrey Courtney, who helped to train the naval navigators and Royal Engineer officers who would land in COPP canoes. In the Mediterranean they would be joined by SB Section canoeists.

After being flown to Gibraltar that October, the COPPists spent two weeks making periscope recces for 'Torch' as the Admiralty refused to let them land. But the profile sketches that they made of the hills behind the target beaches later helped the landing craft coxswains find their landing points. The canoeists, who included some men from 101 Troop, made one close approach to these target beaches a few days before the landing, the naval navigators familiarizing their commando paddlers with the lead-marks, or rather the vague outline of bluffs and dunes by which they might find the landing points. A sudden storm broke, and the most easterly canoe was swept beyond its submarine rendezvous, leaving Lieutenant Geoff Lyne, RN, with his SBS paddler Private Thomas, to be picked up by a French trawler. Lyne, however, managed to slit the canoe buoyancy bags to sink it with the marked chart of his landing points. On the night of the landing, 7/8 November, five teams took their Folbots into the beaches. Dropping a kedge 200 m off the beach, each team set up its signal light and RG beam at about 0015 hours to mark correctly the limits of each landing strip. What mishaps there were in making these landings were not the fault of COPPs. Indeed, after 'Torch' there was a proposal to train 50 teams for this sort of work, but there were never enough navigators nor Royal Engineer specialists available for more than ten such parties, some with ten and others with eleven officers and men.

Norwegian Operations

Meanwhile in Norway the weather is so notoriously fickle that few raids succeeded except during the brief months of summer, for the wild northeasters blowing off the Arctic wastes can freeze salt water at times. Yet within hours softer airs off the warmer Atlantic turn snow to slush and bring a wet coldness that is more dangerous to a raider's survival than dry cold. After several anti-shipping raids in the ice-free Inner Leads during 1941, more ambitious small raids were mounted in 1942 and 1943.

In mid-September 1942 a Free French submarine lay off the Norwegian coast some 200 km south of the Lofoten

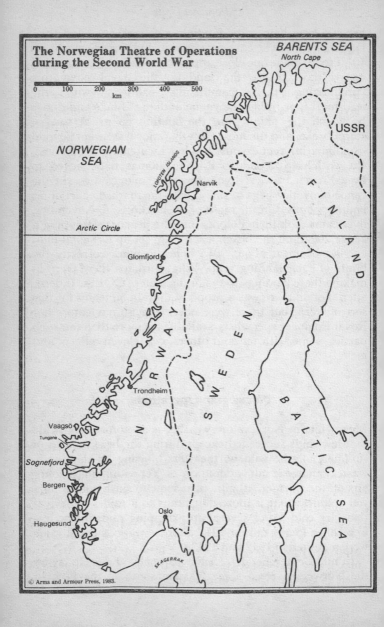

The Norwegian Theatre of Operations during the Second World War

BARENTS SEA
North Cape

0 100 200 300 400 500
km

NORWEGIAN
SEA

USSR

LOFOTEN ISLANDS

Narvik

FINLAND

Arctic Circle

Glomfjord

N O R W A Y

S W E D E N

Trondheim

Vaagsö
Tungane

B A L T I C

Sognefjord

Bergen

Oslo

Haugesund

S E A

SKAGERRAK

© Arms and Armour Press, 1983.

Islands. Aboard were men of 2 Commando and several Free Norwegians who were trained in demolition, for their target was the hydroelectric power station near Glomfjord supplying the largest aluminium plant in Norway. To reach it they must cross a high coastal ridge of mountains to a laying-up base high above a lake near the aluminium plant. Captain J. B. J. Houghton, of the Queen's Own Cameron Highlanders, landed on Friday 18 September with a Norwegian to recce this route, and in four hours they had confirmed that there was a way across the so-called 'black glacier'. The rest of the party, sixteen men led by Captain Gordon D. Black of the South Lancashire Regiment, landed that night. They marched throughout Saturday, and just before dusk could see in the distance the pipelines carrying water to the power station reservoir. From here there was only one way to reach their intended base, by crossing the steep sides of a 'mountain' rising up above the lake. Their Norwegian guide knew of a narrow path along this face, but there were many loose boulders on the route – any rock falls would attract the attention of German sentries. The path was nevertheless successfully negotiated, and on Sunday morning they were in good cover a few kilometres from their target. They spent the day preparing their charges, and an hour before midnight Houghton and a Norwegian moved off to deal with the sentries.

German guards in Norway were more difficult to approach, perhaps, than those in less remote places. During 1942, SOE had mounted a number of raids, usually scattering parachute-troop badges behind them to suggest that the raiders had come from Britain, rather than let German retribution fall upon the Norwegian inhabitants. That Sunday night, however, the sentries were not vigilant enough. Reaching the guardroom, Houghton and his companion rapidly overwhelmed the Germans, shooting one before he was able to raise a general alarm. Then, with the captives at pistol point, the raiders blew up the power-house machinery and cut a sizeable section of the pipeline. The men all reached the covering party and together they began to make their escape. But German search parties and aircraft were out in force by daybreak, one of the raiders was killed in a fire-fight that Monday morning, and by midday they had all been captured, the two officers being taken to Germany where they were later shot.

The effect of their demolition was to cut production at the aluminium plant for several months, apparently. Later, the pattern of such raids against German-controlled factories would be more in the province of SOE than SBS, yet the Glomfjord raid had shown what a few men landing from a submarine could achieve. Other commando raids were to attack German sources of war materials, with fifty men of 10 and 12 Commandos landing from four MTBs on Stord Island in January 1943 to destroy completely its iron-ore workings and equipment, only one raider being killed before they successfully withdrew.

During 1943 the Allies succeeded in convincing Hitler that they would probably land in force in Norway. He therefore had several divisions in readiness to defend the key cities of the south, while some of his best divisions held the Russians from reaching Norway through Finland. SBS and SBS-type raids were, however, mainly directed against the coastal shipping that supplied these troops and carried Swedish iron-ore from Narvik in northern Norway to German ports. These raids in 1943 began with sixteen men of North Force landing from two Norwegian MTBs in Sognefjord on the southwest coast, where they spent eight days. Despite the cold and ice of the winter on this long (190-km) fjord, which runs almost halfway to the Swedish border, the raiders mined a number of coast roads and collected detailed information on the local defences before pulling out on 3 March. No doubt, their obvious presence also lent credence to Hitler's view that a major landing might be made there.

Not all such raids were successful. German guards on the swing-bridge crossing another fjord, for example, prevented six commandos seizing it to allow MTBs into the fjord where ships were sheltering. And in late April came a major disaster for these small raiding forces. Six men of 14 Commando in a Norwegian fishing coble were towed by an MTB to a point some 10 km off southwest Norway in Operation 'Checkmate' and disappeared. They had been training with Sleeping Beauty submersible canoes and the somewhat scary one-man submersible known as a Welman midget craft. 14 Commando's earlier attempts to raid the German torpedo stores near Norway's most northerly point, North Cape, had all failed. Operation 'Carey', for example, mounted against Tungane (Rugsundöy) in these northern waters appears to have been abandoned because of rough weather when a party from 14 Commando planned to land on 11 April. The Canadian Red Indian commandos in these teams, as well as British and Norwegian canoeists, had hoped to make deep-penetration marches; but even forty years later, with all the advantages of sophisticated equipment, SBS operations are notoriously difficult in these remote areas over 600 km north of the Arctic Circle.

On 'Checkmate' the weather in Haugesund proved bad enough although we know that the raiders got ashore. And on a related raid, if not this one, two Welman craft were taken as well as submersible canoes. The Welman was designed to be launched from a special carrier ship that could flood-down like a small floating dock, or it could be put over a ship's side by a derrick. There were even plans to adapt submarines to launch the craft. In 1943 they were towed on occasions, but however they reached the target area their lone pilot would have his hands full. In addition to the joy-stick controlling the boat, he had to keep her trimmed at the level he wanted under the surface.

When the coble going into Haugesund was unable to find a fishing fleet, her raiding crew had problems. Since 1940 there had been a steady decline in the numbers of boats off the Norwegian coast, for as Allied MTBs became increasingly active, the Germans placed heavy restrictions on who might fish where. There was, therefore, much less chance of an agent at sea being slipped aboard for passage to a Norwegian port or for one of North Force's cobles to hide among other boats on a fishing ground. In the event, the raiders were betrayed and were captured with their equipment.

Little is known of the Welman attacks but in all probability at least one of the two craft entered Bergen. The Welman pilot who made his approach to Bergen harbour, over 80 km north of Haugesund, must have been near the surface, for he had to see his target in order to set the instruments that would enable him to steer under the enemy ship. The heavy glass window-ports would have broken the surface with half a metre of hatchway above them – a difficult but not impossible object to see in the wavelets of a sheltered bay. (If the sea was at all rough, then the craft ran the risk of porpoising in and out of the waves, quickly drawing attention to itself.) Having run inshore at a depth of 20 to 25 m, bringing the craft to the surface made sure the pilot's dead reckoning (his calculation of distance covered at 1.7 knots for four hours or more) was correct. He checked the bearing of the landmarks he expected, made mental adjustments for any extra distance the currents had set him, and chose a target. He also pumped out any excess bilge water so the trim of the craft would not be upset later.

His gyroscopic direction indicator, once set on his chosen enemy, maintained the bearing of the target as he dived to approach it. He must not go too deep or he would risk fouling the heavy keel (285 kg of it) on the bottom. Yet he had to pass through or under the boom nets, risk being 'pinged' by shore Asdic operators listening for echoes from underwater craft, and calculate carefully the time needed, at his chosen slow speed, to put him under the enemy. All this time he must be allowing for such currents as there were just before high water. There would be twenty minutes at slack water for him to get under the ship and place the charge from the Welman's bow. Then its 250 kg of explosive would be held to the hull of the target by large magnets – thus it was a limpet-mine on a grand scale.

Having nosed his way by feel to a position where he might be under his quarry, he released compressed air into the bow tank. This forced the great limpet against the enemy hull before he swung the wheel of the rod holding the charge, shifting the trim weight forward by a second wheel to compensate for the loss of weight now the charge was no longer on the bow. Then he withdrew. The time fuse on the great limpet would set it off five hours later. All – it seems a great deal – he now had to do was come out, still submerged, to rendezvous with his parent ship.

No proof of a successful Welman attack has been traced, although limpet-mines were reported on several ships in Bergen. The most likely outcome of these difficult attempts was an accidental surfacing of the craft where sentries could see it. Alternatively, with the craft wedged on the bottom, or water coming in through a broken window, the emergency drill was followed and the heavy keel detached allowing the craft to surface.

SBS men trained on these Welman craft in the waters off Rothesay in the Clyde estuary, although Norwegian pilots made the raids described. In 1944 a number of different special forces operatives would also train in the Welman. Since 23 February 1943, the 12th Submarine Flotilla had been based at Rothesay with a collection of strange submersibles: the Norwegian and Royal Navy's charioteers rode large 'human' torpedoes; the Welman craft proved trickier to control; and the midget X-craft submarines prepared to place their charges under the *Tirpitz*.

Other small raids to southwest Norway were taken over by Timber Force, which began training in the spring and was drawn mainly from Commando units and Norwegians. The Force never made any significant raids, however, although some of its small operations were successful in the early months of 1944.

3 Island Raiding
The Mediterranean, 1942–3

The main historical stream of SBS sabotage raiding comes from the Squadrons in the Mediterranean in 1942–5. These army commando units had been operating since late 1941 as part of the forces under David Stirling's all-embracing Pegasus wings and dagger badge of the SAS. On the night of 22/23 October 1942, canoeists of 2 SBS put ashore General Mark Clark, the second in command of the land forces in 'Torch', for a meeting nearly 100 km east of Algiers. The American general did his share of paddling, finding 'a number of new muscles' after his exertions in a canoe with Godfrey Courtney. The meeting had been arranged by the American Consul, Mr Murphy, who with a number of so-called 'supervisors for the distribution of food in the Vichy colonies' had established clandestine contacts with anti-Vichy resistance movements in Algiers. The villa was visited by inquisitive French police during the day, but they were successfully hoodwinked and the staffs concluded their plans to coordinate anti-Vichy forces with those of the invasion, before the senior staff officers and their canoeists got off that night. The skipper of HM Submarine *Seraph*, Commander J. Jewell, RN, had to bring his boat practically to the surf's edge to make the rendezvous, for in a strong onshore wind General Clark capsized at least once, as did others fighting to get their canoes through the waves. The fruits of the conference were in part a token resistance by some French forces, but, as was predicted, the French navy fought hard. SBS canoeists joined COPP navigators to guide in the assault waves on 8 November, and the landing forces were ashore, albeit with some mishaps but no seriously heavy casualties.

Jellicoe's Squadrons

After the US First Army had established a firm grip on Algeria, they were held in December by Axis forces in Tunisia, while to the east the British Eighth Army was also nearing Tunisia. The Allied advance was delayed for several months, but SAS squadrons probed the Axis positions from the south. David Stirling with 25 men made a long recce patrol some 500 km around the southern edge of the German and Italian defences, with the intention of joining up with First Army. He had a further 200 km to cover when he was betrayed by hostile Arabs, attacked by German armoured cars and captured. He carried in his head much of the future plans for his SAS squadrons, but fortunately some time passed before the Germans realized who they had caught. However, for his adjutant and the few other staff of the Special Air Service Regiment, many questions took time to resolve. Some were small queries, such as which squadron was to have the new jeeps? Others were of greater significance: where and how, for example, were the squadrons to be used when the desert war was won? The tangle was not to be resolved for some months.

The reorganization of SAS squadrons took place in Azzib, north of Haifa, where they became part of the Middle East Raiding Forces based in Palestine. 'A' and 'B' Squadrons from North Africa were formed into the 1st Special Raiding Force (SRF) under the command of 'Paddy' Mayne. These 16 officers and 238 other ranks made a series of parachute and seaborne raids in Sicily and Italy before returning to Britain to form 2 SAS Regiment in the SAS Brigade. 'D' Squadron, commanded by George Jellicoe from March 1943, was renamed the 'Special Boat Squadron'. These 230 men moved from Azzib to south of Haifa on 1 April 1943. There, on the long sandy beaches of Athlit below the old Crusaders' castle, they began training. In addition to these canoeists there was a small staff called (unkindly perhaps) 'base barnacles', for without storekeepers, RAF parachute packers and cooks, no SBS unit can function for long after coming back from one operation and having to prepare for the next.

The Dane, Anders Lassen, and Philip Pinckney, with their considerable experience of SB-type raids from England, now joined the Squadron. Lassen was to serve the rest of his short life most valiantly in the SBS, but Philip Pinckney was only with them a few weeks before transferring to Mayne's SRF. He had an understandable dislike of sensational journalism, having once bundled all the notebooks and cameras of one press party into the sea. The SBS never have – and still do not – like lurid exaggerations of their exploits. In plain words, however, Philip Pinckney's last raid seems inadequately described, for he parachuted into the Brenner Pass with the intention of blowing up a railway tunnel linking Italy and Germany. Caught after escaping from the scene, he was later shot by the Germans.

Lassen had been with the Squadron some six weeks when he went with 'Dinky' Sutherland's 'S' Squadron to Crete. They landed in this Operation 'Albumen' near Cape Kochinoxos on the south coast on Tuesday 22 June 1943 to try again to destroy German aircraft at Kastelli and Heraklion. This summer they were better equipped than in 1942, for they were able to set up a firm base, or at least a defended one, near the coast. On Wednesday, Lassen set off with a patrol, to reach Kastelli over a week later in an approach march on which 'very little of interest took place, but very little ever *does* take place during approach marches: they are merely boring'. John Lodwick, the novelist, wrote this of his days with the Squadron, and might well have added: should the invisible raiders cause any incident on their approach to the target they inevitably find it more heavily guarded than it might have been. By the following Tuesday, Lassen's patrol had covered over 250 km through the mountains and was in a position to make a recce. Below him at the centre of a wide valley lay the airfield. The Cretans had told him that guards permanently ringed the perimeter, and he could see their tents by the edge of the airstrip. This year there would be no chance to infiltrate the wire between wandering patrols.

The next night at 2230 hours, he and Gunner Jones cut their way through the western perimeter, while on the west of the airfield Sergeant Nicholson and Corporal Greaves prepared to cross the wire. Lassen and Jones had gone some 70 m along the perimeter road, pausing every few minutes to listen for any patrols, when they heard singing and found some Italians sitting round a fire. Moving off the road, the raiders were about to skirt round this festivity when Lassen was challenged. Bluffing his way past this and the next sentry, Lassen found that a third was not to be duped. His rifle was levelled at the Dane, who pointed towards the singers, giving him time to come a step nearer the sentry and draw his automatic. Two quick shots at close range into the stomach doubled the guard in an agony of death, but roused his companions to a lively response. The singers, no doubt, and other sentries fired, but Lassen and Jones flung a couple of grenades and moved towards an apparently quiet spot.

This apparent quiet was deceptive, for Lassen had to shoot another sentry who challenged them, bringing a shower of Verey lights summoning help from the guards on the eastern perimeter as Lassen and Jones withdrew. Yet they found time to lay charges on a tracked vehicle before leaving through the wire. Nicholson and Greaves, hearing the small battle to the west, had made their way unseen to place charges on two aircraft; as the firing across the field became more intense, they lay low for ten minutes. They then resumed their destructive way, being fired on, but nevertheless putting charges on a pile of fuel drums and two more Stuka dive-bombers before getting back through the wire despite guards and searchlights.

The patrol did not, however, rendezvous as planned, for Lassen and Jones were betrayed next day by a villager. They then only escaped German patrols by moving each night and hiding by day, not daring to enter any village for food; they had nothing of substance to eat for over three days until they reached 'S' Squadron base. Lieutenant Ronnie Rowe, Scots Guards, had Guardsman D'Arcy (who had made those early parachute experiments some eighteen months earlier) and two other veterans in his patrol. They had had no luck on the deserted Timbaki (modern Timbakion) airfield on the south coast. But Lieutenant Kenneth Lamonby and Lance-Corporal Holmes destroyed 200,000 litres of petrol near Heraklion despite the presence of dog patrols, there being no aircraft on the airfield.

These raids had reduced some of the German air effort that would be directed against the Allied invasion forces landing in Sicily in the early hours of Saturday 10 July 1943. That same morning on Crete, Sutherland had all his Squadron's patrols back at their base, where a number of somewhat undisciplined Cretans had joined them. Axis forces no longer wasted time in combing the mountains for raiders, however, for they knew that the SBS patrols must leave by sea. The Germans therefore had men on the coast that Saturday, and four found 'S' Squadron. Sutherland had spread his men out along a small valley, while Lamonby tried to control the Cretan volunteers: the less fighting there was before the MTB came in the better. Two Germans surrendered to Guardsmen D'Arcy and Conby without any fuss, but a second pair of Germans were attacked somewhat noisily by Cretans, who were only dissuaded with reluctance from pursuing their quarry, while Lamonby stalked them. He shot one but was killed by the other. The Squadron nevertheless got away from the coast in MTB 361 before any major force of Germans arrived. Reaching Cairo a few days later, Sutherland was on his way to hand over his two prisoners when he decided to stop for a drink. The Germans went with him into Groppi's, an elegant café in Cairo, causing no comment. Among all manner of French, Polish and other Allied uniforms, the two Germans passed unnoticed.

The German forces in the Mediterranean that autumn were by no means to be passed without notice. Once they had evacuated Sicily, which they did in reasonable order, bringing 60,000 of their soldiers and 75,000 Italians across the Straits of Messina in mid-August, they established a strong defence line in Italy. Here the Allied landings at Salerno that September coincided with the Italian surrender, but with Allied forces in Britain preparing to invade France having a priority in the allocation of landing craft, not to mention air squadrons and other supporting arms, the campaign in Italy was destined to be a long affair. While the British and Americans were fighting in Italy, their Allies – the Yugoslavs under Tito, the Albanians and the Greeks – were fighting one of the bloodiest series of campaigns in the Second World War. Since they were in many ways closer to guerrilla partisans than regular forces (in their tactics although not in their strategy), the SBS became closely involved in these operations.

Into the Aegean

In May 1943, 10,000 Yugoslavs were killed or captured in the fifth German offensive to be mounted against them since 1941. In Albania, SOE had made contact with some partisans, but these tribesmen were ill-armed and, with their leaders captured, resistance to Axis forces had fallen largely on the Russian-trained Enver Hoxha after his return to Albania late in 1941. In Greece, the British Secret Service (MI6) had contacts, and from October 1942 SOE had been working with ELAS, which was formed from Communist and non-Communist guerrilla bands, although it was the military wing of the Communist EAM organization. But the Greeks carried their civil war into exile with them: only briefly could the British persuade the Communists to work with the liberal-republican EDES.

The uncertainties of such differing political persuasions coupled with the possibilities of Italian garrisons surrendering in Rhodes and other islands off the Turkish and Greek Aegean coast, all lent themselves to interesting possibilities for the SB Squadrons. The fifty men of a reinforced 'S' Squadron were therefore sent to the island of Kastellorizon, some 100 km east of Rhodes and close to Turkish territorial waters. The Turks, however, took no action; later they were to turn a blind eye to SB activities off their coast. Landing on the day after the Italian armistice, Sutherland found that there was little opposition from the 300 Italians in the garrison. This boded well for a capitulation in the key island of Rhodes, where Jellicoe parachuted in that same night, 9 September, with a senior British interpreter and a signals sergeant. The Italians were not expecting them and fired as they floated down, the gusty wind fortunately making them difficult, swinging targets. This saved them from more accurate shots, but all made heavy landings, the sergeant breaking his leg on this, his first jump. With difficulty they established their identity in the small hours of the next morning, before leaving with the good assurances of the Italian admiral in command, as well as useful details which he had provided of Aegean minefields.

Meanwhile, Lieutenant-Colonel (later Brigadier) D. J. T. Turnbull, later to command Raiding Forces, Middle East, had flown to Simi in a captured Italian seaplane. This small island north of Rhodes was one of several the staff planners intended to be occupied by Mayne's SRF, with 240 men of the LRDG, who had taken to seaborne raiding, and SB Squadrons. This would be an interim measure before 8 Indian Division came to garrison these islands. But it was not to work out as planned, for while Jellicoe was returning with 'S' Squadron in a small fleet of armed local fishing boats, caiques, the Italians in Rhodes and many other islands handed over their defences to the Germans. They had little choice, probably, for on Rhodes, Jellicoe had been unable to guarantee that any major Allied forces would arrive for some days.

The Aegean and Adriatic Theatre of Operations
during the Second World War

'S' Squadron was welcomed by the islanders of Kos, when Jellicoe stepped ashore in the colourful harbour below the vineyards of Kos town. He stayed only long enough to ensure that the Italians had surrendered before setting off the same Tuesday morning (14 September) for Leros in an Italian MAS motor torpedo-boat, which pitched across short, steep seas as soon as she was clear of the island. The voyage took most of the forenoon, but they landed at the pier by the Governor's castle and George Jellicoe began more talks, this time with Admiral Mascheroa, who was being advised by a Colonel Fanetza. The colonel had already disrupted Jellicoe's plans the previous Friday: en route from Rhodes, Jellicoe had intended to visit Simi, but the colonel had diverted the Italian MAS boat in which he was travelling. However, Jellicoe was given a tour of Kos, when he was able to pick the DZs for his men to drop to the following day, had a sumptuous meal and reported by radio to Turnbull and Cairo, before flying back to Kastellorizon. Then, after five days on the move, he slept for fourteen hours.

Sutherland's men selected, if not fully prepared, defensive positions for the Indian Division companies that were intended to garrison Kos. The Squadron also made similar arrangements on Leros and Samos, a large flat island over 50 km across the sea north of Leros. Reinforcements from the other Squadrons were on their way, however. Major J. M. ('Jock') Lapraik, having brought 'M' Squadron from Palestine via Kos and Leros, turned south in his caiques for Simi, which his little fleet approached on the evening of Friday 17 September. Lapraik had taken over the Squadron from Maclean when the latter was sent to Yugoslavia ten weeks earlier; a lawyer, he had served in Abyssinia and the Western Desert. Now he would need both his diplomacy and nerve to take Simi. He sent Anders Lassen ashore in a canoe to make the first contact – the Dane's language, when 20-mm cannons fired at the approaching caiques behind him, is said to have stunned the Italian gunners into silence. Be that as it may,

'M' Squadron got ashore and Lapraik negotiated the conditions of surrender for the 140-man garrison. His 50 men
then improved the 'somewhat ornate Italian defences'. The
local inhabitants (mainly Greeks, as were those in most of
the Dodecanese) took exception to the continued presence
of the Italians, who still ceremoniously raised their Fascist
flag every day. But the major coped with all such civic
difficulties and organized raids during the following twelve
weeks.

One of the major's protégés was the lanky New
Zealander, Lieutenant Dion ('Stud') Stellin, renowned for
his appeal to the ladies. The lieutenant led two recce patrols
on Rhodes, the first only four days after 'M' Squadron
reached Simi. In both, he found the Germans alert and
active – once, he and his two companions only escaped
capture by the help of a wedding party who hid them under
a load of stinking straw, no doubt from mucking out animal
sheds. They completed their three-week second raid in mid-
October and rejoined the Squadron. Meanwhile Lassen
had been on Khalki, a few kilometres west of Rhodes, where
he so inspired – or terrified – the garrison of twelve policemen, they were later to resist German patrols.

Inevitably, however, the Germans had to recapture the
islands if their presence in the Dodecanese were to be a
constant reminder to the Turks of the risks in joining the
Allied cause. There was a shortage of boats to ferry the
Germans from Rhodes to the outer islands, in part because
the Greek fishermen were working for the British: 'M'
Squadron alone had six caiques. But, by bringing craft
through the northern Aegean, the Germans were able to
land in strength on Kos on Sunday 3 October, after their
parachutists had taken its only airstrip. By 9 October they
had already attempted to land on Simi, but were at first
driven off by 'M' Squadron's Bren gunners. When the
German assault companies later got ashore, Lassen and
Guardsman D'Arcy, among others, captured or killed six of
them. This – and Lassen's automatic – encouraged the
Italians to resist; those who did not were likely to be shot by

the Dane, as were Fascists calling on them to surrender.
Nevertheless, by 0800 hours the Germans held half the
higher parts of Simi town, until a well-organized
counterattack dislodged them about midday, when one of
the SBS caiques also went out to intercept the schooner
from which the landing was being directed. The schooner
was forced to alter course, and then came under fire from
SBS Brens raking her crowded decks. The Germans withdrew, having lost sixteen killed, six captured and leaving
thirty wounded, against which the SBS had one killed and
two wounded. There were, however, more SBS casualties in
air attacks, and 'M' Squadron were ordered to withdraw on
12 October. A week later Lassen returned to find no
Germans on the island: both they and the SBS were destined to return.

'S' Squadron was on Leros at this time with men of the
LRDG and three battalions of British infantry from the
Royal West Kent Regiment and the Buffs. They were
supported by a British light anti-aircraft battery and several
well-organized Italian units. From a kilometre across the
water on Kalimnos, German heavy machine gunners
occasionally fired bursts at the Leros beaches, before a more
serious series of German air attacks in the second week of
November was launched to soften the defences. At dawn on
the 11th, assault craft came in, not noticing an SBS caique
in their wake, bringing back a recce patrol. Successfully
evading the Germans, they rejoined 'Dinky' Sutherland's
men on the island, and were in positions covering a likely
DZ for paratroops when, at midday, 15 Junker 52s dropped
600 men. These were driven into the hills, while the SBS
snatched most of the weapons from the parachuted containers. Next morning, men of the Brandenburg Regiment
a number of them trained canoeists, established a beachhead, but failed to join up with a further 200 parachutists
most of whom were killed or injured in a disastrous drop
high winds scattered some into the sea and others fell to
their deaths when their 'chutes failed to open, probably
because they were damp.

The Stukas continued their bombing, and that afternoon the British headquarters began to negotiate terms after the Brandenburgers had fought their way house-by-house into Porto Lago. Jellicoe withdrew 'S' Squadron that night by sea, lying-up next day on Lipsos to the north, before sailing back to Kastellorizon through neutral Turkish waters. There, dumps of fuel and other supplies were hidden at points near deserted beaches. The Germans had lost 1000 men killed on Leros and the British about 400. Samos was evacuated without a fight meanwhile, as its relatively long flat coastline would not have been easy to defend.

On 26 October 1943, HQ Raiding Forces Middle East was established in Cairo under the command of the square-jawed Lieutenant-Colonel Turnbull. He met Lapraik there in late October, and together they planned the first of the bloodiest series of raids in SBS history. A foretaste of these came that November when 'M' Squadron returned to Simi, after several recces of the island. Its garrison was small: a German major with 18 men and two Italian captains commanding 60 Fascist militia, plus ten 'cooks and bottle washers' and the island's small police force. That at least was the strength before Lapraik's patrols went ashore on about 20 November. The moon was full, yet Bob Bury got his patrol into Kastello, moving quietly over the rubble of streets shattered in earlier bombing. In the outbuildings of the Governor's castle they at first found no one, but for all their caution and slow movement they made sufficient noise to rouse a machine-gun detachment. Bury threw a grenade at them and heard the groans of wounded men. His sergeant hit seven on the nearby pier, at 30 m with a captured Schmeisser; one crawled away, but died in a second burst of fire. Bury shot another man before detonating over 10 kg of explosive, bringing down part of the castle residence. To cover their retreat from this noisy attack, they left another booby-trap charge in the street, where their pursuers accidentally exploded it. Lapraik and three others fired the local boat yard, attacked the power station and killed another eight men, while their covering Bren-gun teams had a fire-fight with the harbour guard. By the time the SBS withdrew, nearly all the small garrison had been killed or wounded, setting a pattern for the raids to follow.

Before these, Jellicoe reorganized the Squadrons, for 'L' and 'S' Squadrons had lost many of their original teams. The regrouped organization absorbed the Sections being trained at Athlit under Major Ian Patterson, a Parachute Regiment officer to whom Jellicoe had promised a free hand when he was recruited on Kos. Like David Stirling, Patterson was a perfectionist – he sent four officers and fifty men back to their units almost as soon as he arrived. As second in command of 11 Parachute Battalion, Patterson had seen action and knew the value of resolute men in small operations, an attribute men of the SB Squadrons would need in considerable measure in the coming months. Their work was not pleasant, to put it mildly; and, some forty years later, some still have grim memories with unnerving nightmares.

The strategic position of the Aegean had for some months been a personal concern of Adolf Hitler. On this, as on his fear of an invasion through Norway, the Allies had played a deceptive series of games. These were to convince Hitler that Germany might well be attacked by Allied advances through Greece and across the plains of Hungary, where Russian armies could link up with American and British forces. To further such deceptions, a bogus diplomatic mission of men from SOE and the American Office of Strategic Services (OSS) went to Hungary, the British Secret Service making sure Hitler knew that they were there. Towards the end of 1943 – in part no doubt because of the activities described earlier – Hitler had sent Rommel to report on German defences in the Balkans.

These defences in the early months of 1944 had an outer ring of eleven garrisoned islands in the Dodecanese, forming a front facing the Allies on the northern seaboard of the Mediterranean arena. They were reinforced early that year by a crack brigade from XXI Mountain Corps, stationed on the Greek mainland, and the less well trained infantry of

999 Division. These units came under the command of General von Klemann whose headquarters was on Rhodes. To transport his forces he also acquired a fleet of L- and S-lighters capable of carrying vehicles to a beach and land them over ramps, plus some Magda barges from the Ems Canal in northwest Germany to carry combat stores. There were shortages, but the loss of Sicily freed a number of Junkers transport seaplanes for use in supplying the German division in Rhodes. Eight hundred men defended the radar station on Karpathos (Scarpanto), the 42-km-long, barren island between Crete and Rhodes, with its satellite small islands Saria to the north and Kasos to the south; on Leros the garrison was raised by 4000 and on Kos by 2000; on the smaller islands of Simi and Tilos, companies each of 150 men were landed; and 200 men were sent to Astipalaia midway between the southern Dodecanese and the Cyclades. On Crete the ruthless General Otto Müller ruled with an iron hand. In the northern islands the Italians were disarmed and the local Greeks given some measure of independence, a ploy to ensure that Greek and Italian would not present a united opposition to von Klemann. For a time, small German garrisons were scattered in the islands, but in the spring of 1944 von Klemann's policy was to garrison single islands in strength for several weeks and then move these companies to other islands.

An island war, and indeed most SBS operations, are dependent on the Royal Navy. They, in the person of the Flag Officer, Levant and Eastern Mediterranean (FOLEM), worked with Colonel Turnbull to provide the craft – in both senses of that word – by which the SBS could raid the German-held islands. His coastal forces under Commander R. E. Courage, RN, included motor launches and MTBs skippered by men with experience of amphibious raiding. There was also a fleet of requisitioned caiques with officers who had been yachtsmen in peacetime, like Lieutenant-Commander Adrian Seligman, a good navigator and raiding enthusiast. Royal Navy submarines were already blockading the port of Athens, Heraklion in

Crete and Porto Lago Bay (Leros). The RAF was also a part of the overall planning, with squadrons of Beaufighters from Cyprus attacking German sea transports.

Air and naval attacks soon took their toll of these German transports, which were no longer in sufficient numbers to evacuate the larger garrisons had the Germans wished to do so. The SBS could help to reduce even further the size of these fleets of small boats in harbours; could attack outlying garrisons which, in turn, exposed German shipping in rescue attempts; and, when the shipping was destroyed, could so unnerve the isolated larger garrisons that they would surrender.

In the first phase, on 20 January 1944, Ian Patterson sailed from Beirut with the schooner *Tewfik*, 180 tonnes, registered in Port Said. Carrying over 2000 kg of explosives, she was escorted by a small flotilla of caiques and MLs, the ships commanded by Adrian Seligman. They reached the Turkish coast and sailed into one of the forty anchorages the Navy had reconnoitred as suitable bases for operations against the Dodecanese. The Turks, whose help for the Allies in the Second World War has sometimes been underestimated, continued to allow the use of their neutral waters despite German aerial photographs of the ships 'breaching her neutrality'. As *Tewfik* dropped her hook, therefore, Seligman made sure his hidden gunners knew what was to be done if the craft were attacked. Meanwhile, a brief recce of the scrub and few trees of the low headland above them confirmed that no one was about. The steeply shelving shoreline here on Kastellorizon enabled the craft to be moored close under the scrub.

Life was varied at this anchorage, and later at Yeti Atala, or elsewhere along the 300 km of Turkish coast running northeastward from this island of Kastellorizon where 'S' Squadron had landed the previous September. Further up the coast, even in the grand bay of Kos, were staging points nearer the SBS's quarry but on the mainland. Here a well-camouflaged caique could lie hidden off a tiny beach, preferably with some offshore island to help screen her. Nearby would be one of the few freshwater streams on this otherwise barren coast, where the men were only allowed to land to answer calls of nature and never to go inland. At *Tewfik*'s first anchorage with Ian Patterson's Squadron was Lassen, stripped naked and soaking in the sun with some impatience, his usual companion canoe-paddler Guardsman O'Reilly, forty-two years old, sipping tea laced with rum. Here too, Marine Hughes, still serving as were a number from the early days, ate his peaches and ham sandwiches (if there were any to be had from an ML's galley) to relieve the diet of octopus the Greek cooks served for the evening meal.

Lassen's impatience was cut short at the end of January 1944, when he and five men sailed in HDML1083 for Khalki, the island west of Rhodes where the previous November he had pressed twelve Italian paramilitary police to resist the Germans. This, reports later confirmed, they did to some good effect, but by January six Italian Fascists formed a local guard, as Lassen discovered on 31 January when his Greek interpreter contacted the mayor. With his usual boldness, Lassen then called on the Italians at the police station, where – since they at first refused him entry – he had the door broken open. His small raiding party found nothing of value in the office and were about to blow the safe when a motor boat was reported entering the harbour.

The patrol quickly prepared to ambush her, for the Germans could be expected to land 'if only in their mania for taking snapshots'. Two of these would-be photographers were killed in the burst of fire from O'Reilly's Bren; the other four surrendered. Lassen, getting too close to the landing point, no doubt, was hit in the foot by a bullet from the Bren, much to O'Reilly's distress. He was indeed a great deal more distressed than Lassen, who had to reassure his guardsman friend with a liberal tot of rum.

The launch provided more rations, including four live pigs, for *Tewfik*, and the prisoners gave a good deal of information. Their interrogator, the Squadron's Intelligence Sergeant named Priestley, was an Afrikaans-speaking South African, although of English origins, whose insistence on the truth was firmly persuasive, albeit without physical violence. Another South African, Captain M. E. Anderson, was meanwhile on Astipalaia (known to his patrol by its Turkish name of Stampalia). With them was the signaller, Stephenson. He had met and befriended a Cretan named Manoli Kankakis, who was now an interpreter serving as a private with the SBS. Both spoke fluent Greek and together they reassured the peasants in a village on the southeast of the island, near the patrol's first hide in a cave. Many worthies then made their way up the hillside next day, the local doctor and a priest among them. They provided much intelligence, and the patrol later sank all the Axis caiques on the island.

Recce teams, usually a corporal and two or three men, had been watching the coasts of several islands, when the team on Tilos learnt early in March that two German P-lighters would be calling at Nisiros on their way to Kos. Nisiros, lying between Tilos and Kos, is a circular extinct volcano rising to over 750 m. The island has two harbours, the pretty little port of Mandracchio in the northwest, and Palo, 10 km away on its east coast. In early March 1944, these were not garrisoned, enabling Patterson to land in comfort and take billets for himself, Stephenson and four other men. Lieutenant R. Harden took two marines of this scratch patrol to Palo in case the lighters landed there. Harden would need help to attack them, however, for they often carried ten to fifteen men and each craft had 20-mm quick-firing AA cannon.

About 0700 hours next morning Harden sent one of the marines to Major Patterson: the lighters were mooring in Palo. The major's first response was to send Stephenson in 'civvies' with a Greek to pay a visit to Palo quayside. But before they could come back with news of the crews, then strolling around the little town, these men re-embarked and the lighters sailed. For a while Patterson thought that he had been thwarted of his quarry, and cursed himself for not having attacked them when many of both crews were ashore. But his fury abated when the lighters were seen moving into the blue waters of Mandracchio, each dropping her kedge astern as she came alongside the quay. They had not been in port very long before Patterson learnt that they intended to take children from the local orphanage, to the great distress of the nuns who ran it. He was therefore able to arrange a little pantomime – but the children would not be in the audience. They were secretly taken up the mountain, while their pathetic luggage was stacked in deception by the porch of their home.

The Germans had arranged to collect the orphans at 1500 hours – they would be by no means the only foundlings the Nazis virtually kidnapped in the Balkans – but the orphanage on Nisiros that afternoon had a remarkably turbulent 'priest' in Ian Patterson, dressed by a friendly Italian in the cloth of the church. The ruse worked, to a point, for Dick Harden and several men were scattered in cover around the drive. Patterson got behind his visitors in the bustle of welcomes, and had shepherded the officer and his twelve armed men indoors to the large dining room before a premature 'Hände hoch!' ('Hands up!') startled them. They fired in too much haste, for the pseudo-priest and Dick Harden, only 10 m away, escaped. A fight at close quarters followed. A foot flung at the crutch of one German left him squealing in pain; a knife thrust at another doubled him in agony. The 'priest's' gun jammed and he was seized by a broad-shouldered NCO who had the advantage, for the vestments of the church are not designed to give any freedom of movement in close combat. But a US Navy observer with the patrol fired his pistol into the German's head, scattering his brains in grey flecked globules over Patterson. Indeed the American, Lieutenant-Commander Ramsaur, was so close to the 'priest' that it was touch and go as to whose brains he would blow out.

Several Germans jumped through the window but only into the arms of SB sentries crouching outside. Then the fight was over. Two Germans were dead, seven lay wounded and, with the other three, were taken prisoner. But there was no time to lose, for the children and their guards would be expected back at the quay. Leaving a medical sergeant and Greeks to guard the captives, Patterson – stripped now of his vestments – ran towards a hill 300 m from the lighters it overlooked in the harbour. In this commanding position he had the Bren with five full magazines ready to fire as Harden and his two marines, Corporal Long and Lance-Corporal Clark, ran on towards the quay. They were 150 m from it when another two Germans could be seen by Patterson entering the orphanage, sent no doubt to see what had delayed their comrades. One came out quickly shouting as he ran down the hill, but his cries were stifled by a burst of Bren fire. Two magazines were then fired at the sunbathers on the lighters' decks, who had not heard the earlier rumpus. They were not to be intimidated by relatively long-range fire and rapidly brought a machine gun into action. One German, spotting the marines nearer to hand, fired at them with his Schmeisser.

Dick Harden and his two marines were forced to take cover, but continued to fire at the boats as opportunity offered, hurling the occasional '36' grenades, while they worked their way under cover along the quay. The Bren's accurate fire, meanwhile, kept the Germans from their 20-mm cannons and any chance of getting ashore. By this time Harden was getting low on ammunition, but he did have some one-pound sticks of plastic explosive from the charges he might have used to sink the lighters had he got aboard. He began to throw a stick at a time. The resulting damage cannot have been great, but was sufficient to force the crews to surrender. Two had been killed and six of the surviving eight wounded. Like the men at the orphanage, they had fought with the courage for which they were famous, as men of an assault engineer battalion.

Allied crews hauled the captured lighters out on their kedges, taking over 40 tonnes of food, more live pigs and plenty of brandy back to *Tewfik*. The patrol went with them, except for Stephenson. He was left with the wounded prisoners, who would be picked up that night by an ML. She duly arrived and was near the Turkish coast at about midnight when her skipper saw two lighters, apparently in distress. Assuming that these must be the captured vessels, he put his boat alongside one – no easy feat in the dark on a blustery night, and all the more chancy when the ship proved to be full of Germans. Stephenson, never slow to react to the unexpected, at once clambered on to one of the lighters followed by two sailors. Firing his tommy gun, he headed aft for the bridge, but the flashes of gunfire brought a third lighter to the rescue of the others in this convoy, which turned out to be escorted by a number of well-armed caiques. The forward 20 mm on the ML was hit by a 50-mm shell from one of the larger of these escorts, killing two of the ML's crew and setting her flare locker afire before she sheared off. The Germans ceased firing for several minutes, giving Stephenson and the two British sailors just enough time to reach the lighter's twin Breda machine guns on the bridge wing. From these they fired burst after burst along the craft's forward deck until, out of ammunition, they jumped over the side and swam over a kilometre to the Turkish shore.

When they arrived riding mules next day at the anchorage, all Patterson's patrol were back at base, having suffered no casualties. The British losses were the two sailors killed on the ML and a number of seamen wounded, but the Germans had lost 47 men, including 26 killed by their own Bredas on the lighter and four killed on Nisiros. Not surprisingly, when 'S' Squadron relieved Patterson's men on *Tewfik*, the island garrisons were watchful. More raids followed in late March to June, but they were considerably curtailed from the end of March, as SOE and OSS did not want the Dodecanese garrisons unduly stirred up: these secret services were putting agents ashore.

The Squadrons therefore were to raid in April against the Cyclades islands. Here in early April 'S' Squadron attacked all the major naval coast-watching stations on the islands, destroying the radios by which they had been sending warning reports of Allied sea and air movements. These raids were all successful, the numbers of the enemy killed or taken prisoner accounting for the garrisons, although usually they fought fiercely despite often having been trapped in their billets off watch at night. The Germans then reinforced the islands with more Mountain troops, but they could not expect to hold the many islands in the Aegean against the invisible raiders from the sea, as 'S' Squadron proved in early May. Fourteen of them got ashore on Paros, Lassen leading them, and on Naxos Captain Clarke's patrol carried out the Squadron's first joint action with Greek partisans, killing or wounding eighteen Germans.

Such mayhem, however, brought the almost inevitable response from Hitler, for he did not have the flexibility to give some ground in order to preserve a stronger force to defend the Fatherland. Four thousand reinforcements joined the Cyclades garrisons at this time; and Lapraik's Squadron had to look for less heavily defended targets, for the purpose of their actions was as much to draw Germans into the side shows as to kill them, leaving fewer to perform in the main ring in the mountains of Italy. Therefore the SBS were to be sent to raid the northern Sporades. But before Allied ships ventured across the Aegean, to 450 km northwest of Rhodes, the last of the Axis navy's destroyers in these waters must be disabled. The Allies had nothing more powerful in these waters, nor at that time did they have ships to spare for escorts, apart from the MTBs of FOLEM's coastal forces. The destroyers were believed to be either in Crete or Leros, for they were known to escort lighters in supply convoys between several major garrisons.

4 Beneath the Atlantic Wall
Raids and Recces on the French Coast, 1942–4

By this date the thread of the modern SBS's reconnaissance history had reached an interesting stage, and we must backtrack again to follow the Allies' interest in intelligence on the occupied French Channel coast in 1943, with a policy of deceiving the Germans about the true invasion intentions by bombing the defences of every likely landing point from Cherbourg to the Belgian border. Equally deceptive were the number of recce raids made by canoeists and men in powered dories, which in theory were better equipped than the earlier skiffs and Goatley boats with only paddles.

Forfar Force

The Germans had begun building a so-called Atlantic Wall in 1942, and by August that year had ports like Dieppe well defended. But along the beaches the building of great concrete gun emplacements with walls 10 m thick and the reinforcing of beach-side houses as machine-gun nests took a long time, except in the Pas de Calais. Here, less than 35 km from Dover, an invasion could well be expected, an idea the Allies encouraged by creating a fantasy American army under General Patton. Only its radios, with their constant stream of messages, were real enough.

In part to conceal the slow progress in raising this 'wall' of defences along the Channel coast, the Germans removed all French civilians from their homes up to 25 km from the shore. This also restricted intelligence work by the French Resistance for de Gaulle's forces and SOE, whose agents

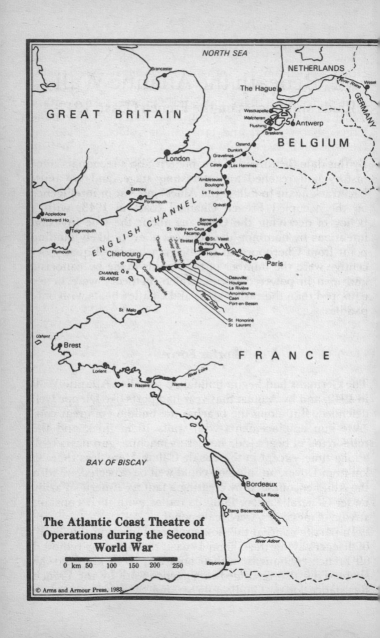

The Atlantic Coast Theatre of Operations during the Second World War

0 km 50   100   150   200   250

© Arms and Armour Press, 1983

could not wander freely among the lines of beach obstacles below the Atlantic Wall. These were becoming formidable. Heavy, angled timbers, with mines and impact-fused shells, spiky hedgehogs of steel girders welded to form six-pointed three-dimensional stars and 2- to 3-m stakes each with a Teller mine atop – all could hole an assault craft or even the larger infantry craft and tank landing ships. To look at these beach obstacles and perhaps take a prisoner or two, Forfar Force was formed under Lieutenant-Colonel Ewart W. Fynn, with men from 12 Commando and the SB Sections in Britain. To look at the new coast batteries, they would need to climb cliffs, an art they practised in Freshwater Bay on the Isle of Wight, where they were based.

Cliff climbing, in the days before helicopters were in general use, had exercised the SBS almost since their early days in Arran. Some dubious and some successful aids were tried out at Freshwater cliffs in that summer of 1942. Rockets, based on the line-throwing rescue device used by the Navy, successfully carried grapnels 100 m up one cliff face, while the climber, Sergeant (later Captain) Joe Barry, showed how pitons should be used. (He was to become well known to many marines after the war, for he taught climbing techniques to Cliff Leaders – now called Mountain Leaders – a qualification that includes skill for those deep penetration recces for which North Force had trained.) Then a balloon was tried – for the cliff climbers 'did not want to waken seagulls', and the noise of the rockets, if not of hammering in pitons, 'wakened the dead'. But the balloon proved even more frightening: one commando with his foot in a stirrup was almost carried into the great blue yonder above the cliff top.

On the French beaches the men of Forfar Force found that the short summer nights distinctly limited any penetration of the enemy-held coastline. Ten of them landed in a dory on 3/4 July not far from Onival, on the outskirts of Dieppe. Their MTB, which had launched the dory from a special davit on her stern, was to return to collect them half an hour at least before daylight if she was not to risk being caught by German air patrols. She and other small MTBs could get within 800 m of the coast without being noticed on German radar, but that January MTB 344, for example, had completed almost six months of work with SSRF and other raiding parties; she therefore needed a major refit. Therefore some of the large C-type MGBs had to be used instead on raids but being slower had to work in pairs for mutual protection off defended enemy coasts. Also, as they could not come close inshore without risk of radar detection, they were normally only used when powered dories were available.

Once they had climbed the cliff at Onival, the raiders found a minefield, and it took them well over an hour to clear a 100-m path to the coast road. There they waited with growing impatience to spring an ambush, but no one appeared and they abseiled down ropes to the beach, getting off in time for their rendezvous. All they could bring back were some clippings of the beach wire. Fynn determined to stay ashore for a longer spell on 'Pipeline', a raid near Eletot, on the craggy coast north of the Seine estuary, where he led his men ashore during the night of 1/2 September. The robust dories could stand the hammer of landing on rocky coasts far better than inflatables or canoes, and they apparently towed in a dinghy with some stores including three days' rations, unloading the boats before hiding them in the rocks under the cliffs. In addition to two radio sets, they brought five homing pigeons, perhaps more reliable message carriers than the battery radios. Certainly a pigeon might get past enemy patrols, who by this date had begun to intercept and locate many French Resistance wireless sets by radio direction-finding vehicles. Maybe they also detected Fynn's transmissions, because two German aircraft flew low over the cliff that Saturday evening. But the raiders were not spotted.

Fynn sent out a number of patrols, the men camouflaged like snipers in combat jackets, with netting hoods laced with scrim in greens and browns over their berets, to match the greasepaint stripes across their faces – a make-up that startled a fisherman, although he accepted their British chocolate as passports. And on the third day he brought them some picture postcards: not ordinary scenic views, but cards marked to show German positions along that coast. Fynn also saw something of the troops manning these, possibly Ukrainians, and noted that 'they were in a depressed state'. Encouraged by such findings on Friday, he wanted to stay until the Sunday – his diary reads a bit like a holiday record. But peregrine falcons nesting in the cliffs caught all the commandos' pigeons on the wing, and the MTB took them off as originally planned, after 70 useful hours ashore. Fynn made sure that the Germans would discover their visit, just to ensure that the Germans knew it had been a British raid and not the local resistance fighters. As they launched their dories, a bangalore torpedo – an explosive tube to cut enemy wire – was exploded on the beach.

The night after Fynn's party landed near Onival, a captain and nine men of Forfar Force parachuted on to a stubble field near St Valéry-en-Caux, 25 km west of Dieppe. Parachuting proved one way of getting over the problems of climbing a cliff. The crews of two Whitley bombers flying at 600 m took the flak and distracted enemy searchlights, while a third flew in low before climbing to some 220 m for the parachutists to jump. They landed at about 2200 hours, but Captain Oliver B. Rooney found that not all the men were with him on the stubble field. Where were the rest? As Rooney bundled away his parachute in the light reflected from the enemy searchlights, he realized that some men had drifted beyond the field. For three hours the small party searched for the missing men until they had found them all, including one who had damaged his shoulder on landing. As so often seemed to happen, the scatter of a parachute drop had delayed the start of an operation: there were now only four hours left before dawn, and they must reach the beach half an hour before then.

The captain led his men towards a cliff top nearby where they found a suitable rock to secure their climbing ropes,

which snaked out down the cliff with little noise. The
strongest climber went down the first rope, checking the
cliff was clear of entanglements at its base, and the injured
man was lowered to him. The rest made a quick recce of the
cliff tops before following him. On coming down the rope
too fast, one man misjudged the distance in the dark and
fell. He was knocked out for several minutes, but recovered
before the captain led them off along the beach. They were
further from their rendezvous than they had expected, and
the crunch of their boots on the shingle made a
frighteningly loud noise. But time was passing and they
must chance a sentry's challenge as they plugged away with
growing weariness along the beach. They had covered
nearly 5 km before they at last found the dory, far nearer to
the lights of St Valéry's small harbour than was comfortable in the growing daylight.

To make a bad situation worse, the engine refused to
start. Stripped to the waist, the dory crew struggled to get
the boat off the beach. Ten men with all their kit could be
carried, just, in a powered dory, but now they would have
to paddle her. Off came their combat jackets, all but the
Bren gun and the ammunition were ditched on the beach,
and with the sky showing the first streaks of dawn they
began a rhythmic if somewhat frantic paddle. There was no
sign of the MTB, no answer to their recognition signals
flashed from the bow. Water slopped into the boat as she
swayed with the paddlers' efforts, the water came up to
their knees and some men had to bail as others paddled.
Then they saw the signal light from the MTB flash 'hurry'.
She was still some way off and had been unable to get to her
usual 800 m from the beach because of shallows – the dory
appears to have drifted out of position before beaching,
forcing the raiders to make their march over shingle and
preventing the MTB making a close approach. The sun was
up by the time they were hauled aboard and on their way to
Newhaven in Sussex. In all, it had not been a very profit-
able expedition: they brought back no prisoners, for the one
searchlight control position they found was deserted, but at

least the night glasses picked up there proved to be of a new
type.

While Forfar Force patrols were making these two raids,
a third party went to Ushant, the island 20 km off the tip of
Brittany which had been raided several times by the SSRF.
By September 1943, however, this coast, which covered the
approaches to the naval port of Brest, was well guarded.
Two Rangers (the American equivalent of British commandos) landed here with the eighteen men of Forfar Force, but
the raiders were unable to identify the German unit
garrisoning the island. The sentry who challenged them
was set on fire, probably by a phosphorus smoke grenade,
and they had to withdraw before the garrison could
surround them. Another attempt to snatch a sentry, this
time from the pier at Calais, also failed. Two SBS canoeists
in a three-man canoe approached the harbour, but were
seen and, in the glare of a searchlight, were forced to paddle
clear of the area. Their orders were to make a capture
provided they were not caught themselves: in the circumstances, therefore, they had no option but to paddle home.
At least they had the satisfaction of seeing RAF fighter-
bombers go out to attack a German convoy the canoeists
had passed in the Channel.

Layforce II

These raids had cast a wide cloud of deception from Ushant
to St Valéry, even if they had not collected much military
intelligence. The Combined Operations planners now decided to reinforce the deceptions, being less concerned to
collect detailed intelligence of defences than to keep the
Germans guessing. Forfar Force and 12 Commando were
disbanded that November, and the job of deception raids
passed to Layforce II. The men of this force, commanded
by General Laycock's brother, Major Peter Laycock, were
drawn largely from French commandos of 10 (Inter-Allied)
Commando, a polyglot unit of Britain's Allies from overseas

that included X Troop (formerly No. 3 Troop) of German-speaking refugees, given British names and military backgrounds. This Troop, under Captain B. Hilton-Jones, was to make a particular contribution to small-scale raiding. The deceptions of Layforce II began almost immediately they were formed, when Combined Operations Headquarters planned 44 such raids: only seven were in fact carried out. These were costly in lives, lives that were sacrificed for sand samples and details of minefields that were never analysed for future planning: by December the Allied commanders had decided that the invasion would be made on the Bay of the Seine beaches.

For these raids the dories carried S-phones, radio-telephones with a range of over 10 km at sea, but which at greater ranges could be used as homing beacons. On the MTB a dial pointer showed whether she was steering to left or right of the dory's homing transmission, but not how far they were apart. A series of raids was carried out over the Christmas holiday of 1943. At Gravelines (west of Dunkirk) the operator on the MTB's S-phone heard the code word 'Maroon', indicating that the dory was in trouble. The MTB moved closer inshore and saw some men swimming. One nearly made it to safety, but was drowned. The others failed to reach the Carley float that the MTB had launched, and swam back ashore. They escaped, but the British crew of the dory were both captured. Another dory landed ten raiders at the foot of the cliffs near St Valéry, but they could find no route to the cliff top and came off. This was a disappointment, for as far as they knew this was a genuine raid for intelligence: indeed, on other occasions some most useful intelligence was gained. At Quineville, on the Cotentin Peninsula, and at Biville (near the planned landing points for American assault craft) raiders found a massive steel obstacle, which they christened 'The Belgian Gate' for it resembled an overlarge farm gate on a 4-m base. Other landings in the Channel Islands cost the lives of two Frenchmen as they hurriedly tried to map a minefield before the sun rose, and a third was killed as a dory was machine gunned when sailing away from this beach.

The last raid Layforce II mounted was the most ambitious. On the night of 24/25 February 1944, six men in a dory were landed on the Dutch coast to reconnoitre a long stretch of beach running north from Scheveningen. They got ashore – the dory crew saw flames and heard shouts – but the six were not heard of again until 1945, when their bodies were found in a shallow grave. Five had died of exposure and the sixth had drowned.

COPPists in the Channel

Nigel Clogstoun-Willmott had meanwhile been working on new ideas for reconnaissance and found that the 16-m-long X-craft could be adapted for his purpose. Much of the control gear by which its four-man crew laid their charges was removed; in its place on a couple of craft extra navigation equipment was added, for the COPPists needed to be able to pinpoint landings. These were becoming more complex in some respects than they had been when COPPs surveyed the Sicily beaches, and a specially equipped Landing Craft, Navigation – a converted LCA with radar and other navigation aids – was being built to help pinpoint beach 'berths' for flotillas of assault craft.

COPPists by May had been putting the final touches to their training at Brancaster, Norfolk. Here Professor J. D. Bernal had found a beach with characteristics that closely resembled those of the Normandy beaches. He had also – as Experimental Scientific Adviser to Combined Operations HQ – learnt of peat workings near the beach at Arromanches, where the Allies planned to tow one of their floating Mulberry Harbours after the D-Day landings. Information about the loads this peat and the nearby clay could carry was most important to obtain, because a steel 'mat' roadway was to be laid for vehicles coming out

S.B.S.–D

of the Mulberry Harbour. COPP 1 and 2 were sent to investigate.

They could not use their X-craft because the Calvados reef runs off the coast at La Rivière where the British 'Gold' beach would meet 'Juno'. Here, 7 km east of Arromanches were known to be peat workings that had been in use since Roman times. Their conditions would give some idea of similar workings elsewhere on the 90 km of coastline where the Allies had chosen to land. All the raids over the Christmas had been made when there was little moonlight, and on New Year's Eve there was no moon. But the weather was rough as two LCNs of COPP 2 were towed across the Channel by MGBs. As the little craft snatched at their tow lines, the crews suffered the first pangs of sea-sickness: Major (later Major-General) L. Scott-Bowden, of the Royal Engineers, had worked with COPP 1 for some time, yet he was sick, as was his sergeant, Bruce Ogden-Smith. Smith had been in the SSRF before joining the SBS, and as he struggled into his heavy swimmer's suit he made sure the wrist bands were taut. His buoyancy, an inflatable stole like some lady's mock fur, he fully inflated – tonight there would be no swimming with just one's head above water. In the seas crashing on the beach, he would need all the buoyancy he could muster, and the suit's kapok lining alone would not carry him high enough in the water.

After two swimmers got into these one-piece suits, with their rope-soled feet, they laced up the lower part of the legs, which had the effect of making these into 'boots'. Over the suit they fixed the tools of their trade, including a wristwatch in its waterproof container and a waterproofed torch with an ultra-violet lens, used to read maps in a case with a cover treated by fluorescent chemicals. (The Germans do not appear to have used goggles that might pick up either ultra-violet or infra-red light, but American coast-watchers did so in about 1943, looking for agents signalling to U-boats.) By the time the little convoy had reached the edge of the German radar scan some 10 km or more offshore, the swimmers were nearly ready. The LCNs

Hood

Brandy flask

Leather pads (elbow)

Gradient reel

Wristwatch in plastic watertight container

Army prismatic compass

Body sounding lead

Leather pads (knee)

Emergency ration and 2 star red signals

Spare underwater writing tablet and lead pencils

Underwater writing tablet holder and card

Waterproof wrist compass

Spare pocket

Weighting leads

The leg is of diver's twill. Rope sole feet are an integral part of the suit.

SURFACE SWIMMER'S SUIT, 1943–4

This surface swim suit was made of rubberized Grenfell fabric with the opening at the neck sealed by metal clips holding folds of the integrated black rubber neckpiece to make a watertight fit. Buoyancy was provided by the suit's kapok lining, and an inflatable rubber stole blew up through a mouthpiece and tube. The suit was worn by SBS, COPP and other swimmers in 1943–4. Line drawing by John Walter.

setting a course for La Rivière bucked the waves, their blunt little bows in a steadier motion now they were under their own power. In this weather it would take them an hour or more to reach the beach, or at least a point a couple of hundred metres from it and well clear of that 'Rommel's asparagus' of beach obstacles.

The navigator, Clogstoun-Willmott, made a final check on their position about half an hour before midnight. The swimmers then went over the boats' side. The waves buffeted them, but the tightly fitting hoods of their suits kept them dry, with only their faces and hands bare to the sea and rain. This was being driven by the wind, which must have discouraged even the keenest of sentries from keeping too sharp a lookout.

The swimmers swam and crawled nearly 200 m to the beach, where they moved across the sand to find the rocks and earth samples the 'boffins' required. On the stroke of midnight the sergeant tapped the major's shoulder: 'A Happy New Year', he said. This New Year was little over an hour old when they made their way back to the beach. They had seen no one and despite the buffeting were reasonably dry, for these new surface swimming suits were a great improvement on the type that drowned Norman Teacher. The LCNs also had better equipment than had been available in Sicily, but on this New Year's Day they were by no means without their faults. One craft's echo-sounder failed and the crew were reduced to putting a pole over the side to judge the depth of water. That pole was almost lost as the sailor attempted to stay with the rolling LCN. The other craft lost an anchor. They had lain 500 m out watching a lighthouse flash its warning of the reef before braving its shallows again to collect the swimmers, and it was here near the beach that the anchor was lost. At low water, this incriminating evidence must suggest to the Germans that there had been a recce. With grapples and some difficulty, the missing kedge anchor was found and the swimmers brought safely aboard before the LCNs headed out to meet the MGBs. But in the inky black darkness of that wild night the two craft became separated and might well have had to make their own way back to Dover. Eventually they were both found by the MGBs and escorted home.

Their alarms and excursions had not been in vain: the samples of rock and sand proved to the scientists that the old peat workings had turned to rock. Such details could not be deciphered from aerial photographs for, as the commander in chief in the Mediterranean wrote to General Eisenhower, 'The estimation of beach conditions and gradients by air photography and the study of wave velocities have now reached a fine pitch of efficiency, but where sandbars exist there is no substitute for swimming reconnaissance.' He could have added that on heavily guarded beaches there was no other way to get sand samples. Two weeks after the 1 January recce, the need for swimmers was emphasized when a mysterious coloured 'stain' was noted on one beach. What was this? The planners had to know, for this patch of discoloured sand, or clay or whatever, lay on the American 'Omaha' beach, not far from where they would tow in their Mulberry Harbour. American intelligence officers discussed it with the British and Clogstoun-Willmott volunteered to get samples, in what became operation 'Postage Able'.

This time COPP 1 used X-20. Clogstoun-Willmott navigated the little submarine, whose skipper and crewman had also made room for Scott-Bowden and Ogden-Smith. Five men, around whom 'everything was moist with condensation in such small unventilated spaces', would live in a space of less than 5 m by 3 m with a headroom of 1.5 m. You were always crouching in an X-craft. They slept on top of the batteries, in the driest compartment with room for two men huddled together, occasionally disturbed by a watch-keeper checking the specific gravity of the acid in the batteries. Or a man thin enough to snake his body around the engine might sleep in that compartment, where wet clothes were drying in its draught and warmth. A brief nap was possible coiled around the periscope mounting, but the bunk provided for sleeping was usually chock-a-block with

gear. Their diet was mainly sandwiches washed down with
orange juice followed by hardboiled eggs, chocolate, boiled
sweets and condensed milk.

On the first night, Monday/Tuesday 17/18 January,
Scott-Bowden and Ogden-Smith again clambered into their
special suits before going 'up top' to squeeze past the skipper
on his tiny platform and lower themselves into the sea. Again
they swam nearly 200 m, but this night, although dark, was
calm. The array of defences here began with those 'Belgian
Gates', which by 1944 had been officially called 'element-C',
and further up the beach, but still below the high-tide mark,
were timber ramps. The swimmers passed the first of these
before beginning to take sand samples. These were gouged
out with a notched auger tube; if that sounds technical, the
device was nevertheless typical of SBS equipment –
cunningly designed for simple uses. The hollow half-tube
had notches every three inches (75 mm) along its gouge to
check by feel the depth of insertion, Ogden-Smith pushing it
into the sand or earth to pull out a plug, which he carefully
eased with his finger into the first of twelve waterproofed
cases. The cases, normally used for batteries, were each filled
in turn and put back in his bandolier.

The major meanwhile had fixed their guide line to a brass
staked ring at the precise spot their survey began and
skewered the line to the sand every metre or so. Then,
moving along the line, they could feel the first knot exactly
50 yards from the ring. Here Ogden-Smith was taking that
first plug, feeling those notches on his auger to get the depth
of plug he wanted. It was a simple method needing no light,
for he had only to feel his way to the next knot to take the
second sample. 'Only' of course is a relative term, for with
cold fingers on a winter's night any work is difficult, even
without the need for silent movement when enemy sentries
were about. The major had pegged the line on the compass
bearing which later would show on a map exactly where
each sample came from. They had taken about ten of these
going nearly 500 m up the beach past a number of
'hedgehog' obstacles, and were by the wire well above the

tide line when they sensed that someone was moving along the beach.

They had moved as cautiously as their bulky suits would allow them, for only a few hundred metres away in either direction were German bunkers. The footsteps – undoubtedly those of a soldier, although not one of a patrol – continued on towards the swimmers' marker line. They waited for him to pick it up and follow it in their direction, but he never appeared to have noticed it. The meat skewers had kept it tight to the sand.

They rejoined X-20, climbed out of their suits and had a hot drink, for the submarine's 'electric kettle' or an electrically heated glue-pot, warmed water or soup. The craft moved offshore and westward along the coast, where in an almost dead calm she came inshore again next day to make a periscope recce this time, with Clogstoun-Willmott noting the positions of beach obstacles, German bunkers and the state of defences on roads running up from the beach. These 'beach exits' (in the jargon of Combined Operations) were blocked by concrete walls with concrete pyramids spread near them to prevent tanks climbing past the blocks. The swimmers went ashore again on Tuesday and Wednesday nights finding the samples the Americans wanted. On Thursday X-20 again came inshore, but the Germans were active, firing machine guns, probably in practice bursts, but uncomfortably close to the tiny periscope. That night she left the French coast in a storm after the calm of the previous days, and all the crew's seamanship was needed to get her back with her interesting samples.

Next morning, Clogstoun-Willmott presented the jars of coloured sand to an enthusiastic American intelligence officer. So far as is known, the colour made no difference to the load of tanks or vehicles the sand would carry on a beach roadway. What was more important were the precise details of obstacles, road blocks and gun positions in the defences. X-20's long recce had not been noted by the Germans, but the greater the number of deceptive raids that were carried out, the more likely the Germans were to wonder why none had apparently been made to recce the Seine Bay. The Chief of Staff of the British Twenty-First Army Group, Major-General F. W. de Guingand, pondered the fact, for this was the Army that would spearhead the invasion. Without obvious raids in the Seine Bay, he explained in a memorandum, the Germans must be suspicious in this game of bluff and double-bluff; as for other intelligence raids, these were no longer required since 'the Allies have very complete details of the German defences'. The deception raids therefore ceased in February 1944.

But aerial photographs, SOE agents' reports and periscope recces had failed to yield any details of 'element-C'. One nasty clue to beach defences was also on record: after overshooting his target, one bomb-aimer saw not only the explosion of his bombs in apparently empty sea, but also a line of secondary explosions, possibly from mines. Someone would have to land and examine a 'Belgian Gate'. Hilton-Jones's X Troop of German speakers with a few Royal Engineers would, the planners thought, be able to carry this off without jeopardizing the secret of the Bay of the Seine. The dory crews were specially picked from Royal Navy and Royal Marine commandos; and with Hilton-Jones's men as Hilt Force, the raiders were divided into parties of eight to make half of the ten raids planned, all to points well north of the Seine Bay. They were nevertheless uncomfortably close to the Pas de Calais where the Allies had been pointing the finger of their invasion for some time, and had any of this series of raids codenamed 'Tarbrush' gone wrong it might emphasize the point of this deception. The real invasion was due to be launched within six weeks of the night of the first two 'Tarbrush' raids, 15/16 May, to Bray Dunes near Dunkirk and Onival where Forfar Force had made a raid the previous summer. Each MTB would make an Asdic sweep to 'ping' any German patrol boats before launching her dory – for this was the most heavily guarded part of the coast.

The MTB going to Onival fixed a land surveyor's thin steel wire to the East Bullock buoy as a known point, reeling it out several nautical miles as she headed towards the French coast to be certain of her navigator's dead reckoning. The distance was right, but Lieutenant G. Lane, of the Buffs, and his party were landed at the wrong place, for the MTB's radar had failed. Luckily, they came off without mishap, but found neither any unusual mines nor 'element-C'. At Bray Dunes, Lieutenant Groom, a sergeant and a signaller were brought in by dory to launch a small inflatable, leaving their signaller with the dory. This was linked to the inflatable by a stout cod line, which the two paddlers reeled out as they went ashore not 100 m from a man smoking a cigarette on this pleasant May night. The smoker had been flashing a torch around the ground near his feet, with occasional beams seaward, but he did not notice Sergeant Moffat with a waterproofed mine-detector. This had an ultra-sensitive amplifier and gave Moffat a searching swing of a metre or so across their path. Later he took off the top two sections of its pole, so that he could crawl back under the outer pieces of sea-moss-covered wire, still sweeping for that mysterious mine right into the incoming tide. The only shrill sounds of contacts he heard, however, came from the waterproofed Teller mines fixed to wooden stakes and other obstacles.

Having taken some infra-red photographs, they followed the tracer-tape that they had laid in order to move back to the inflatable. This in turn was barely afloat, but a couple of tugs on the cod line signalled the dory crew, who gently hauled on the line to bring the inflatable quietly 100 m or so to the boat. The dory engine started with barely a whisper – so well silenced was the exhaust that it could not be distinguished from night sea noises by a man even as close as 50 m away. The little boat made only a slight disturbance in the water, and had been in view from the MTB for five minutes before her Asdic picked up the noise of the dory's tiny propeller. Again, however, they had found no 'element-C', and the photographs (in the Public Record Office) show only the usual obstacles.

At Les Hemmes near Calais the 'Tarbrush' party found only the usual obstacles, but came out at 0410, fifty minutes before dawn, after a difficult rendezvous. The excitement was not yet over, for on the run home their MTB was fired on by another Royal Navy boat, an incident that indicates how difficult it was to correctly identify vessels at night, especially when they were travelling at 35 knots.

Lieutenant Lane and his party returned to Onival two nights later, landing this time at the right place. But there their luck ran out. Two of the raiders became involved in an exchange of shots with German patrols, while the other two saw one of these patrols fire on another. Verey lights, flares and the shouts of men were followed by a scream: to the three men in the dory this sounded like the cry of an injured man, but they saw only a few flares and then all was quiet. Two heads then appeared off the dory bow and Staff Sergeant E. Buff and Corporal King were hauled aboard. Lane and Lieutenant Woodridge had gone in another direction when they landed, a fact that the signaller in the dory now reported to the MTB. His signal was probably intercepted, for soon afterwards star-shells illuminated the sea near the boat and she was forced to withdraw.

Bryan Hilton-Jones went ashore to search for the two officers, but had only a few minutes before he had to return to the MTB or she might be exposed to shore-battery fire in daylight. Lane and Woodridge, he learned later, had launched the inflatable only to be caught by a German patrol boat after ditching their camera and tell-tale gear. The 'element-C' was eventually found to be a framework of iron girders '10 feet square supported on a frame base 14 foot long'. At points on the framework of 150-mm girders were mines, no doubt the cause of the mysterious explosions the bomb-aimer had seen. They would be broken up by underwater swimmers on D-Day, each of these nearly three-tonne obstacles requiring 36 charges.

On D-Day, 6 June 1944, X-20 lay near La Rivière marking the edge of Calvados reef, her shaded masthead light and box-radar beacon guiding coxswains heading for 'Gold' beach to leave her to port (that is, keeping east of her). A second X-craft marked the western limit of 'Gold', her COPPist, Midshipman Robin Harbud, working a 'bong stick'. This mechanical hammer, worked by cranking a handle, sent underwater sound waves that were more easily pinpointed by ships' Asdics than could the old RG light on a camera receiver. Harbud had to sit astride the X-craft's casing and as the weather became rough, he was washed off the bow, just managing to catch the skipper's outstretched leg as the midshipman was swept past the X-craft. X-20 also had difficulties in the rising seas, her skipper unlashing himself from the small air-vent mast, also being washed overboard and almost lost.

5 Fighting Recces
Final Campaigns in Europe, 1944–5

With the Allied invasion safely ashore on the beaches surveyed in Normandy by COPP, we can return to the Aegean, where that June two SB patrols went north, in part to provide some protection for MTB anchorages, as commandos did in Norway. These boats, however, did not operate as had been planned: for at the last minute the problems of maintaining them in the Aegean proved insoluble. Even so, Captains James Lees and Bob Bury had some sport in these islands, although, as Paddy Mayne would have said of such hunting, 'a bit here, a bit there'. But at Kalimnos a raid on the last day of June met heavy opposition.

The stage was now set for the SBS finale in the Aegean: a raid by 210 officers and men led by Colonel Turnbull against Simi. The 81 SBS hands (the rest being Greeks of the 'Royalist' Sacred Squadron) landed successfully at three points on the night of 13/14 July (Thursday/Friday), but two Greeks carrying heavy packs fell into deep water before landing and were drowned. The main force, commanded by the colonel, moved unseen to a forming-up point overlooking Simi castle, which was mortared at dawn. Two motorized Ems barges returned to the harbour at this time, after finding five Royal Navy MLs offshore. Attacked by SBS ashore and by fire from the MLs, they surrendered. On Malo Point, the Germans retreated before 'Stud' Stellin and the Greeks cleared some 75-mm coast-gun positions. From the castle the garrison maintained accurate fire on the bridge leading to the port and boat yard, but by 0900 the main forces had closed to within 600 m of them.

To the south, Stewart Macbeth and Bob Bury had cleared a platoon of Germans from a monastery, but were having difficulty in persuading them to surrender. They did not understand Bob Bury's first note of truce; a second carried by a Greek girl, proved more successful, and 33 Germans gave themselves up. At the castle there was a stalemate by 1000 hours, so the colonel sent a German petty officer to offer terms. After much shilly-shallying, these were agreed two hours later. The German commander had radioed at 0700 hours that morning for air support, but it arrived too late – when three Messerschmitts flew over dropping anti-personnel bombs, the port had surrendered.

Bill Cumper supervised the ensuing demolitions with his usual brisk efficiency. Nineteen caiques (some of 20 tonnes) gun emplacements, fuel depots and the inter-island tele phone cable were all destroyed before the force withdrew with 151 prisoners, after distributing the 30 tonnes of food that had been brought for the islanders. Stellin and his patrol remained there to watch developments, seeing next day the Germans bombing the island before sending in two armed launches. These Stellin ambushed with accurate fire as they tried to enter the castle harbour. But the last SBS were safely in the hills before the next air raid, and by 1500 hours the Germans had reoccupied the town. An ML picked up the New Zealander and his men that night, and she was able later to surprise an E-boat with such a weight of fire – every man had a machine gun – that this powerful coast craft was set ablaze. The comparatively small MLs normally carried 20 mm and four, not fourteen, machine guns. It was a fitting end to the campaign, for the SB Squadron had left many successful marks on the Aegean. As an American journalist wrote of them after going on one raid, 'They're tough . . .'

'Earthworm' Section

We have yet to look in detail at the Royal Marines' con tribution to this raiding, but by early June RMBPD' curiously named 'Earthworm' Section had been in the Mid dle East for some weeks, based near the SB Squadron a

Athlit. They had brought Cockle Mark II** canoes (the two stars denoting an improved version of the craft used in the 'Frankton' raid). But with a marine-ply deck and bottom, making it stronger than a Folbot, the Mark II** was collapsible in that the rubber-proofed canvas sides could be folded by lowering hinged struts. When stacked aboard a submarine, *three* of these craft required little more space than a single assembled Folbot. Their first operation, in early April, was to be on hand in case a mutinous Greek cruiser and other ships in Alexandria had to be sunk: fortunately, they were not called on in the event. Nevertheless, this broke the monotony of training – after living in their own billets at Southsea, the SBS hutted camp had few attractions. The RMBPD later moved to their own beach camp at Mahariyah, a tiny village near the Squadrons' base. In early May they moved to the forward base at Kastellorizon, from where half the Section were flown to Malta. To the Army Squadrons, with a number of marines like Hughes in their ranks, the new arrivals must have seemed inexperienced and perhaps overequipped, for they brought some 60 tonnes of stores with them. But they quickly became acclimatized to the warmer and clearer waters off Palestine, which were pleasant to swim in by comparison with the Solent.

Captain (later Major) W. Pritchard-Gordon, RM, one of the two original volunteers selected by Hasler from some twelve young officers two years earlier, now commanded 'Earthworm'. He took five canoes for raids being planned against supply ships in Cretan harbours. They embarked on the submarine *Unruly*, with her small crew of 27 already experienced in Mediterranean operations, and sailed on 17 May. Yet, despite an extended voyage of seventeen days, they found no targets against which to launch the limpeteers.

Lieutenant J. Richards, RM, the second in command, had more luck. His three canoe teams were taken by ML from Kastellorizon to lie up on the Turkish coast where they could attack either Leros or Rhodes, depending in which harbours aerial recces would reveal German destroyers. For several days the marines lived in a camouflaged caique at Sertcheh, an anchorage in the Gulf of Mandalya, some 90 km north of Rhodes and 60 km east of Leros. They each had a personal cache of gold sovereigns (and the caique skipper had considerably more) in case bribes should be necessary. Gold is often a quieter method of persuasion than firing a pistol.

On the afternoon of 16 June, ML360 arrived with recent aerial photographs of Porto Lago on Leros. This showed *Anita*, an ammunition ship, under the lee of a cliff on the north side of the harbour, 2.5 km beyond the boom across the entrance. To the northeast lay the supply ship *Carola* and a flak-boat, while near the old Italian naval base to the southeast were the two long-sought 1000-tonne Italian destroyers and some smaller escorts.

That evening ML360 moved along the coast to a second and more convenient anchorage, where she lay up next day, Friday 17 June. In the evening, a moonless but starry night, she sailed 'on silent engines' carrying the canoes. Each canoe carried eight limpet-mines with $4\frac{1}{2}$-hour time fuses, a 24-hour ration pack for each man and the now-familiar charts, for the raiders had been studying these for several days. Silenced Stens, canoe camouflage nets, fighting knives and other items of standard SBS kit were also in the canoes. Less well known were the bird-call whistles that they carried for mimicking seagulls, ducks, owls and crows – a means by which RMBPD canoes could signal to each other.

They rafted together under the shadow of the cliffs at the entrance to the bay, less than an hour after leaving the ML, which lay with engines silent until the canoes were 3 km away. *Shrimp*, crewed by Corporal Horner and Marine Fisher, crossed the boom first, heading for *Anita* and the two other ships beyond her, the furthest 3 km up the bay. *Shark* followed her fifteen minutes later, with Richards and Marine Stevens heading for one of the destroyers and three escorts nearby, on the south side of the bay. She was followed five minutes later by Sergeant King and Marine

Ruff in *Salmon* – who were spotted and challenged twice. A light flashed from a patrol boat, but she did not follow the canoe. Thirty minutes later they were again hailed, this time from the shore, being noticed perhaps because the canoe, leaking badly, needed strong paddle strokes to move her through the water. They had to stop at one point, clinging to an empty barge, while they bailed out the water from around their knees. King took this opportunity to make out their target, a destroyer 50 m away but inboard of the line of other moored craft. Men were in her waist a mere couple of metres from the water, so the canoeists placed six limpet-mines under her stern, one beneath the depth-charge rack. A plain hook on the end of the paddle now served for the hook on the original special rod. To reach the destroyer at all they had been forced to back and weave out of a jetty sentry's view; now, half-full of water again, *Salmon* headed back for the boom.

Corporal Horner, meanwhile, was hailed as he came under the stern of *Anita*. 'Brandenburger Patrola! Patrola!' he answered – a welcoming reply for the hands on deck, who threw down a rope ladder. But Horner turned *Shrimp* for the shadow of the cliffs and later withdrew. Had he and Fisher been caught, the entire venture could have come to nothing, for ships in the bay would have sent down divers to check for mines.

Richards and Stevens, 600 m away across the bay in *Shark*, had found the escorts, but could not make out their main target, a destroyer. By the first escort they could hear voices and a dog barking, but no one was on the deck. Two limpet-mines were placed on her; then, despite men chatting on the ship's decks, limpets were put on the second; and with some difficulty, for the magnets could not grip, on a third. An hour had now passed since they crossed the boom. There was still time to search for the destroyer, and they found her beyond the escorts, tied alongside piles in the bay. Under her bows the canoe, steadied as Richards reached down with the paddle hook, was sprayed by urine as a sailor pissed over the side. They moved clear of this cascade to put one limpet 10 m from the bow and a second below the bridge. By this time, it was less than three hours to dawn, and they had to paddle south to Kalimnos a good 2.5 km away, in order to hide the canoe and themselves before first light.

This they and the other two canoes managed success-fully, buoyed up by the sound of several explosions and spending Saturday with a few alarms in hiding before they made their rendezvous. Later they were to learn that both destroyers had been damaged. The German patrol boats had also depth-charged parts of the bay looking for a British submarine, as the three escorts had been sunk. The de-stroyers, after being towed to Greece for repairs, were sunk by the RAF. Now that these had been put out of action, the SB Squadrons could be ferried comparatively safely on raids in the central Aegean.

Crete was not to be overlooked in 1944. The SBS struck in July after suitable recces under the guidance of officers from Force 133 (the SOE command working into Greece, the Aegean and Bulgaria). The airfields were no longer targets worth hitting in view of the island's new-found isolation, for by this date Allied armies were north of Rome and the Germans had long since removed virtually all of their bomber squadrons. But there was still plenty of fuel on the island that might enable the garrison to use some mobile reserves should the Allies need to land in strength. Seven main fuel dumps, therefore, were the principal targets, each circled by coils of barbed Dannert wire strung over anti-personnel mines. Such defences did not deter SBS patrols.

Guards who interfered were reluctantly shot; others were killed by charges laid to prevent pursuit. In one case – after treating with a Ukrainian in the German Army – eleven were killed at supper, as later were the occupants of a staff car. The Ukrainian was rewarded with a passage back to Egypt. All went well except for two of the intruders, John Lodwick and Bombardier Nixon, who had laid some charges when the other two in this team were confronted by five guards. A running fight developed in which one German was knifed as he struggled with Private Stewart. Another was repeatedly shot by one of his companions, an 'own goal' that can happen to any troops in close fighting at night. But Lodwick and Nixon were caught next morning when a dog patrol found them hidden among the drums still inside the perimeter wire.

SBS prisoners were usually given a rough time when caught in the Mediterranean theatre, but not shot more or less out of hand as they were in northwest Europe. Solitary confinement, mock executions and a starvation diet weakened both men, yet in October they escaped from a prison camp in Yugoslavia, returning to the Squadron exactly 134 days after capture. George Jellicoe, always a little sharp in his wit, welcomed them with 'Ah! You're back. Damned slow about it weren't you?'

While they had been away, the Squadrons had moved to Monte Sant' Angelo in August 1944, at that time a town of 25,000 impoverished people, where the black market thrived. Here on the Gargano Peninsula, among virgin woods on its granite surface, the Squadrons prepared to raid islands in the Adriatic. Lassen's Squadron at Karasovia became embroiled in a fight between Yugoslav partisans and 400 Axis troops before the patrols could re-embark without loss. 'Dinky' Sutherland's Squadron, some parachuting, some landing from boats, made several small raids, but these were often hampered by partisan politics. In fact, by the autumn of 1944, in the view of one experienced commando officer, Major (later Colonel Sir) Alfred Blake, 'Attacks mounted jointly with partisans were almost inevitably going to break down.' The commandos and SBS (at this time wearing SAS-type badges) worked to a plan – albeit fairly loosely in the case of the SBS – while the partisans relied on weight of numbers with little subtlety in the way they attacked German garrisons.

Only the independent ways of Lieutenant Ambrose McGonigal, from Eire, seemed to bring any marked success. He and four men spent September and October in southern Yugoslavia, taking largely independent action against German rail and road convoys. Allowing the local partisans to tag along if they wished, he never made details of his plans known to them. Maybe they thought that this aggressive Irishman found targets only of opportunity (as they usually did); more likely, McGonigal's first-rate interpreter, Captain Eden, had much to do with smoothing the way for this small patrol, swimming, so to speak, in a maelstrom of mistrust.

The War in Greece

Further north in the Balkans, the Axis allies were now spinning to destruction, for the Romanians had begun negotiations for a separate peace that summer, believing a joint Allied force of Russians with British support were about to land at Constanta, only 200 km from Bucharest. This was a cleverly contrived deception, which unnerved the Romanian dictator Antonescu, forcing Hitler to keep Romania in the war by stationing four good divisions, three of them Panzer formations, in the northern Balkans. But by September the Russians had advanced into this region and were fighting in Bulgaria, where they could cut off Axis forces in Greece to the south. These were therefore withdrawing northward, XXI Mountain Corps having to fight its way north against constant harassment, first by Greek and later by Albanian and Yugoslav partisans. This withdrawal was covered by a few thinly manned garrisons along the western coasts of Greece and Yugoslavia, opening a wide door for British forces to land in Greece. British troops seized Kithira, the large island off the southern tip of Greece, in late August, Lassen's Squadron having been sent there with orders to recce the approaches to Piraeus. He landed a patrol on Aiyina, an island with a naval base in its port that was full, the patrol reported, of 'drunken and disgruntled Germans recently evacuated from Crete'. This was duly noted by the headquarters of the British Command, Balkan Air Force, responsible since June 1944 for all special operations in this region, including Yugoslavia, Albania and Greece, and for supply drops further afield in Poland, Czechoslovakia and northern Italy. This Command set up Bucket Force in mid-September, with the SB Squadrons as its nucleus, for operations in Greece. Jellicoe, now promoted to Lieutenant-Colonel, took command.

In September 1944, Ian Patterson and 58 men parachuted on to Aroxos airfield on the Akra Papas Peninsula, south of the entrance to the Gulf of Corinth. They were not opposed, but enthusiastic Greeks bearing lemonade and bottles of the powerful ouzo spirit delayed proceedings – almost as much as their compatriots, who tried to loot the 1.7-m-long containers dropped for the SBS with reserves of ammunition, rations and other combat stores. Jellicoe flew in next day by Dakota: he would mastermind the advance towards Athens along the coast road on the southern shores of the Gulf.

Patterson's men first met resistance at the town of Patras which was the largest town on the road to Corinth, over 120 km to the east. That September 865 Germans and a Fascist Greek battalion – 1600 men in a so-called 'security battalion' – increased the local population. These Greeks, fearful of the retribution from ELAS partisans surrounding the town, were not prepared to surrender. Patterson, therefore, arranged to enter the town under the Red Cross flag of this society's local representative to tell the German commander that he was surrounded. The ELAS forces did not appear to be very active, but Patterson's men staged a good display of mobile fire power. Moving unseen from one hilltop to the next, they created the impression in true Beau Geste style of being on every hill, while their few mortars flung bombs into the town – if somewhat at random, for 'mortars had never played an important part in SBS weapon training'. After his meeting, Patterson reported to Jellicoe that the Germans were playing for time, so the colonel decided to work on the Greek security battalion. Protracted negotiations eventually succeeded, and the

Greeks silently left the town, accepting Jellicoe's promise of fair treatment, and presenting him with problems, for they had to be fed. The German commander did not even realize they had left.

The Squadron had meanwhile taken delivery of a number of jeeps, equipped, like SAS jeeps in the Western Desert, with machine guns. These would provide the mobility that Patterson needed. He was also reinforced by a couple of companies of the RAF Regiment who had been landed with a few armoured cars. Mixed SBS/RAF mobile patrols – light in manpower (each totalling twenty men) but carrying a heavy punch in fire power – penetrated the town, and by the evening of 26 September the garrison were withdrawing by sea. SBS Bren gunners and a captured 77 mm were brought into action to prevent this, but the intense fire of 20-mm and machine guns from the Siebel ferry leaving the harbour forced the SBS to break off the action.

In the following week, despite effective German demolitions of cuttings and mining of the coast road, Patterson reached Corinth, where another Greek security battalion surrendered on 7 October. Patterson's men found a ferry but with some difficulty, for the Germans had sunk most of the boats in the canal. Once across this waterway, however, several small patrols went north to ambush stragglers until they met the main German rearguard. Now with 70 men, Patterson found these Germans were still ready to fight, sending fighting patrols among the SBS positions. Some Germans were ambushed, but in this mood there was no way in which 700 of them could be persuaded to surrender. Fortunately, help was at hand. Despite heavy casualties through parachuting in near gale-force winds, 4 Independent Parachute Battalion dropped to take over from Patterson. Meanwhile another small patrol in a caique had reconnoitred the Bay of Salamis: these were the first British troops to enter Piraeus. It was to Athens that Patterson now pressed on, landing with Jellicoe as the last Germans withdrew from the city. The senior SBS officers rode off on two bicycles to the centre of the city to find the mayor. Later the whole of Patterson's Squadron took over billets in the luxurious Hotel Grande-Bretagne.

They were not allowed to sleep between sheets for more than a couple of nights, however, before they were on the move again. Jellicoe had now been given command of Pomp Force, 950 men in all, consisting of 4 Parachute Battalion, SBS, a Troop of parachute-trained Royal Engineers, some 200 men of the RAF Regiment and a battery of Royal Artillery 75-mm guns. The Force went northwest 150 km towards Lamia, their progress again slowed by the efficient cratering of roads and other demolitions by German engineers, with occasional misdirected attacks from the RAF – although the Spitfires more often caught the right targets: German lorries, half-tracks and horse-drawn wagons jammed on the steep bends where the road came out of high hills, or strung out on the 10 km of open valley road leading to the town. A litter of packs, opened ammunition boxes and even water-bottles strewn by the roadside marked where the attacks had succeeded. There also the inflated bodies of dead mules sharpened the smell of destruction, as burnt oil, granite dust and the sickly sweet scent of burnt human flesh were carried on the gentle breeze from burning wreckage.

The pursuit followed a relentless pattern of strafing from the air and harassment by Pomp Force when Jellicoe's men could catch up with the rearguard. These Germans made their first serious stand at Kozani where hills commanded the road as it passed below the 2112-m-high peak of Mount Siniatsikon. Here, some 160 km from Lamia, Patterson led half of Jellicoe's force in a frontal attack on the town while the parachute battalion, under Lieutenant-Colonel Coxon, led the rest past it to Florina, a further 60 km into the mountains. The men attacking Kozani – SBS, RAF Regiment and some paras, supported by a battery of 75-mm guns – were checked in part because a Greek security battalion refused to surrender. Patterson went forward in his jeep, noting 'the bad marksmanship of the enemy'. This enabled the Para companies at dawn next day to clear some trenches overlooking the road with the loss of only fifteen men, although seventy of the defenders were killed. SBS patrols in heavy rain got forward nearly to the town's outskirts, but were pinned down there for two hours, as their support fire from the 75-mm guns could not be ranged properly when radio communications broke down. The Germans were able, therefore, to withdraw in reasonable order, their mobile guns shelling the RAF armoured cars and SBS jeeps as they tried to follow them. The Greek battalion, however, did not get far before they were badly mauled by ELAS guerrillas, who spent less ammunition in attacking Germans than they did against Greek collaborators and against Royalists.

At Florina, Pomp Force regrouped, a convoy of jeeps with their twin machine guns and the mobile '75s', circling north towards the Yugoslav border. There, drawn up on a hillside some 1000 m above a narrow valley, they caught a German column coming out of the hills. The result was devastating: 'It took a long time to count the German dead.' British forces were not allowed to cross into Yugoslavia, but Captain 'Papa' Milner-Barry, Transjordan Frontier Force, crossed into Albania. 'Papa' had served with the Squadrons since April 1943, and his venerable years – at least to the Squadron who regarded men of thirty-five as 'old' rather than in their 'middle' years – had been enhanced by experience as an oil company executive when he worked for Shell in Palestine. His tact almost matched that of Lieutenant J. Stewart F. Macbeth, and both officers were used by Jellicoe on missions requiring a more subtle diplomacy than fire power. Stewart Macbeth, recruited to the SBS by Maclean in November 1942, possessed considerable charm and, as Jellicoe's liaison officer, from time to time 'smoothed many ruffled feathers' at Army Headquarters.

'S' Squadron had been in Albania since late August, and by October they were in Korcë, a hill town in the southeast of that country. Here Milner-Barry met Sutherland and a link-up of the Squadrons was arranged. Lassen, in the Sporades, was given his majority that month. A 'majority' in the Squadrons was sometimes a fleeting promotion, for Jellicoe had been known to reduce even Patterson to captain's rank for exceeding what Jellicoe felt was his subordinate's authority. This was a means, perhaps, by which the colonel kept some measure of control on his highly independent senior officers – although, knowing them from their actions, one can but doubt whether the loss of a major's crown would have concerned them a great deal.

Turnbull's raiders, who were mainly Greeks, were also in the Sporades, but the Germans had recently evacuated most of the islands. On Volos an SOE agent, immaculate in his uniform of a Sapper major, appeared with a large number of Italian prisoners who had been under his control (if not command) for over a year. The Squadron moved on leaving the Navy to cope with the problems of feeding this multitude. Other more intransigent difficulties lay ahead for the SBS as they sailed into their first brush with the Greek civil war. The patrols had been making a coastal recce through the islands when the caique carrying Bob Bury and his men entered a large bay and immediately came under heavy fire. The helmsman of the caique was hit, but Bury realized that this was not fire from German rifles. He therefore determined to land, but without recognition signals or any obvious means of making clear that his men were British, he could only stand at the helm and shout as he swung the caique's bow deliberately towards the beach positions. The nearer he could get to the riflemen the better the chance of their understanding him, but as the craft moved more slowly now towards the shore he made an easy target, standing openly at the helm. The firing did not stop in time, and he fell, mortally wounded. His sergeant took command, bringing the boat on to a beach across the bay. The riflemen turned out to be Royalists expecting an attack from ELAS bands. Bury had taken part in many raids, including the one that had blown up the governor's residence on Simi the previous winter. Always unselfish and devoted to his men's wellbeing, he was buried next day, the Greeks forming a sad funeral procession. He was twenty-four.

With the departure of the Germans from the Sporades in October, Lassen's patrols were sent to reconnoitre Salonika. They sailed in two schooners, one with a jeep camouflaged among her deck cargo. Their escort of two MLs left the sailing ships in the Gulf of Thermaikos Kolpos, and they sailed on as apparently ordinary trading vessels among several entering the Potiahia canal. There they lay alongside the German hospital ship *Gradisca* coming in with the garrison from Leros (apparently fit men to the SBS observers). The Germans had no time to check Greek ships, however: they were busily evacuating the area, as ELAS guerrillas roamed the hills inland.

Lassen paid those irregulars a visit. Disembarking the jeep, he and Lieutenant Martin Solomon, RNVR, a drinking partner of the Dane and his naval liaison officer, made a grand tour of the area. They left the quay at 0700 hours, and drove fast to be clear of any possible German attention before they reached the ELAS lines. These in places were only 100 m from German strongpoints, but the guerrillas had no intention of letting Lassen near the enemy – until he made clear to their colonel that he would go where he wanted to go. Not that there was much activity on this front, for as German units withdrew, ELAS forces merely occupied the now-vacant trenches, claiming nevertheless that they had liberated more Greek territory. The reconnaissance party were back by late afternoon, the jeep's odometer showing it had run 130 km that day. In the evening Solomon and Lieutenant J. C. Henshaw, a German speaker who had served as a regular soldier in the Guards before being commissioned, set out again in the jeep. Their recce took them along the coast road to a battery still manned by Germans, to whom Henshaw wrote a note calling on them to surrender, as they were surrounded by British troops. This was carried to the commander by a Frenchman (most likely a conscript in the Todt Organization). But apart from a couple of drunks there were no prisoners to be taken that night; instead, two tanks, some self-propelled guns and lorried infantry came down the road. The SB officers dived for cover, taking their befuddled prisoners with them but leaving Lassen's jeep by the road. This was too dear to Lassen's rough heart to be lost by such overboldness. Having spent the night in a wood, Henshaw went back to the road, and was relieved to find the precious vehicle intact. As he drove it away, the explosions of German demolitions covered the sound of the engine.

Before the week was out, the Germans were withdrawing the last of their Salonika garrison. This had been going peacefully enough, with ELAS occupying suburbs as German troops withdrew, but the SBS played a more realistic role. The patrols arrived in the centre of Salonika on four fire-engines, probably the only vehicles with petrol in their tanks when the Squadrons found them, and not usually expected to carry armed men. Greeks leapt on to the running-boards in a frenzy of welcome, characteristic of citizens liberated throughout Europe. What they did not expect was sudden action, which sent them scurrying into the cover of nearby buildings. Henshaw, Lassen's second in command, led part of this attack and caught the demolition teams off guard: 'He killed eleven Germans, Lassen eight.' Salonika fell to SBS action this Monday 30 October, with the German demolitions far from complete. Sixty Germans had been killed in the sally from the fire-engines. Others had seen the jeep in the hills and SBS patrols on the islands and along coast roads, not surprisingly estimating their strength as being 'at least 1000'. Yet these 40 men of the SBS who had sailed from Piraeus barely a week earlier were the only British uniformed land force in the area. Off the coast, however, COPP 10 were preparing to make further beach surveys, having earlier made surveys of Anzio, off Piraeus and in the Adriatic, since their arrival in the Mediterranean on 1 June 1944.

In reply to Lassen's signal on 30 October 1944 to say he was there, Jellicoe replied: 'Give your ETA Athens.' The estimated time of arrival was a day or two hence, but the Squadron, with Patterson's men from Yugoslavia, would have a few days of leave among the Greeks with whom they got along well at that time, for most of the former swimmer-canoeists spoke a smattering of Greek. The fact that they had not used many canoes and done little operational swimming in recent months owes more to the changing nature of the war in the Balkans, than their SAS parentage at that time. The Squadrons of those days were an army unit, and tended to be more 'gung-ho' than their seaborne descendants perhaps, the difference between them being that nuance of professionalism which required a reconnaissance team to be sure they got their intelligence back and the sabotage raider who does not worry overmuch about how he will get out.

Further battles developed in Crete in early December 1944, when Lassen's Squadron went to Crete strictly 'to watch over and report' on the German withdrawal. The garrison of 13,000 men were pulling back to the area around Maleme airfield, Canea and Suda harbour, a perimeter 30 km in length and 15 km deep along the northwest coast. The SBS patrols landed at Heraklion on Sunday 3 December to report and to protect food supplies to be distributed to the townsfolk. Yet, two days later teams were inside the perimeter doing the job of a modern Forward Air Controller: spotting targets for air attack. Henshaw even contacted the German provost marshal, whose military police had been unable to stop starving troops' forays to rustle sheep from outside their lines. The exchange of prisoners that Henshaw had hoped to make was not completed, while the Greek partisans (a ferocious bunch on Crete) were hanging about the edge of the German defences.

Henshaw thought the Greeks could be more aggressive, persuading them to put in a night attack under covering fire from SBS Brens, while Lieutenant Ian Smith put a stop to the sheep rustling. But civil war in Crete was reaching a stage where no one could travel safely in the liberated four-fifths of the islands. The SBS were strictly neutral and were on speaking terms with both ELAS and their rivals, the EDES. This state of affairs changed with the deaths of Private Corithwaite and Captain C. Clyne, and the wounding, for the third time, of Captain Charles Bimrose, all at the hands of one Greek marksman. Corithwaite had been the motorcycle escort for the two officers' jeep when it was attacked, far from the German perimeter. The man responsible must have clearly seen that they were British and unarmed. Despite these factors, an ELAS court later pronounced the Greek to be insane, after which the SBS in Crete kept their relations with this organization to a minimum during the rest of their time on the island.

In Athens the civil war flared into open rebellion against the British. Patterson's men, about to fly to Italy, were sent back into the city from the airport on 8 December. They found the city controlled by ELAS, except for an enclave where 4 Parachute Battalion guarded a perimeter around the Allied Headquarters. At first, guard duties were shared with ELAS platoons at key buildings, but at the waterworks, while off duty, an SBS patrol was surprised and disarmed. They were later marched north for three days and held for nearly a month before being released when the British drove ELAS out of Athens early in January 1945. The sixty men of 'L' Squadron had lost three killed and twelve wounded in four and a half weeks of street-fighting in Athens, where they tended to use Brens and PIATs (against buildings) to dislodge men sniping at the SB road blocks. This was the first brush for their SAS line of descendants against urban terrorists.

Such actions are not the only risks, however, facing light, mobile troops such as the SB Squadrons. Patterson flew out from Athens in a Dakota, which was loaded with wounded and heading for Brindisi in Italy, but the aircraft crashed when making its approach on instruments in bad weather, and all the passengers were killed. The major's men had felt great affection for him. The strong sense of personal reliability he had looked for in the volunteers he trained had produced an efficient unit, one to which men were proud to belong. Many of them wrote at this time to Patterson's mother expressing their sorrow at his death.

The Adriatic Raids

In mid-December, George Jellicoe left the Squadron and
was succeeded by David Sutherland. Lassen was reorganiz-
ing the patrols at Monte Sant' Angelo and new volunteers
were being trained by Marine Hughes and Sergeant 'Brown
Body' Henderson (the naturist) among other 'old' hands.
While Major Lapraik and Bill Cumper had completed their
secondment to Raiding Forces Middle East, this force had
made – including its early SBS operations – 381 raids on
some 70 islands since its formation in late October 1943
But the Aegean now being clear of Axis forces who might
impede the Allies, the Squadrons began operations in the
northern Adriatic. Here 2 Commando Brigade had helped
the partisans to clear German garrisons from the Dalmatian
islands during the summer of 1944. The Brigade's 43 (RM)
Commando had been in the Montenegro mountains o
southern Yugoslavia and 40 (RM) Commando in Albania
but were both withdrawn to Italy that December when the
partisan Communist governments rejected any direct Brit
ish help. In January 1945 40 (RM) Commando were sen
back to Corfu, nevertheless, to protect the Greek islanders
from attacks by various factions.

By February 1945, the 30,000 men of the German XX
Mountain Corps had extracted themselves from the winte
battles in these southern mountains, while their main Army
Group retreated north along roads from Greece. The
Mountain troops, seasoned in island defence from their
time in the Aegean, now held a number of large islands of
the northern coast of Yugoslavia and the Istrian peninsula
On the northwestern coast of the peninsula lies Trieste, the
port on the Italian-Yugoslav border over which nation
have fought for generations, which the Yugoslavs coveted
that spring. It was a region of varying loyalties, the Slovene
peasants welcoming the partisans; but many Italians had
lived in the region, which had been part of Italy since 1919
The partisans' base at Zadar was also being used by Roya
Navy coastal forces, when 'S' Squadron arrived with 20

parachutists of the RAF Regiment in January 1945. They found that the Yugoslavs, often to be seen carrying rusty Mauser rifles, tended to strut about in pairs, having imprisoned most of the citizens who were Italian. British forces were not allowed into the town, and nor were their billets very hospitable, so 'Nobby' Clarke (who had succeeded Sutherland) transferred the Squadron to Uljan island nearby.

Recce teams from this base found strong garrisons on Losinj, Cres and Unije, islands in the Gulf of Fiume, where the metalled roads and wooded hills contrasted with the scrubland on the much smaller Aegean islands. The Adriatic defences were also more sophisticated, with anti-personnel minefields, wire entanglements and alert sentries. The recces complete, 'Stud' Stellin with a party of 20 landed on Cres to take out a coast-watchers' post with its powerful radio. Fire from PIATs, Brens and SMGs on the post and nearby billet brought a quick and bloodless surrender from the twelve Italian Fascist soldiers in the post who did not have time to destroy their codebooks and their radio.

The next target was the Villa Punta, a fortified house overlooking a beach on Losinj. This rambling old villa, with its large garden and outbuildings, was held by 45 Germans, who appear to have reinforced its cellars as protection against air attack. Ambrose McGonigal planned to clear the building by drawing the Germans to the back (seaward) side, while his main body – if that is not too grand a description for some seventeen men – broke in through the front door. One of his three lieutenants (for this patrol had four 'chiefs' to its thirteen 'braves') led a team along the beach. There, coming up against barbed wire apparently, they were heard by an alert sentry and fired on. Nor were the Germans content to wait for an attack to develop, for they sent a small fighting patrol to attack the intruders. As these men ran out they were met by fire from SBS Bren gunners on the walls of the garden, and some were driven back into the house.

McGonigal then led his teams into the attack, breaking into the front of the house while Bren gunners kept the Germans from firing back through the windows or lobbing grenades from them. In pairs, the SBS began clearing the house passage-by-passage, room-by-room and through the nooks and crannies of the outbuildings, a difficult job in daylight, when working to a planned if flexible timetable, so that covering fire from outside would not strike the rooms being cleared. At night, with a scratch plan of action, the job was verging on the suicidal. Lieutenants Jimmy Lees, Thomason and Jones-Parry got into the building, but the difficulties for the Bren gunners in identifying friend from foe led to some confusion. The dark of the passages was lit by the occasional flash of a grenade, while the sudden noise of firing – the ripping burst of a Schmeisser's rapid fire, answered by the slower staccato of Sten or tommy gun – seemed to reverberate from all directions. The shudder of explosions and the acrid smell of smoke added to the confusion, after spells of deathly silence broken only by occasional bursts of Bren fire raking the wooden shutters. After one such pause, Jimmy Lees had reached the last room along one passage on the ground floor. He moved into its dark unknown following a burst from his SMG, but the bullets failed to cover this large lounge, for a German shot him from behind a sofa. Lees was to die next day in a German dressing station, for the rest of the patrols did not find him.

Jones-Parry had meanwhile sent out a message telling the Bren gunners not to fire on the north side of the house. Then he saw two or three men in a corridor, threw a '36' grenade at them, which failed to explode, and followed it with a phosphorus bomb. This sprayed the walls with flames as he fired his Thompson through the explosive's thickening white smoke. He and Marine Kitchingham moved down the corridor, but there was no one to be seen: Sergeant McDougal then stood guard at one end of the passage, the lieutenant listened and cautiously tried a door. It opened into a dark and apparently empty room, for there

Folbot of 101 Troop with two Army commando canoeists in Scotland, 1941. Note the Bren gun on the canoe's bow.

The schooner *Tewfik* moored off the Turkish coast in July 1944 when she was the forward base of the Special Boat Squadron.

An Underwater Swimmer's Suit (UWSS) Mark 1 used experimentally for breathing oxygen during trials in October 1943.

Some items carried by canoeists in 1944: – silenced .22 pistol, 9-inch fighting knife, bird-call whistles, magnetic clamp for canoe's painter and emergency rations.

An SBS Jeep with heavy machine gun is cheered by liberated Greeks in Patras, September 1944.

This 14-foot paddle board could be parachuted with the swimmer to an enemy coast and, being low in the water, was difficult to see from the shore.

Raiders lay charges under the tracks of a railway near the coast of North Korea, which carried combat stores south.

Swimmer-canoeists take a Klepper canoe down a fast-flowing river during operations in Borneo in 1963.

was no answer to his burst of fire. At a second door, he and the marine could not hear any movement, Jones-Parry repeating a quick burst of fire as Kitchingham threw open the door. Jones-Parry leaped into the darkness, but the marine must have heard some unexpected noise – he moved from behind the door jamb half into the room. 'Are you all right, sir?' he called. 'Yes,' the lieutenant replied. It was a fatal exchange of words, for a German hidden in the dark fired at the voices and the marine's dim outline in the doorway. Jones-Parry's arm was shattered and a bullet lodged in his spleen – nevertheless, he managed to reload his SMG, sling it around his neck as he knelt on the floor, and fire a final burst one-handed, traversing the wall where the shots had come from. There was no answering fire, only groans, as the lieutenant crawled past Kitchingham slumped in the doorway. He was dead, shot in the head.

As Jones-Parry staggered from the building, Thomason's team were also working their way from room to room, and had to send messages to the Bren gunners that their fire was hindering the house clearance. But now, with the villa on fire, there seemed little likelihood of many of the garrison escaping. As McGonigal had only eleven more or less fit men, the rest being seriously wounded, Lees dying and Kitchingham dead, he withdrew the patrols. The 3-km march to their motor launch was an agonizing walk for the badly wounded – Jones-Parry, for example, had lain down on the road 'very weak now' – but they were determined to get back to the boat.

This action at Villa Punta showed the difficulties of dislodging determined men from a defensive position: despite their bravery, the SBS had been unable to win a conclusive victory, for at least twenty Germans survived in the cellars and outhouses. The Italian Fascists were not so determined, however, and several later surrendered to recce parties, but at the bridge linking the islands of Cres and Losinj in the Gulf of Fiume, there was no surrender on 18 March. The 80 Germans holding this vital junction fought off Captain McGonigal's force of 38 despite a carefully integrated plan of attack. A canoe team, Sergeant Holmes and Rifleman Lecomber, landed south of the bridge to ensure that any German reinforcements from their direction would not arrive unexpectedly, while the main force was landed from two MLs some 10 km from their objective to make a concealed approach that took three hours to reach Osor, the village by the bridge. The first part of the plan was to take out the strongpoints surrounding the main German defences. In one of these, a machine gun was found unmanned, but nearing the second there was a scuffle and, although only one of the five guards escaped, a general alarm was raised. The high walls around the gardens of the houses protecting the bridge were all topped by wire entanglements. Lieutenant Henshaw, the commissioned guardsman who had entered the Germans' last enclave on Crete, realized that a way must be found through the German wire. He drew much of their fire as he crossed open ground to reach it, and had cut some strands before being killed by a grenade. Other teams were also checked. With at least eight German machine guns covering any final approach to the bridge, the SBS teams were only able to fire on the occasional German as he moved forward to bring up more ammunition. Fire was called in from the ML's 20-mm cannon, but even this failed to dislodge the defenders. McGonigal by this time was forced to accept that the bridge could not be taken by direct assault, so with ammunition supplies running low he withdrew his men. The German positions had held, despite nearly half the garrison being killed or wounded. McGonigal had lost Henshaw killed and three wounded.

Future SBS raids were therefore confined in this region to ambushing trucks on the islands' roads at night and recces by day. Lieutenant Ian Smith, a regular officer who had served in the Squadrons since the previous summer and who was McGonigal's 'mucker', turned one recce into a fighting patrol. His target-of-opportunity was the German garrison of Osor, or at least those off duty after guarding the bridge. They were sunbathing peacefully in a courtyard until eleven magazines of .303-inch rounds from SBS Brens at 800 m caught them, killing nine. In later raids the lieutenant collected numbers of Italian Fascist troops who had deserted, but the Germans held firm until late March. Then, with British support, Yugoslav partisans working along the mainland coast cleared in a week the three major islands near the coast.

The island wars in the eastern Mediterranean were now virtually over. There were, however, two more operations in which the Squadrons had a hand. On 11 March the Squadrons' Intelligence Officer, Captain Daniel Riddiford, who had escaped from a German prisoner-of-war camp in 1943 through the Fiume-Trieste area along the coast of the Istrian peninsula, returned there. Teams from LRDG had already established coast-watching observation posts, reporting the course of German supply ships along this coast. It was a dangerous game which most people associate with the war in the Pacific islands, but it was played quite frequently in the Mediterranean where, incidentally, some RMBPD marines had been trained specifically for this type of work. Two LRDG coast-watchers caught that March on the Istrian coast were shot out of hand when the Germans discovered their radio.

Riddiford found that the 43rd Division of Tito's army on the peninsula was commanded by a man with 'a good grasp of military values . . . [but] who kept very much in the background', no doubt because he was subject to political directives. The Royal Navy's coastal forces were fighting a series of running battles off the Istrian coast, in part to help this division by denying the Germans the opportunity to resupply their forces by sea. Such battles delayed the landing by patrols of 'S' Squadron in March, and when they were landed on the southeast coast at the third attempt, German ships were close by. Once ashore, however, the SBS became a pawn on the chessboard of Adriatic politics: virtually interned, they were not released until after the Allies had captured Trieste. Had the Squadron followed its usual aggressive course, no doubt the Slovene population (which had lived under Italian domination for a generation) would have found the even tenor of their ways disturbed.

Operation 'Roast'

The Squadron's final major action in Europe was fought around the muddy wastes of Lake Comacchio, where there had been deliberate flooding as part of Field Marshal Kesselring's defences south of the River Po in northern Italy. The lagoon was divided from the sea by a narrow strip of land known as the Spit, and the bleak, stagnant waters extended westward some 20 km, vast areas no more than 60 cm deep and in places a mere 15 cm over flooded fields. Crossing such shallows was difficult even in COPP 2's canoes, as they surveyed the dykes that crossed these flood-waters. Four SBS canoe teams worked with the COPPs, examining potential landing points as they had done in Normandy. For several nights before D-Day night here (1/2 April), the canoeists probed the defences despite the flares dropped by the RAF while bombing the town of Comacchio 5 km to the north. Other flares were fired at irregular intervals from heavily fortified defences on the Spit, which were held by a force of Turkomans stiffened by a fusilier battalion of 42 Jäger Division – 1200 men in all.

In the ensuing assault, Operation 'Roast', four SBS and four COPP canoes provided the lead lights for the stormboats that brought a Commando Brigade across the dykes. In fierce encounters during the next two days, the commandos succeeded in advancing 12 km, almost to the Valetta canal, which crossed the northern end of the Spit. This advance began to draw Kesselring's reinforcements from positions further west, where the British intended to make their main attack. To ensure Kesselring continued to believe that the main assault would be at Comacchio, the Commando Brigade's advance would need to be exploited. Preparations were put in hand to mount Operation 'Fry', for which 'M' Squadron provided 60 men and the Italian Resistance force's 28 (Garibaldi) Brigade a like number, supported by 42 Field Company of the Royal Engineers, who would clear mines as necessary in the target area. This initially was four islands of firm ground above the flood-waters southwest of Comacchio town. A dyke road linked them and the mainland through salt pans south of the town. As far as the British knew from earlier reconnaissance and local informants, the Germans had some 50 men in and around a fortified house with defence positions on Island II, Caldirolo, and were using some sheds on the island for shelter.

Lassen, whom the Commando brigadier had known for several years, took command of the assault on the night of Thursday/Friday 5/6 April. A preliminary strafing of the islands by the RAF early that evening drove the Germans from the house, but there was always the chance that the defences could be reinforced. Lassen's force was divided into four groups: two, consisting of partisans with his HQ, made for Islands III and IV in punts, while a third landed west of Island II to block the dyke road; the main group landed a kilometre east of this island. There, while partisans blocked the north and south sides of the dykes with machine guns, ready to hold off any reinforcements from the mainland, the SBS launched their canoes. There was a channel along the dyke's north wall that enabled the canoeists to approach Island II, which they secured rela-tively easily, enabling the whole force to establish a firm defence in case they should be attacked that morning. But the Germans made no serious attempt to dislodge them. The canoeists set out again after dark on 6 April to land on the northern shore at two points 500 m apart and 5 km due north of the islands.

On the following night they mounted three raids. One patrol landed near the coast road, repeating the ambush intentions of the previous night, cutting the telephone lines, booby-trapping these breaks and putting mines on the road a kilometre east of the previous raids. The second and third patrols were to create an even more forceful diversion, the second team looping south to land near the salt pans with the intention of alerting the Germans to the possibility of a major assault in the morning striking at the heart of Comacchio.

There had been no opportunity to recce these southern defences of the town since the Allies seized control of the lake the previous week, and Lassen had decided on a bold stroke for the third patrol. They, under Lieutenant Turnbull, would make an advance along the dyke road towards the town. At the last moment, Lassen decided to go with them, and they paddled their inflatables across the still waters of the lake, the sound of their approach being covered by the rustling of the reeds in the gentle breeze. They had moved 500 m along the narrow ribbon of road when Lassen, in the lead, was challenged. Fred Green answered in Italian that they were fishermen. (A curious choice for cover, as the only fish caught in these brackish waters are eels.) He was then called forward by two men in a listening post, but as he stepped into the centre of the road shots were fired. O'Reilly, Trooper Crouch, Sergeant-Major Leslie Stephenson and Lassen took cover over the edge of the embankment half a metre above the flood-waters. Green joined them and Lassen pointed out a pillbox some distance up the road, no doubt with a telephone link to the outpost that had challenged them. He worked his way in the lee of the dyke to the roadside opposite this strongpoint, tossed a couple of grenades and killed the four machine gunners.

There were at least two further defence posts up the road, and machine gunners were also firing at the raiders from away to the left. Crouch was killed and O'Reilly badly wounded, but Green and Stephenson dragged him to the cover of the dyke. Lassen went on alone. They heard a shout of 'Kamerad'. As he had neared the third defence position he had stood up, only to receive a blast of close-range fire. Mortally wounded, he crawled back to the others: 'Steve . . . try and get the others out,' were his last

words as the sergeant-major tried to stem Lassen's wounds.
Even as he lay dying, he still mustered enough energy to
throw three grenades to cover his men's withdrawal behind
the dyke. Two other raiders were killed before the group
reached the inflatables, carrying O'Reilly. Anders Lassen's
body was later found by a partisan patrol on the road where
he had died, aged twenty-five. For his courage and leadership he was awarded a posthumous VC.

The following night there was a further raid, the
attackers going ashore on a watery promontory 7 km west of
the town. But the Germans had already reinforced these
defences, so on the Tuesday the men took their canoes in a
feint near the shore north of the islands. The preliminaries
to the main attack by the British Eighth Army, over 30 km
west of Comacchio, had begun by this time and would
sweep through the German Gothic Line at Argenta.

Islands of the Scheldt

While the Allies were chasing the Germans from Greece,
they had also cleared German armies from northern France
and had captured Antwerp on 5 September 1944. Its dock
cranes and railways could clear 100,000 tonnes a day of
much-needed supplies for the invasion of Germany, but the
port lay over 60 km up the River Scheldt, and its estuary
islands (including Walcheren) were strongly held with over
thirty coast guns of sufficient size to sink any ship
attempting to clear sea mines in the river. By mid-October
the Canadian Army was advancing along the coast to pull
these teeth, but was prevented from crossing the narrow
kilometre-long causeway on to Walcheren. Plans prepared
six weeks earlier for an amphibious assault by 4 Commando
Brigade were updated, including SB-type recces.

A gap in Walcheren's age-old sea dykes at Westkapelle
was blown by nearly 260 RAF bombers on 3 October. This
75-m cut was extended by further bombing when other gaps
were also made on the eastern dykes. The resulting floods,

adding to some controlled flooding by the Germans, made most roads on the island impassable and flooded some anti-aircraft gun positions. What the British did not know was the state of the Westkapelle gap after several weeks' tides had flooded and ebbed through this breach. Therefore on the night of 15/16 October, MTB 621 dropped a dory from her stern davit about 1100 m west of the dyke. The shallows here are difficult for larger craft to cross, but the dory had not left the MTB when a signal light winked a challenge from the shore. Although there was no moon, the night was calm and probably the suspicious movement was seen from the coast, if not in the clutter on the fringe of the radar scan. The dory was hoisted back aboard and the boat moved away at half speed before four searchlights caught her, almost certainly directed by radar.

A second attempt was made a few nights later. This time the dory was launched undetected in a rising wind. She got inshore and launched her inflatable carrying Captain C. R. Steven, and Sergeant Joe Barry (one-time cliff-climbing instructor on the Isle of Wight). They paid out the buoyant line, 170 m of 'orange cotton floating rope with luminous rings every twenty feet' if they used standard line. Certainly they had so much paid out that the dory's small anchor warp 'strummed like piano wire' under the strain, for the seas were now breaking around the inflatable dinghy and in the pitch dark against a strongly running tide they were swept south of the gap. They hauled in the line at about 0100 hours, rejoining the dory, but the signaller could not raise the MTB on the S-phone by 0230 hours. In worsening weather, therefore, Steven headed for Ostend, south along the coast. They made the 55 km back in seven and a quarter hours, after coming close to the mole at Zeebrugge and almost hitting a pier there. The Germans held this port and a sizeable pocket of land, with experienced troops whom the Canadian First Army had cut off from the main German forces. The MTB had meanwhile waited off Walcheren until nearly dawn and had then run back to Ostend at some risk in the early daylight.

A third attempt by this party from Keep Force three days later also had to be abandoned. The dory got inshore in a haze of sea mist, but then she was seen – on radar, possibly – as the inflatable was about to be launched. Verey lights went up from the beach defences and the whole area was quickly flooded in light. The dory made an emergency rendezvous with the MTB while her crew were taking checks on the offshore currents, and when these were completed she sailed. The beach searchlight came on again, possibly at the sound of her engines. In the end, a dory did get inshore, according to one account, before dawn on the day of the assault, 1 November 1944. Even so, the crew were unable to check the state of the beach obstacles, as they were fired on and had to withdraw.

At Flushing on the south of the island, where 4 Commando would land, a party originally brought together for the 'Tarbrush' raids was in the leading LCP (Survey) equipped in many ways like an LCN, their dory having been damaged by shelling before they sailed from a jetty in Breskens. As they crossed the 3 km of river, fires started by RAF bombing and artillery bombardment lit up the sky over Flushing, silhouetting the Oranje Mill, a clear lead mark 100 m west of their intended landing point. Sergeant Barry was with them and has written that 'the Navy took us to the wrong breakwater', to the left of the intended landing, near the base of a breakwater at its western (outer) side. The second LCP(Sy) went too far to the east and collided with the breakwater. A third craft, an LCA carrying the scout section of 4 (Army) Commando, went aground on obstacles, but the men swam ashore. They scrambled up a rubbish dump slipway in the sea wall, cut through the wire and captured 26 Germans in dugouts without a shot being fired. But the more easterly LCP(Sy) attracted some tracer, fired at first too high to cause any damage, while Barry reached the incline of the slipway to find the scout section already there. No climb was required up the harbour wall, no doubt to his disappointment – certainly, he was not pleased to be greeted with 'We've been here ten minutes'.

The 'Tarbrush' party – now in an LCA – sailed for Breskens, but near the breakwater they were hotly engaged by German machine guns. One 'Tarbrush' officer was killed, as was the craft's engineer in the unarmoured space aft. She drifted on the current, her ramp still down, bullets 'beating a tattoo on the armoured sides of her well' as she slowly swung towards the gun. Seeing this danger, Corporal Jones, the party's dory mechanic, dragged the dead engineer from the aft compartment and restarted her engines before more damage was done.

This was the last 'Tarbrush' operation and indeed the last major seaborne landing in northwest Europe, 4 Commando Brigade with 155 Infantry Brigade having cleared Walcheren in four days. But there were river crossings. In one, at twenty-four hours' notice, COPP 5 was called in to survey the Rhine banks near Wesel for mines on the night of 22/23 March. Here, after successive nights of bombardment, no artillery cover was available, because the batteries were being moved forward, an interesting comparison with the United States Navy's Underwater Demolition Teams. They, for example, at Okinawa recced beaches while naval bombardment kept the Japanese gunners from firing on the swimmers. On the Rhine, despite the lack of covering fire and bright moonlight, COPP swimmers checked the west bank before 1 Commando Brigade crossed to it in tracked amphibians and storm boats the following night.

6 More than Cockleshell Heroes
The Royal Marine Boom Patrol Detachment

While we have been following the main stream of beach reconnaissance and Special Boat raids, the Royal Marines were pursuing their traditional roles of raiding. They had been in action in Norway and elsewhere in 1940, but during the amphibious landings in Narvik fjord Captain H. G. Hasler's landing craft had put ashore men of the French Foreign Legion, Poles and young Norwegians, his Landing Craft Company having been one of several marine units, as well as their detachments on ships, who saw action in Norway in May 1940.

After his return from Norway, 'Blondie' Hasler, promoted to major in the Royal Marines, worked on new types of canoes and other intriguing gadgets for swimmers, work he did as a part-time member of the Development Staff of Combined Operations Headquarters. On 27 June 1942 he was given permission to form a special detachment of marines to help in these developments and to carry out 'at short notice any other form of specialized small boat operations'. This Royal Marine Boom Patrol Detachment was ostensibly to operate its Boom Patrol Boats 'with or without canoes', as one memorandum stated, in work on harbour booms to protect Allied shipping in North Africa. But Boom Patrol Boats were not what they seemed, and the memorandum went on to emphasize the Detachment's underwater work and transport by air, with the intention of 'evolving new methods of attacking ships in harbour'. Their methods specifically would not duplicate raids by the SSRF or the SBS.

The Bordeaux Raid

The RMBPD's first raid, however, was a conventional anti-shipping attack against blockade-running Axis vessels preparing to take the latest German fuses, radio and radar equipment to Japan. These ships lay alongside the quays of Bordeaux over 110 km up the River Gironde from the Bay of Biscay. To attack them with an assault landing would have required over 20,000 men, for there were German forces in the area; while air bombing would have caused unacceptably large numbers of French civilian casualties. SOE, however, had also made tentative plans to attack these ships. In the event, the RMBPD raid was to become one of the war's most famous feats of daring: the 'Cockleshell Heroes' raid.

No written orders were issued, but Hasler had trained his No. 1 Section in Cockle Mark II canoes during the first week in November to launch these 'Cockles' by a new method. The loaded canoe with its two paddlers, weighing in all over 215 kg, was hoisted up from the casing of a T-class submarine by tackle fitted to a 1.2-m 'extension girder' from the muzzle of the submarine's 4-inch gun. The gun then traversed to lower the canoe into the sea. All the men of RMBPD were highly trained swimmers, selected for their knowledge of motor-car engines among other things, an indication of the Detachment's involvement in more technical equipment than canvas canoes after their first operation, codenamed 'Frankton'.

At about 2000 hours on Monday 7 December 1942, five Cockle canoes were launched from HMS *Tuna* on a clear night, but as a sixth was brought on deck it was holed too badly to be put in the water. They were to paddle by night and lay up during the day, moving independently in two small groups. If necessary, each pair of canoeists could reach the target alone, for they carried marked maps, eight limpet-mines and rations for five days. The return trip would be another matter: Hasler doubted if they would be able to make it all the way back to the estuary by canoe, for

over this time the winter weather would probably turn
rough. The maps gave some idea of just how dangerous the
raid would be: long stretches of the river banks were shown
to be patrolled by Germans, and there were lookout towers
at many points as well as anti-aircraft batteries.

As in every canoe operation, the most dangerous element
was the sea. The surface was calm as they paddled inshore
but an Atlantic swell lifted the canoes, sending them surging forward as they moved north from the submarine on a
course that would round the point at the estuary's mouth.
The tide was helping them as it flooded towards the river.
Then, after three hours, they heard the roar of broken
water. Soon, just over 2 km ahead, they saw the white froth
of a tide race, where short steep waves tumbled over each
other. The tide was flooding strongly, and Hasler 'rafted
them together' for a brief word of guidance on crossing
this wild water. The next minute each craft on its own went
into these overfalls, paddlers struggling to keep the canoe
bows into the seas and avoiding broaching-to across them.
One boat, *Coalfish*, did not get through this confusion of
seas, and the other four turned back. But there was no sign
of her. No sooner had they started north again when *Conger*
was capsized in a second tide race. She had to be scuttled,
and her crew, Corporal Sheard and Marine Moffat, clung
to the stern of *Catfish* and *Crayfish* while these were paddled
to within 2.5 km of the lighthouse at Pointe de Grave. Its
light had suddenly been switched on, and lit the scene every
few seconds with a brilliant harsh light, under which
Sheard and Moffat set off to swim ashore. Already numb
with the cold, they never made it to land.

Daylight was not far away now, so Hasler led his surviving three canoes to the shore side of some moored boats.
They had been paddling by this time for over seven hours in
an arrowhead formation, but moved in line-astern using
single paddles behind Hasler to pass the boats. Two got
through, but *Cuttlefish* went missing. Her crew, Lieutenant
J. MacKinnon, RM, and Marine James Conway, had lost
touch with the others, but they paddled on independently

as planned. For three days they made their way secretly up the river, but on Thursday night, as *Cuttlefish* was nearing Bordeaux quays, she suddenly jarred against a submerged object sharp enough to slit her bow. In seconds, the crew realized that she was going under despite her buoyancy bags. Scrambling ashore, they set off on the roundabout escape route to Spain.

Catfish, crewed by Major Hasler and Marine Bill Sparks, and *Crayfish,* with Corporal A. F. Laver and Marine W. H. Mills, came ashore after the first night's 36-km paddle at a point where the river bank lay over a kilometre from the main channel. Here they hid the canoes under lightweight camouflage nets behind reeds. Even so, they were seen by French fishermen. The four marines had taken turns in keeping a lookout, ever ready with Hasler's silencer-fitted Sten gun to fight off German patrols, but the Frenchmen mistook them for Germans. That Tuesday evening the canoeists had a struggle to drag their boats across the mud, and were several hours late in catching the flood tide. On Wednesday night they were keen to make up for this lost time, and launched their canoes before it was dark. A French farmer saw them and 'was rather upset' when they would not stop for a drink with him. Despite this urgency, however, they were not as far up the river as they had planned to be by Thursday morning, so they were forced to spend an extra cramped day in their canoes – there was nowhere to hide them on the bank. Hasler put off the attack to Friday night, and on Thursday evening they paddled another 14 km to hide within striking distance of the target ships.

All Friday they lay behind a tall bank of reeds out of sight from passing ships and the crews of two vessels moored 700-m away on the opposite bank of the river. The men were even able to smoke as they relaxed before checking their gear and restowing it; each man would carry only one pack on his escape. Then, at 2100 hours, they set the limpets' time fuses to go off in nine hours, at 0600 on Saturday morning.

The canoes set out fifteen minutes later, when the moon had set. There was not much time, however, before the flood tide would turn. *Catfish* moved up the west bank, while *Crayfish* crossed to the east. But Laver and Mills found no ships on Bordeaux's eastern quays and the canoeists came back on the ebb tide to place eight limpets on the two ships opposite their last lying-up point, the 5645-tonne *Alabama* and a second ship. Whether the ships attacked were later correctly identified has not been proved, but the suggested targets tally most closely with what is known of the number of limpets laid. *Catfish* had better luck, Hasler drifting her on the flood to halfway along a line of moored ships, as Sparks got the limpets ready on their 'placing rod'. He reached this two-metre rod below the surface, as Hasler steadied the canoe enabling the corporal to make sure the mines' magnets were firmly gripping the steel hull of the 7840-tonne steamship *Tannenfels*. Three limpets were fixed to her before the canoe was drifted further upriver to an auxiliary minesweeper, *Sperrbrecher 5.* Hasler fixed two limpets to her before the tide changed and *Catfish* moved back on the ebb down the line of ships. With the canoeists crouched in their camouflage jackets and the boat's course steadied by a single paddle, they appeared like some log drifting on the tide. A sentry's torch snapped on, wavering over the length of the canoe . . . the marines stock-still in this revealing beam of light. Yet the canoe drifted on silently, beyond the beam and the sentry's attention, but the canoeists remained still for five more minutes to be sure that they had not been discovered. The ebb was beginning to run strongly as they came to an oil tanker moored outside another ship, *Dresden*, 8567 tonnes. They had to pass cautiously along the side of the tanker, for at her bows the current flowed fiercely and the canoe could have been trapped between the two hulls. At the stern there was a better opportunity to place the limpet-mines, two on *Dresden* and their last one on the 7132-tonne tanker *Portland*.

Downstream they joined *Crayfish* and began to paddle hard, caution giving way to urgency, for they must be well clear of Bordeaux by 0600. After fifteen minutes the canoes went separate ways. The major and Sparks landed that Saturday morning, apparently scuttled their canoe below the low-water mark, and successfully came out on the French Resistance's 'Pat' escape line. Their only mishap – despite some close shaves – was the loss of 'Blondie's' fine moustache, which he was obliged to shave off when one of the ladies of the escape line thought it too easily recognizable as a British appendage.

On the Friday night, meanwhile, other activities about Bordeaux had been more dramatic. Unbeknown to the others, Sergeant Sam Wallace and Marine Bob Ewart of *Coalfish* had been able to keep afloat in the maelstrom of the first overfalls, and had carried on paddling until the current forced them inshore. There they capsized in surf off the beach and were captured by an anti-aircraft gun crew. Wallace, the oldest of the Section at twenty-eight, and Ewart, at nineteen, were taken to Bordeaux for questioning, but they revealed nothing. Although their canoe had been found, Sam Wallace had probably destroyed their map, for the Germans made no extra effort to guard the ships. Both canoeists were shot about midnight that Friday. At about this time, a local resistance group were preparing to make a detailed recce of the quays. This they were completing at about 0600 when the charges – to their surprise – exploded. Four merchant ships were damaged, but the limpets on the auxiliary minesweeper possibly dropped off the ship's side. The official history of Combined Operations describes the result 'of this brilliant little operation' as a good example of the 'successful use of "limpeteers"'.

Successful as the raid was, only the ships themselves were damaged, being empty of cargo according to German reports. These also obscured for a time the true fate of the captured canoeists. Wallace and Ewart had been shot without any court martial on the orders of Admiral Bachmann, who commanded German naval forces in western France.

MacKinnon and Conway, after their canoe had sunk, successfully reached La Reole, some 50 km from the river, but were betrayed while in civilian clothes in a hospital; Laver and Mills were picked up by French police two days after the raid and handed over to the Germans. All four were shot in Paris, probably on 23 March 1943, a few weeks before Graham Hayes of the SSRF was also shot in Paris. All these deaths were at first falsely shown in the records, those of the RMBPD being described as taking place 'in harbour near Bordeaux'.

The Boom Patrol Boat

The RMBPD also made the Leros limpet-mine raid, but the majority of the 73 men in the Detachment were working on some startling developments. The Boom Patrol Boat was something more than its name implied. Before the RMBPD was formed, Hasler with two commandos had been working on the development of a captured Italian speedboat of the type that had sunk the cruiser HMS *York* off Crete in April 1941. These explosive boats, each powered by a 120-hp engine, had been launched against ships with some success, and Combined Operations Headquarters intended to develop one similar to it. Eighteen feet long, carrying over 225 kg of explosive, it could be launched from an aircraft and skim in towards its target. When certain it would hit the enemy ship, the boat's pilot bailed out: pulling a lever, he released a 'flutterboard' that fell clear of the stern to open out as a raft. Connecting the pilot to the board-raft was a buoyant line, along which he was to swim. It was not a new concept, for similar ideas had been used by the Italians in 1918 as well as in 1941. Vosper Limited, the boat builders, worked on the new hull while the Admiralty developed various firing mechanisms to explode the charge: on impact, with a bumper at the bow; by time fuse; or when it sank to a pre-set depth. This last hydrostatic fuse was for use after a small explosive charge broke the boat in two, the bow going off, they hoped, under the target ship.

Hope was perhaps the essence of these complex experiments. Canoes were only involved in recovering the Boom Patrol Boat's pilot. Difficulties in finding a really powerful light marine engine were solved with the American 140-hp Gray 'Fireball': the boat at speed on the multi-chines could then jump a harbour boom, as the outdrive through a universal joint enabled the pilot to raise the counter-rotating propellers, the boat weighing over 1.75 tonnes. In a carrier, it could be fitted under the bomb bay of a Lancaster, stern forward because the Royal Aircraft Establishment at Farnborough, Hampshire, had discovered, when working on air-dropped sea rescue dinghies, that this helped to keep a craft stable as it fell. The parachute packs were slung in the bomb bay, and after several unsuccessful drops a parachute system was evolved using three 'chutes, each 15 m in diameter. All this development work took time, however, and in December 1942 Hasler had men working on underwater swimming as an alternative method of anti-shipping attacks.

Hasler's recruits for RMBPD had originally been intended to crew the explosive boats; their canoeing was something of an afterthought, when Hasler considered that the boats might need outside help to cross the boom protecting an enemy anchorage. His second in command, Lieutenant (later Captain) J. D. Stewart, RM, was an 'HO' officer who had served with Hasler in a landing craft company in Norway in 1940. The other officers and men, 36 all ranks, he chose after two interview sessions at the RM Small Arms School, where officers were training, and at the Plymouth headquarters. The two young officers he selected were not sent to him, the colonel commandant sending Bill Pritchard-Gordon and Jack MacKinnon instead, an apparently arbitrary decision with which Hasler was later to find no fault. The men, all from Plymouth, had to be, in Hasler's order of priority: eager to engage the enemy; indifferent to their personal safety; intelligent; nimble; free from strong family ties or dependants; able to swim; and of good physique and eyesight. For a while the young officers and men trained together before they were paired in canoes and in the two specialized Sections: No. 1 in canoes, No. 2 in parachuting and the underwater swimming needed by pilots of explosive boats.

They lived during this summer of 1942 in requisitioned boarding houses whose landladies only knew that their lodgers patrolled the long boom stretching from Southsea to the Isle of Wight. On this round trip of four hours they dropped small (2-kg) depth-charges, to discourage their German counterparts from attempting to cut holes in the nets, while providing the curious with a plausible reason for having a Boom Patrol Detachment at Southsea. The landladies shared in the plunder of chickens, a welcome supplement to rations, which a nimble man could acquire without disturbing the rest of the Home Guard's brood. But one doubts if the ladies received any of the beer removed unnoticed from behind the bandstand after a swimmer had climbed the outer piles of Southsea pier. This was a climb, incidentally, that the band and others thought impossible, for wire coiled round each pile was supposed to make it unscalable.

In fact, European underwater attacks were to become the only effective seaborne way of reaching important targets afloat in harbours as, after the Bordeaux raid, the Germans tightened up their harbour defences. They had found *Conger*, lost in the estuary, 80 km to the north when it was washed ashore; they had also salvaged *Catfish* and *Crayfish* from the river. They knew something, therefore, of the methods of 'limpeteers'. A more subtle approach was needed. The midget submarine X-craft and charioteers riding torpedoes provided this but the Boom Patrol Boat never went into action. Lieutenant David Cox, RM, nevertheless made the first experimental drop on Saturday 10 June 1944 from 1500 m over the sea off Harwich.

In the darkness of the bomb bay, Cox clambered into the boat, fixing a triphibious complex of harnesses over his underwater swimming suit. One harness clipped him to the explosive boat, while a second held his reserve parachute – although there seemed little chance to use it if the boat plunged into the sea. The system of electrical releases, tested by warning lights, proved correctly set. Then with a '5, 4, 3, 2, 1 . . . Now!' over the intercom, the boat dropped clear of the bomber into daylight. As the pilot 'chute opened, the boat shuddered and the stern swung upwards. She was dropping vertically when, seconds later, there was a violent jerk. Cox needed all the grip in his cold, bare hands and the harness to hold him in the boat. Then the second and third 'chutes opened more gently and the boat floated on even keel. One ominous 'crack' above his head made him aware there was still the chance of the parachutes breaking free, but they held, landing the boat without too much of a splash. Water slopped into her, however, and on the choppy sea he was unable to run her at her potential 30 knots.

The Boom Patrol Boats were stood-to for several operations but never dropped, one raid against ships in Bergen, Norway, being cancelled finally in February 1945 when German smokescreens successfully hid the U-boats in the harbour. A second of RMBPD's developments, the submersible 'Sleeping Beauty', proved equally frustrating. Yet such experimental work provided a strand in the history of SBS roles which they cherish today.

The 'Sleeping Beauty'

The first operational 'Sleeping Beauty' was delivered to RMBPD in Southsea in July 1943, and by mid-1944 some twenty Mark II craft had been built. These were the type used by Lieutenant-Colonel Ivan Lyon in his second raid on Singapore, Operation 'Rimau'. The craft, however, had only a range of 20 km submerged, although at 4.5 knots on the surface they could cover three times this distance. They had therefore to be taken to within 7 to 10 km of their targets. They were such good sea boats that they could ride through the 2- to 3-m waves of a Force 5 blow, according to one report. But they were never used in training in anything stronger than Force 4 winds and operationally their use was restricted to raids in conditions not exceeding Force 3. Yet this craft was relatively short at 4.20 m with the pilot-swimmer being comfortably seated aft. When under power the craft made less disturbance than one being paddled. Under the water she would be small enough to be almost as invisible to sonar sweeps as to the naked eye on the surface, where her low silhouette and small size should enable the pilot to get reasonably near to his target before diving. Then, at 10 m below the surface for normal cruising, he could make about 6 km an hour; in the confined area of a harbour he would edge his way at much slower speeds.

The pilot, secured in the cockpit, his chin level with the cockpit coaming, would lay back in the way the grand prix racing driver does in the 1980s. His feet stretched forward, fingers round the hand grips each side of the joystick, as he eased it forward when the craft began to flood, until the air pressure in the buoyancy tanks equalled the surrounding water pressure to give the canoe neutral buoyancy. The trim tank in the bow was partly filled with water by a couple of pumps of the handle by his left hip, and as the engine started – hopefully at the turn of the switch – the 'Sleeping Beauty' nosed gently under the sea. In the Far East, daylight penetrated the sea to some 7 m or more, but once the depth gauge of the panel behind the joystick read thirty feet the natural light was dim. Should the current force the bow further down, even though a pull on the joystick set the hydroplanes to raise the craft's trim, the pilot would use a 'puff of high pressure air' to increase the buoyancy. With the craft steadied now on even keel, the speed could be increased. Once outside the enemy harbour, the raider would plan to bring the canoe near his target ship and, with a line to a magnetic clamp fixed to her bilge keel, he could move beside the ship and place his limpets without losing contact with the canoe.

When he calculated he was near the harbour entrance, he would cut the engine speed, easing back the joystick before briefly opening the ballast tanks' air valves. He controlled these with his thumbs, keeping down the rate at which compressed air was allowed to enter the tanks in order to minimize any sudden bubbling cauldron of water disturbing the surface. With some practice he would be able to do this so neatly that even a sea bird would not be disturbed as he surfaced. He could even porpoise to catch a brief glimpse of his bearings.

It proved 'hair raising in the extreme, stooging about half submerged in the heavy swell off Luma Voe'. The cold here in the waters around the Shetland Islands was intense in the winter of 1944–5, when Hurst's MSC Section of marines was practising attacks. Their projected raid against U-boats in Norway gave an edge to their training: Lieutenant Stan Hurst, Sergeant 'Taff' Evans and Corporal Jock Marriott had even loaded their craft and the two intermediate carriers in HMS *Minna* ready to sail for Flekkefjord on the day the raid was finally abandoned. Their intermediate carriers were a group of the specially designed Mobile Flotation Units commanded by one of the officers who had a major hand in SBS developments, Lieutenant-Commander G. C. S. Montanaro, DSO, RN (formerly a major in the Royal Engineers).

Since they began experimenting with their explosive Boom Patrol Boats and the 'Sleeping Beauties', they had been training hard for various operations. Hasler had found that he needed a small carrier boat to take his canoes inshore and had developed the 'Country' craft, officially an 'Intermediate Carrier'. Launched from a destroyer's davits, this adapted 25-foot naval cutter could make 6 knots on her silently running diesel engines; with a range of over 600 km, she could carry two Cockle canoes. Her low silhouette and pink-grey camouflage made her virtually invisible to the naked eye at 8 km. But the ten 'Country' craft with which the RMBPD trained in the spring of 1944 did not go to the Far East. Nor did the air-dropped container codenamed 'Suitcase', which was considered impractical by the Canoe Committee of Combined Operations HQ. Throughout the later years of the war, this body of specialists had provided a means for all combined operations small units to exchange information on canoes and their development.

During the formation and early operations of RMBPD they were part of Combined Operations, but in June 1944 they were placed under the Admiralty's Director of Operations and moved to Teignmouth. (Later, to get ahead of our story, they moved to Appledore and the tri-service training and experimental wing of Combined Operations, later known as Amphibious Operations commanded from a headquarters in London.) The Admiralty planned to use the Detachment's section of 'Sleeping Beauties' (or Motor Submersible Canoes, as the Admiralty referred to them) against the new Type XXI U-boat, a fast 1600-tonne craft with a Schnorkel that enabled it to remain submerged for long periods. But the Director of the Admiralty's Anti-U-boat Division cancelled the operation, for in the appalling winter weather of 1944 the MSCs would not have been able to travel submerged that October the distances required.

A plan to drop canoes into the Etang Biscarrosse lake 75 km southwest of Bordeaux presented difficulties, for the modified 'Suitcase' containers, now designed to carry a single canoe, were likely to drift into the pine woods surrounding the lake. Nevertheless, the four Luftwaffe Viking 222 aircraft based there, the largest flying boats used in the Second World War, made a tempting target. For this operation, the Detachment had the Matarrasinno inflatable paddle 'board' made by the Dunlop Rubber Company. This little mattress folded into a 46 × 25 × 15 cm package weighing about 22 kg but it needed some modification for the RMBPD – including an air bottle for inflation 'to 5 × 2 feet', and separate compartments for limpet-mines and the civilian clothes that the raiders would wear for their overland escape into Spain. The idea worked well in trials. The small kit-bag of mattress, limpets and other equipment hung by a quick-release line from the parachutist's waist, and he lowered it just before landing. Thus he had his craft with him straight away, a more certain way of mounting a raid from pine woods than having to search for his craft. 'Suitcase' containers, with their extra-large parachutes, might have drifted quite a way off course, and would then have to be humped to the water's edge. The Matarrasinno-type raft was easily carried. However, before sufficient of these could be delivered to RMBPD, the Germans moved their four long-range sea reconnaissance aircraft to Norway. This was the second disappointing operation, abandoned as was the Boom Patrol Boats' Norwegian raid. Nor, as has been mentioned, were the Boom Patrol boats used, although six of the Dam-Busting 617 Bomber Squadron's Lancasters had been modified to carry the explosive boats. Royal Marine swimmer-canoeists, however, were to find better hunting in the Far East.

7 The War Canoes

The War against the Japanese

The warm waters of Singapore harbour stank of diesel oil, garbage and the flotsam of rubbish drifting down from junks moored at the head of the harbour. On the soft night air, the spicy smells from galley fires were scented by two canoeists from time to time, as their adrenalin sharpened every sense. They had heard the distant hiss and clang of a steam crane working on the far side of the harbour, a bustle of shunting engines and other harbour night noises; the swish of some picket boat's wash along the quay walls; the steaming roar of sewage outflows. But here under the towering side of a cargo ship, the gurgle and splash of her generator's cooling water drowned out all other noises in the canoeists' concentration. This waterfall amidships gave some guide to her size, as Ivan Lyon leant gently over the canoe's side to place the first of his limpet-mines. He and his paddler worked methodically, easing the craft along the ship's side, pausing to listen in case the men chatting on the quay should be moving from whatever it was that absorbed their attention.

Silhouetted against the starglow they must have seen the squat figure of a sentry on the outer harbour wall, his long bayonet distinctly Japanese; but he did not notice their canoe, nor the other that was in the harbour that night. Both of these had set out at dark from *Kwike*, a specially equipped fishing junk, and now they were steering for the creek where she lay, hidden behind an island. This trading junk had sailed to the Riau archipelago from the South China Sea, carrying Major (later Lieutenant-Colonel) Ivan Lyon, Gordon Highlanders, with three Australian canoeists in September 1943. On this raid, 'Jaywick', they succeeded in sinking over 37,000 tonnes of Japanese shipping in the busy port of Singapore, making their way back without being detected by Japanese patrol boats. The Riau archipalego's many islands, of which Singapore itself could be said to be the most northerly, provided a legion of creeks and backwaters to hide in – especially for one trading junk among the several thousand on these waters between the southern tip of Malaya and Sumatra.

Kwike rendezvoused with an escort after sailing over 1500 km through Japanese-patrolled waters, to return to her base in Exmouth Sound on the northern coast of Western Australia. From there Lyon flew down to Melbourne to report to the Australian Intelligence Bureaux (AIB). This joint American-Australian clandestine service was primarily concerned with intelligence collected for General MacArthur's forces advancing into the Pacific islands. As MacArthur would not allow OSS agents into his theatre of operations, AIB filled this gap with coast-watchers (an organization first proposed in 1919) and a series of other agents throughout the islands. They also had responsibility for weakening the Japanese where 'practical by sabotage and destruction . . . [damaging their] morale . . . and rendering aid to local efforts in [sic] the same end in enemy-occupied territories', according to the order establishing AIB on 6 July 1942.

MSCs to Singapore

Ivan Lyon of SOE's Force 136, which was organizing clandestine resistance forces, joined AIB after reaching Australia from Singapore. There, as a keen yachtsman, he had made recces of possible island hideouts before the Japanese invaded Malaya, and after the success of 'Jaywick' he formed a larger team of swimmers known as Group X. This had no connection with the SB Sections then operating or Jellicoe's Squadrons, and the modern SBS claim no direct line of descent from Group X. These canoeists from

Australia nevertheless included Major M. J. Ingleton, RM, who (in the versatile way of Royal Marines) had served in the tanks of the RM Armoured Support Regiments, before going to Australia as a swimmer-canoeist.

While in London after 'Jaywick', Lyon had contacted Combined Operations HQ, and they had provided him with fifteen submersible canoes, the same craft that had been developed by Lieutenant-Colonel Hasler of RMBPD. SOE's Sub-Lieutenant Riggs, RNVR, trained in these canoes with RMBPD before taking the craft to Australia where Lyon prepared for his second raid on Singapore.

Lyon set out from Fremantle in Western Australia aboard the minelaying submarine *Porpoise* on 11 September 1944 with 'Sleeping Beauties' stowed 'in place of her reload salvoes of torpedoes', her 32 swimmers of Group X and their back-up team bringing the total aboard to 96 men. In less than two weeks they were off Pulo Merepas, an island near Singapore, making a periscope recce of the beach as they circled the island 1 to 2 km offshore. They saw only monkeys, and Lyon and the skipper were satisfied that the island was deserted. That night, 23 September, a recce party confirmed by 2100 hours that the island would make an ideal secret base, so *Porpoise* closed to 400 m to launch her assault boats. These Coatley-type canvas craft, which had been stowed flat on the after casing as exterior cargo, landed all their stores for a month's stay. The canoes were launched by tackle from the submarine's Samson post, a simple derrick. During this operation, the submariners complained: 'The soldiers could not be made to realize the need for haste with *Porpoise* close inshore.' When she had landed all their gear and stores, she went in search of a junk to use as a canoe carrier – and a desperately long search it turned out to be, for as she cruised submerged along the ten-fathom line in sea 'the colour of tea' junks headed inshore, until she was able to catch one with no sails set on the fifth day, 28 September. This fine-looking white junk was at anchor when the submarine surfaced: men of Group X seized her and prepared to sail her from the east Malayan coast to their secret island. One difficulty was that this trading junk with her crew of nine Malays had no engine; another, one suspects, was her rather striking appearance among the humbler craft in these waters. They did not get far, for she was called on by a Malay coast patrol boat to heave-to off Pulo Sambol, some 20 km from Singapore. The raiders barely had time to ditch their precious secret cargo over the side before taking to inflatables, four parties getting away before the patrol came alongside. In the next few weeks they played a fatal game of hide-and-seek among the islands, for when the Malay patrol reported their interception of the white junk Japanese search parties were sent out to comb the islands.

Ivan Lyon and some of his men were laying up on one island, not long after abandoning the junk, when one of these Japanese patrols came ashore. The canoeists fought them off, apparently making their escape, for they were due to rendezvous with the submarine *Tantalus* early in November after more than a month of island hopping. But they never made that rendezvous. On 4 November – Japanese published records suggest – they were surrounded; several men, including Lyon, were killed, and nine captured. Then official records from Japanese sources, published after the Second World War, suggested that the men died in heroic circumstances, showing 'a valorous spirit' reminding their executioners of men of their Naval Special Attack Corps who attempted similar raids against Australian ports. One survivor reached Timor, an island over 3200 km from Singapore and the most southerly island in modern Indonesia, nearest to Australia. The emaciated officer was struggling to disentangle his inflatable from beach obstacles when he was picked up by Japanese soldiers. Enquiries in the 1980s have unearthed some mysteries. What is clear is that the court records of a Japanese court martial on 5 July 1945, sentencing ten canoeists to death, is phoney. It was written to conceal the war crimes of the general who ordered the execution. There is no doubt that all ten men were executed; but some sources have suggested this took place

The Far East Theatre of Operations during the Second World War

0 km 100 200 300 400 500

INDIA

CHINA

Chittagong
Chin Hills
Tek Naf
River Chindwin
Mandalay
River Irrawaddy
A R A K A N
An Pass
BURMA
RAMREE ISLAND
CHEDUBA ISLAND
Myanaung
River Salween
Sittang
Bassein
Rangoon
BILUGYN ISLAND

FRENCH INDO-CHINA

Hanoi
GULF OF TONKIN

SIAM

ANDAMAN ISLANDS

BAY OF BENGAL

NICOBAR ISLANDS
KAMORTA ISLAND

GULF OF SIAM

SARANG ISLAND

PHUKET ISLAND

PENANG ISLAND
PALAU RAWI ISLAND

Ipoh
P E R A K
MALAYA
Moro Beaches
Highlands
Kuala Lumpur
Port Dickson
Labuan Biki
Malacca
MALACCA STRAITS
Singapore

SUMATRA

BORNEO

© Arms and Armour Press, 1983.

after the canoeists entered Singapore. The truth may never conclusively be proved, yet a nagging thought is that if there was time to ditch the 'Sleeping Beauties' there might also have been time to launch one or two of them. For if – as Japanese reports relate – the white junk was waiting near Singapore, then the craft would certainly have been camouflaged on deck ready for launching.

Did Lyon and the other swimmers get their explosives under Japanese ships? There is a possibility that they did. Yet hastily fused limpets; or possibly an unexpected fall in the density of some warmer patch of water causing a submersible canoe to dive out of control beyond say 20 m; or the difficulties of slipping unnoticed over boom nets, if not in a canoe below them – all or any of these would have taken their toll of these canoeists. The only thing we know for certain is that the Japanese caught them several weeks after the capture of the white junk.

The Small Operations Group

The war in Europe was moving towards victory, but since the autumn of 1943 the main planning effort of Combined Operations Headquarters had been directed against Japan. SB Sections as Groups A, B and C of 72 all ranks had been in the Far East since the summer of 1944 and COPPs 1, 3, 4, 5, 7 – the first to reach India, October 1944 – 8, 9 and 10 all served there. The SB Squadrons, as part of the SAS Brigade, were training for operations in the Far East when the war ended there in August.

Group X was not replaced in southeast Asia, in part because a number of canoe recce and raiding units were sent there from Europe. It had always been difficult to coordinate the various operations of small raiding parties. Those on behalf of the Secret Services, such as collecting agents and delivering clandestine stores, tended to be carried out in such secrecy that even senior officers in other forces knew nothing of them. SOE, although not by 1943 as directly involved in cloak-and-dagger jobs as the British secret service MI6, also had their own sea and air routes in and out of enemy-occupied territory: through these they raised and supplied resistance forces in Europe and Asia. Their American counterparts, OSS, fulfilled three roles: the equivalent of those of both SOE and MI6, as well as uniformed raiding forces for small-scale operations. When Admiral Lord Louis Mountbatten was Chief of Combined Operations in Europe he well knew these problems, and on his appointment in the summer of 1943 as Supreme Commander in southeast Asia he organized the formation of a small headquarters to command all the SBS, COPP and similar small units in the theatre.

This Small Operations Group (SOG), formally established on 12 June 1944, was commanded by Colonel (later Major-General) H. T. Tollemache, a Royal Marine officer with long experience of the operations in the Far East, having served there (among several Far East tours) as a young company officer with the 12th RM Battalion in the Shanghai Defence Force of 1927.

One of the first of the 174 operations by units of SOG was mounted by COPP 7. In the Far East much less was known of the conditions on beaches along the millions of miles of coastline than in the European theatre. There were no guidebooks, no coastal pilot handbooks, no statistics on weather patterns – all of which the planners had used to choose possible invasion beachheads in Europe. Such holiday snaps as could be traced showed beaches near Singapore or other cities (whereas some 100,000 family albums had revealed much about French beaches). The Allies, therefore, expected much of their canoeists. When COPP 7 arrived in India they were expecting to work over great distances, their senior officer, Lieutenant (later Admiral) Geoffrey Hall, RN, and his second in command, Lieutenant Ruari McLean, RNVR, being experienced navigators turned swimmer-canoeists. They operated from the Royal Navy's advanced base at Tek Naf, near what was then the Burma/India frontier. They had made this passage from Ceylon in destroyers before transferring to MTBs, although destroyers or MLs would also take teams to beach areas, where they would sometimes land from surf dories instead of canoes. The 7-m-long surf boat followed a West African design with a high lifting bow and stern. It could land over 2 tonnes of stores. It was powered, but it could also be rowed by its crew of a coxswain and four men, with long tapering oars in rowlocks designed to prevent an oar being forced back through their narrow tapering jaws as the boat hit a 'roller'. The seas at times lifted a boat so steeply that she filled before men leaving a beach could get aboard. Such great seas, building up over the Bay of Bengal, broke over the beaches of the Arakan, that strip of Burma's western coast with jungle-clad hills stretching eastward to the yellow waters of the River Irrawaddy.

COPP 7 made this first recce to these beaches in October, Geoff Hall and his paddler steering a course from their MTB with the help of only a few rough notes on Hall's lapboard. He knew the calculated distance the inshore current would carry him northward, and allowed for this as he told his paddler to count the strokes, a thousand of which would drive the canoe some 700 m. Checking his bearings in the starglow, making the mental calculations for the extra distance a stronger than expected current was setting them northward, Hall guided the canoe to a point outside the roaring surf where it lay for some minutes, being lifted the height of a man or more as the waves rolled past it. Then, having made sure they were opposite the beach to be recced, Hall went over the side and into the water to swim through the surf.

His light tropical swimmer's suit, with its inflatable stole and kapok belt, protected his knees and elbows as he was flung against the beach, despite his efforts to surge in on a large curving wave. Nevertheless, he had pegged in the 'beach gradient line', a fishing line with a breaking strain of 55 kg, and had reeled this out, counting the lead pellets fixed every fathom along its length, provided they had not slipped as he waded back into the surf. The line reeled on out from the drum at his waist while he struggled to keep his feet. There appears to have been no false shoreline shoal, but trying to drop his other line in these waters needed a contortionist's skills. In smooth water he would have plumbed the depth at regular intervals of four or five fathoms from the shore, more frequently if necessary, using a lead weight dropped on an eighteen-foot line shotted at every foot. It was a difficult enough drill, swimming on your back as you paid out the reeled line with your left hand and counted the feet of plumb-line lowered by the right hand; in surging surf it proved impossible. Hall had been struggling now for perhaps ten minutes after being knocked off his feet and rolled in a tangle of lines. He flashed his waterproof torch to Ruari McLean in a second canoe, but before this sos could be seen, Hall was losing consciousness. The more he struggled to free himself, the tighter the lines became round his legs and, although he was in deeper water now, the tangle prevented him from swimming. He went under before McLean, swimming in search of his skipper, saw the torch glow and pulled Hall back to the canoes. COPP 7 would make several other recces, but like the bomber crews of Second World War (as Clogstoun-Willmott has pointed out), they only did a tour of operations before they had to be relieved, or the strain of continued operations would exhaust their efficiency: at that point they would almost certainly get careless, and be drowned or captured. COPP 7 returned to the UK from where four months later they were sent at short notice to Germany to recce the Elbe for a crossing by 1 Commando Brigade.

Other teams working on rivers came from the Sea Reconnaissance Unit (SRU), trained paradoxically to cover great distances at sea. Their Canadian founder and commander, Lieutenant-Commander Bruce Wright, RCNVR, had been a swimmer of Olympic standard. He was to develop his idea of assault swimmers after recalling an article on the Californian divers who went down, without breathing equipment, for the edible abalone. In a series of papers he drew Lord Mountbatten's attention to the value of such swimmers, later pointing out: 'Japanese swimmers in Burma [in December 1941] were used in several hundreds at a time . . . and the Italians [by 1942] were training 2000 of them at La Spezia in the Gulf of Genoa.' During early 1943 he was attached to the RMBPD at Southsea, joining in the Eastney Officers' Mess party the night news came that Hasler and Sparks had reached Spain.

Wright considered the men of RMBPD 'tough but scrawny', lacking the broad shoulders of the Californian divers, so he recruited his own four teams from all three British and Commonwealth services. Each team of an officer and nine or ten men was taught to use the special paddle-boards, which were to be their means of insertion on to an enemy coast. These were in effect enlarged surf-boards, with a gentle upward curve towards their snub-nosed bows. The swimmer, lying towards the back of the board, propelled the craft with steady overarm strokes, a shaped paddle not unlike an artist's small pallet strapped to each hand. He would follow a course by the compass inset in the board, and could cover 30 km or more, having parachuted with his board to a point some distance from his targets. These were to be first in the Aegean, then in the Adriatic, the Black Sea and the Danube; but all the raids were cancelled, in part because SRU teams had many failures with their underwater breathing apparatus, in its infancy in 1943.

Yet Wright's enthusiasm was not to be wasted. His single-window American diving mask was an innovation to the British swimmers, as were the extra-long fins he had made to a Californian pattern. The marines taught him to use Davis Submerged Escape Apparatus for underwater swimming, and the intricacies of their swimwear, with a urination valve fitted in the crutch. (This last was not without problems if 'the-man-you-joined-with' had sunk into the warmth of your body; the answer was to have him conveniently taped to the valve.) More sophisticated was the Welburn propulsion unit strapped to the paddle-board, its 5-cm propeller driven by a totally enclosed motor with batteries to help a swimmer and reducing his silhouette even further, for it could drive the board without any assistance from hand paddles. This power unit could be jettisoned in emergencies, but does not appear to have been put to the test operationally, for on the Irrawaddy in February 1945 simple techniques were needed. In the pre-monsoon heat, on the night of Saturday/Sunday 10/11 February 1945, No. 1 Section had their boards carried into the jungle no-man's-land, a difficult lift for the porters from units of 20 Indian Division, who had to leave the SRU team nearly 5 km short of their laying-up position.

The Burma teak forests give way to a so-called drier zone where the Chindwin joins the Irrawaddy, but the river banks are relatively cool. Throughout Sunday, No. 1 Section appear to have been reasonably comfortable, despite the frequent alerts from birds' shrieks or the chatter of monkeys which might have been warnings of Japanese patrols. Then, after the quick tropical nightfall, the swimmers slid silently down into the water of a back creek; there would be little a Japanese sentry might see, despite the paddlers having to breast the 6-knot current. They recced a narrow beach where the Indian Division would land near Myinmu, and subsequently several other points along 200 km of river. On the night of the main crossing a few weeks later, SRU swimmers guided in the lead assault boats at the four landing sites selected from those recced. Three teams of these swimmers were later to work with COPP parties on the Arakan coast near the An Pass.

COPP 8, led by Lieutenant Freddy Ponsonby, RN, had joined '7' in India, and lost Lieutenant Michael Peacock, RNVR, in a recce to the Elizabeth Islands. Although racked with dysentery, the young lieutenant had been determined to go on that recce on the night of 1/2 November 1944. Having seen others in the party shot at on the beach, Peacock had swum clear of trouble, but weakened by his condition he lost consciousness and was only saved from drowning by the buoyancy of his suit, which kept him afloat. When he came to, it was 0400 hours and there was no sign of his or any other canoe. He therefore swam ashore, and had been trying to find a way of getting back to Tek Naf by sampan when he was discovered by three islanders. The letters he had carefully carried in a waterproof bag proved unavailing: either these islanders did not speak the various dialects in which the offers of reward were made for his safe return, or more probably they could not read. He was handed over to the Japanese but through determination survived their harsh prison routines.

About this time the knowing voice of 'Tokyo Rose', the American-speaking Japanese radio announcer, made much of the capture of British 'war canoes'. Just which canoes these were has not been established, but several SOG units had been active since the last months of 1944. SBS canoeists had reached India that summer, with three Groups joining SOG in Ceylon: initially 'A' of seven officers only; 'B' with four officers and 32 other ranks; and 'C' with sixteen men. In their first raid on 11 September, teams demolished the bridge over the River Peudada in northern Sumatra, cutting the coast road at one point, but other teams failed to find their target bridge. Group 'A' spent November and December in recces of the River Chindwin, which flows from the foothills of the great range of mountains on the Chinese border south to join the Irrawaddy 600 km north of Rangoon. The British Fourteenth Army would fight its way down these rivers in 1945, and in the winter there were operations to prepare for this advance. Many patrols by local hill tribesmen, Chins led by British officers, went behind the Japanese front at this time. Group 'A' and other SOG units worked with them, as did Group 'B' taking over from 'A' in January 1945.

The canoe teams of Group 'C' on the Arakan coast, under the command of 26 Indian Division, landed among the mangroves of Ramree Island (300 km south of Tek Naf). In their fourth recce raid, landing on the small Law's Island off this coast, they spent several days ashore establishing contact with the local fishermen, while the Japanese prepared to evacuate Ramree. Eight weeks later they were making recces of the River Irrawaddy crossings, as was COPP 9 – until the monsoon rains made the river currents too strong for even COPP swimmers. Before then they had some almost amusing adventures, spending one afternoon in a submarine trapped on the bottom of a Sumatran harbour, but Japanese attempts to drop small charges on the submarine failed to damage her. Some weeks later Lieutenant-Commander Geoff Lyne, RN, having clambered ashore on one river jetty, was startled to find a platoon of Japanese in positions ready to defend it. He and his teams made off under cover of the steep bank, to paddle further downstream before crossing to the Allied bank, despite the fusillade of shots fired after them.

Some weeks before SOG had been formed, 'Blondie' Hasler had arrived in Hemmenheil Camp on the northwest tip of Ceylon to train marine canoeists. The 112 men became operational with SOG in February 1945. Known, for security reasons, by the somewhat nondescript title of Detachment 385, the marines' training had included parachute jumps, and as para-canoeists they have a direct line of descent to the modern SBS. A few volunteers had already landed on Cheduba Island that January, when 500 marines from the East Indies Fleet seized this island off the Arakan coast. One of the Detachment's first independent operations was to Bilugyn Island in the estuary of the River Salween some 80 km east of Rangoon. A desolate stretch of mudbanks (fringed with the inevitable mangroves), this island had sufficient firm ground for a possible airstrip; the purpose of the raid was to *suggest* that it had been surveyed for this. Such deceptions here, in the Andaman Islands, 700 km southwest of the Salween, further afield in the Nicobar Islands and Sumatra, would all help to spread the Japanese garrisons more thinly.

A team from No. 1 Troop of '385' led by Captain James F. T. Steele, RM, flew from Ceylon in a Catalina flying-boat staging on the Burma coast. The aircraft had a platform fitted above her hull, and when it put down off the island a 'Y'-type inflatable was made ready by carbon dioxide in under five minutes. (A 'YS', however, may have been used, a similar dinghy but inflated by compressed air.) The gas connections were detached from the two chambers, the floorboards fitted, and Jimmy Steele with three others paddled for the shore. It was dark but not rough as the Catalina took off at just after 2100 hours. The flying boat came back at 0400 hours next morning to make a rendezvous with the inflatable, after the raiders had been ashore for the best part of seven hours. As the pilot skimmed low in his approach to a landing, signal lights near the shore abruptly went out. No reason for this has been traced, but the tide was flooding fast at the time the aircraft landed and the team had probably been signalling from a mudbank. The three-ply fabric of this Second World War inflatable was not as tough as the 'rubberized' skin of a modern Gemini, while the Y-type boat was much lighter in construction than the Army's Intruder inflatable. Possibly, therefore, the buoyancy bags had been holed. Enquiries at the time concluded that all four men had been washed off a mudbank and drowned. Knowing Jimmy Steele, the accident or events – whatever they were – must have been catastrophic for him not to have brought his party out.

'385' was dogged by misfortune that month, for they had more difficulties on the night of 22/23 February, when eight swimmers were landed on the Bassein coast of western Burma, south of the Arakan. They were led by Major Duncan Johnston, RM, who two years earlier had formed Force Viper, with 107 picked marines (mostly coast-artillery gunners) and in ten weeks had fought a long and bloody series of river and shore actions from launches on the Irrawaddy and Chindwin rivers. So he had plenty of experience, as the Royal Marines' motto says, *per mare, per terram* (by sea, by land). His intention this February night on Operation 'Attempt' was to seize the headman of the coast village of Nga Yokkaung and if possible a Japanese soldier from the coast garrison. An officer of the clandestine Force V and an interpreter went with the marines, hoping that the headman could be persuaded to come out voluntarily along with one or two of his villagers.

But there were to be problems from the start. The surf-dory was launched and loaded from HMAS *Plinjor* (ML415) about 2.5 km from the beach, but her engine seized and she had to be rowed to the shore, where the patrol landed. In their eagerness they left the rucksacks of emergency rations in the boat, but 'in good visibility these were recovered by wild gesticulations', the boat's crew bringing her back to the landing point. Not only did the packs contain rations, but also water, escape maps, compasses, air recognition silhouettes of aircraft and medical supplies. This hullabaloo and the fact that the boat had not moved off immediately to her laying-up position at the mouth of the mangrove swamp, no doubt alerted some Japanese defence posts further west on a small headland. At the time the marines did not know this, as they waded through the swamp to a jungle path leading to a dozen mat huts. With Johnston leading, the file stopped every few minutes to listen and observe until, some 800 m down the track, a single shot rang out from near the boat.

The major, suspecting an ambush, led them back towards their landing point. As they came clear of some mangroves near the village, two Japanese light machine guns opened fire on them. To avoid this fire, Johnston led his men south, crossing a deeper part of the swamp with the intention of using the sparse cover below other Japanese positions to hide their movement back to the boat. Some men did not realize how deep the water was, crossing it only with a struggle as they had not inflated their life jackets. Corporal Smith was drowned when swept by the tidal current off the steeply shelving side of one channel; attempts to find his body failed, but several were made despite the Japanese fire, while the other marines got across the swamp to a position 200 m south of the boat. At first they moved cautiously along the water's edge, the major again leading. He had not gone far when he was killed by another burst of LMG fire.

The raiders went to ground. Lieutenant Peter Waugh, RM, with Force V's Major Ferguson then organized them in a series of individual dashes for the boat. No one was hit and they brought the major's body with them, although the boat was under fire. They had to wade, pushing the dory ahead of them until they were out of their depth but clear of the headland. A prearranged Verey light signal was now fired – in theory this would bring down 40-mm Bofors rounds from the ML on the point below the falling flare. But because of damp cartridges the light fell closer to the dory than to the enemy on the point, bringing Bofors shells 'whizzing just over our heads'. The Japanese, not wanting to reveal their positions, ceased firing long enough for the swimmers to clamber aboard the dory. Lying flat, they began paddling out towards the ML, from which a second dory came to tow out the surf-boat. But this second and smaller dory missed her way and was also fired on. Both paddled and rowed, reaching the ML at 0130. Once alongside, the surf-boat was found to have many bullet holes in its moulded marine-ply hull and chunks of metal knocked off the engine, so she was scuttled, the recalcitrant engine being first taken aboard the ML for later examination.

Phuket Island

Japanese garrisons, as this raid had proved, were watchful if none too accurate in their small-arms fire. The alert sentry is the swimmer's most dangerous enemy, and in putting ashore either 'snatch' or 'jitter' parties there were more risks than in recces. And, while the raiders kept the Japanese garrisons jittery, this also militated against possibilities of COPP or other recce parties getting ashore undiscovered – a chance made doubly dicey when several parties were to work in the relatively small area of Phuket Island, off the north Malayan coast. It has a good number of fishing villages around its coast, many tracks and only a few low hills to the north, and was in no way a remote corner of the Japanese empire. Yet in March 1945 two raids, 'Baboon' by a reinforced team from COPP 3, and 'Copyright' by '385', were sent to land on the island.

The teams were led by Major Ian Mackenzie, Royal Engineers, who had guided in the DD-swimming tanks of 13/18 Hussars to the Normandy beaches on 6 June 1944. For the recces he had two RAF officers in his party. These airfield surveyors would check the suitability of several possible sites for use when Fourteenth Army had advanced into Malaya. Alex Hughes's COPP 3 parties would check the beach at points for the landing that the planners intended would capture the island in order to establish these airstrips. The COPP party, aboard HMS *Torbay*, reached the island on 8 March after a 1900-km voyage, making a periscope recce of the north coast where the Papra channel cuts the island from the mainland. At some points, this stretch of water is only 800 m wide. Alex Hughes, who commanded COPP 3, noted a number of tents on the island's beach, the usual native huts and no doubt a few of those quaint jetties with 'sentry' boxes, which were the Japanese coast garrisons' usual form of lavatory over tide-washed sands.

That night, Thursday, a day ahead of the planned landing, Hughes and his paddler were launched from the submarine and went inshore, accompanied by a three-man canoe (a Mark II** with the centre cockpit cover replaced by a paddler's canopy, no doubt, and still able to carry three-sevenths of the normal 160-kg load carried with two men). In this were Flight-Lieutenant Guthrie, RAF, with two Royal Engineers, Captain Johns and Sergeant Camidge. A third canoe carried the Canadian Captain Alcock and his paddler of COPP 3. All three craft reached the beach, but COPP 3 lost touch with the three-man canoe. Navigation and other lights had shown that the Japanese were passing coastal convoys through the channel, and there were barges off-loading at what appeared to be a temporary wharf. The submarine waited as long as her skipper thought prudent, perhaps even a little longer, before moving out into deep water after taking the COPPists aboard. There was no sign of the Sappers and the flight-lieutenant.

While *Torbay* lay off the northern coast that Friday, her sister submarine HMS *Thrasher* was off the west coast. The previous day she had made her periscope recces, taking photographs through the periscope; and Major John Maxwell, RM, made sketches of the intended landing point, as did Ian Mackenzie, who was in overall charge of both submarines' landing parties. He had learnt by radio that Alex Hughes intended to advance his 'Baboon' landings by twenty-four hours, but the major did not change the plan for 'Copyright'. He and the other officers agreed that the early moonrise on Thursday could hamper the submarine when she came in to rendezvous later that night. They would also have to hurry their preparation, while a night recce that Thursday/Friday would possibly reveal more than had been seen by day. As it turned out, they were able that night to plot the position of shore lights, apparently from two camps, and other signs of habitation largely screened from the sea during the day by trees, not to mention barges' and other navigation lights.

On Friday night, therefore, two parties were landing: Alex Hughes and Captain Alcock with their paddlers looking for the Sappers; and Mackenzie with Marine B. P. Brownlie and two other canoes. The conditions were perfect, 'almost dead flat, no swell and clear visibility', although in the distance there were dark storm clouds and flashes of lightning until about midnight. Mackenzie had the canoes on the submarine's casing by 1910 that evening, when she was 5 km off the beach where the teams were to land near Goh Gavia rocks. In the next few minutes all the canoes were loaded and ready to float off, as *Thrasher* trimmed down, making a low silhouette as she moved inshore. She stopped a kilometre and a half west of the rocks, launching the canoes at 1955 hours. They took about ten minutes to form up in a small company behind John Maxwell's craft, in which Corporal R. A. Atkinson was the paddler. (This is not to say that the major was being 'chauffeur'-driven, for he also paddled; but the number two in the boat was usually there to act as the chief muscle power and as guard for his 'swimmer' when inshore.) Ian Mackenzie with Marine Brownlie were in the second canoe, and Flight-Lieutenant Bertie Brown, RAF, with Colour-Sergeant E. C. Smith in the third. The submarine remained inshore until midnight 'in case the landing party encountered opposition', but as no one returned she sailed for deeper water.

No lights were showing near the coast as the canoes came in – an ominous sign. After safely reaching the shore, all three canoes were carefully cached behind the beach among some trees. By daylight, Mackenzie with the RAF officer and Colour-Sergeant Smith went inland to survey a possible site for a landing strip. They saw a number of villagers at a distance, but their presence did not deter the raiders from gathering soil samples or from checking the detailed contours of this, the first site of two to be surveyed. The three men lay up that night, sure that their movements had not attracted attention. What they did not know was that the operation had already gone badly wrong.

The seeds of disaster had been sown on that Thursday night, after the three-man canoe had separated from the pair of two-man Cockles. The Sappers' boat had capsized. The craft's buoyancy bags kept her afloat, but it was an exhausting task for the three men as they tried desperately to push the canoe, by now waterlogged, towards the shore. Their resolve was stiffened by the certain knowledge that should the canoe be washed ashore the whole operation would be placed in jeopardy. At last, they reached the shore. After dragging their load up the beach, wearily they set about hiding it among some bushes. Physically and mentally drained by their exertions, the three had few reserves with which to counter the Japanese patrol that then challenged them. The RAF officer, a little away from the Sappers, managed to hide in the undergrowth while Johns and Camidge fired on the patrol. Both died as Japanese and

Thai soldiers fired into the scrub where the raiders lay hidden. The canoe revealed to the Japanese that a British recce party had come ashore. Now they were on their guard.

The nominal Allies in the Japanese plan for the Orient included Thais, Burmese and Indonesians, whom the Japanese armed and equipped (even, in the case of the Indonesians, giving them some tanks). On Phuket Island Thai patrols had a good deal of independence from their ally's military command, for when Guthrie, the RAF officer, gave himself up on the Friday night he remained a prisoner of the Thais. His wanderings that day without water or food, under a broiling sun in the morning and in heavy rain that afternoon, had totally sapped his energy. (The high humidity inland not only weakens the body, it also – without you realizing it – greatly reduces one's will to do anything.)

His capture on Friday evening alerted the Japanese to the possibility of further landings. They were ready for the COPP landings on the north coast that night, when the two remaining canoes from *Torbay* came in again looking for the Sappers and Guthrie. The four men heard 'thudding over the sand', which they took to be patrols doubling along the beach, maybe moving to positions to cut off any COPPists ashore from a rendezvous, although Hughes and Alcock did not know this. They continued their work of the previous night and safely returned to *Torbay* without catching sight of the missing men.

On Friday, while Mackenzie had been making his first recce, all the island's garrisons were alerted. The villagers, hearing of these goings-on from the gossip of soldiers, were in some alarm of any strangers. So when the RAF officer, Bert Brown, climbed a tree to get a better view and photographs of the second airstrip site, several local villagers became inquisitive. Mackenzie decided the survey could not now be safely continued, and that evening his team began to move back to the canoe cache. They arrived on Sunday afternoon to learn from John Maxwell that a large

Thai patrol with some fishermen had found the canoes and 'made off'. They returned later that afternoon and Mackenzie went forward, unarmed possibly, to talk to them. The Thais made him strip naked to prove he was not armed, but he continued to occupy their attention, enabling several of his party to sneak into firing positions. When they opened up with their SMGs, the Thais ducked, enabling the major to skip into cover and the raiders to escape.

There were many remote clumps of tropical scrub and stretches of virgin forest in the area which offered the party temporary refuge from their pursuers. The raiders therefore planned to lie low until the following night, Monday, when they would signal the submarine, which was expecting them. That night *Thrasher* came in, and waited. The weather conditions were far from ideal. She would have launched her spare canoe to investigate the beach, but a tropical downpour reduced visibility to a few metres and the ensuing storm forced the submarine to seek deeper water. *Thrasher* came in again the next night, and the next, stretching each appointment for longer than had been arranged, for the charging of the submarine's batteries had taken less time than originally expected. The weather was clear on these two subsequent nights, but the lookouts still saw no sign of the raiders nor anything untoward ashore.

Each morning the submarine kept a second rendezvous 16 km west of the night RV, in case the canoes had missed her in the dark. The crew of the submarine must have been mystified as to why the raiders did not make contact, by day or night. The canoe had, of course, been captured, but why could the crew not see the signal lights from Mackenzie's patrol? The raiders were still free on these nights and lying in the area from which they expected to signal the submarine. The general opinion is that they had gone to the wrong beach, for there were few distinguishing features in the flat country behind this shoreline. Nor on the Monday were there any incidents apparently, except for a tropical downpour, which would at least ensure they had some drinking water. Their real troubles began on Tuesday when they were found by Japanese search parties. The raiders had to fight to make an escape, with two Japanese patrols trying to encircle them. But by firing to cover each other's withdrawal, they were breaking out of this encirclement down a track through heavy undergrowth. Marine Brownlie successfully engaged one patrol as Colour-Sergeant Smith moved from the jungle's edge, but the marine was killed when the second patrol appeared unexpectedly on the track behind him. The colour-sergeant was also badly wounded by this time and the rest of the party were scattered. Three days later, on the Friday, a week after their landing, they met up for a last attempt to signal *Thrasher* from the bay. There was no response to the signals from their hooded torch; had they had an S-phone, *Thrasher* might have been not too far away on several nights to contact them.

The party again split up, rightly believing that they had a better chance in pairs of crossing the island undetected, as they headed for the north coast where *Torbay* was known to have her rendezvous before going south again to an emergency RV. At first they evaded Japanese patrols, but in the next ten days had to shoot their way clear of others. In one such brush, John Maxwell was captured, and later in a prison cage he is believed to have met Smith, who had barely recovered from his injuries. The other three had dysentery, were emaciated from hunger and jungle sores, if they did not have malaria. Finally, Mackenzie, who was by this time wearing a pair of borrowed shorts, led them into a Thai village, where all three were taken prisoner. The major was later interrogated by the Japanese but returned to the Thais who treated their prisoners reasonably well.

The submarine *Torbay* had meanwhile made further attempts to find her missing Sappers, Hughes and Alcock taking a canoe along the northern shore one night, before both submarines met off Goh Huyang Island some kilometres south of Phuket. There Alex Hughes swam over to *Thrasher* for a final check on what might be done further to search for all nine men missing on the island, but six days had passed since Mackenzie landed, seven since the Sappers went missing. Their most likely escape would now be 'the emergency escape organization', a series of escape lines set up by MI9 and the American Secret Services to rescue air crew and others from behind Japanese lines.

Thrasher transferred her spare canoe to *Torbay* before they parted, as COPP 3 were to make two further rendezvous at an emergency escape beach on the early hours of Saturday and of Sunday. On both nights two canoes went in, Alex Hughes staying on 'the escape beach from 2330 to 0200'. Mackenzie's men may never have reached this beach, or if they did so it was in the following week. For John Maxwell and Colour-Sergeant Smith, the threat of Tokyo Rose 'that we will behead anyone landing from war canoes', came fatally, if not literally, true. They were shot by the Japanese that summer in Singapore.

The Final Victory

That summer, however, five months after the landings on Phuket Island, would see the end of the Japanese schemes of conquest. By March, Fourteenth Army in Burma and the American forces in the Pacific were resolutely breaking the Japanese grip on the Far East. In the Arakan and south along the Burmese west coast among the mangrove swamps, Mountbatten's main threat was towards Rangoon, but he also sent forces to cut off the Japanese who were withdrawing their divisions from Burma and Thailand with the intention of holding Indochina (modern Laos, Kampuchea and Vietnam) in a war of attrition. The seaborne arm of these pincers was guided by COPPs, while the SRU, their canoes launched from LCAs at times, made recces of landings barely the width of an LCA's ramp, often having to clear felled trees, and other barriers which the Japanese left across the chaungs.

These dark tidal creeks, in places only a few metres wide, ran through mangrove swamps where a canoe might pass with ease at low water but be among the tree tops when the tide was in. Water snakes, crocodiles and deadly tropical diseases infested these waters, where a swimmer had also to contend with the foul swamp mud – a far cry from the fresh salt breakers rolling on to open beaches. Yet COPPists recced the chaungs, leaving their tide gauges hidden on one night's recce to come back the next to check it. Daylight movement was too dangerous, for a single marksman could ambush a canoe as it moved beneath the thick mangrove branches in which he was hidden. Tide gauges did the work of silent observers. These were simple but effective pieces of beach recce equipment. A rising tide pushed a cork float up two guide rods until the ebb began, when this float was held by inverted pins; and there were also downward-facing pairs at the lower end with a cork to be caught at the tide's lowest point.

Not all raids, however, were conducted with such stealth, for marines trailed their coats in decoy raids. HMS *Thrasher*, on her next voyage after the recce to Phuket Island, towed in an Intruder inflatable carrying a spare dinghy and accompanied by two canoes towards Expedition Harbour. These went in from 2 km offshore, the lead canoe prepared for the scout recce anchoring 500 m offshore, the moon being so bright that Corporal James Buxton misjudged the distance and had 300 m further to swim than he intended. He was a powerful swimmer, but without a life jacket he found he sank the moment he stopped swimming. Nevertheless he got ashore, found the coast clear and signalled in the Intruder, aboard which the loud hissing of the second dinghy's inflation could be heard all over Komorta Island, if not throughout the Nicobars. Wags have said it could be heard on Phuket Island nearly 500 km to the east! Be that as it may, the intention was to let the Japanese know the raid was being made.

The original plan had been to stay for twenty-four hours from 18–19 April in this Operation 'Defraud', but during the periscope recces – when each of the eight men in the raiding party had been given the opportunity to study the beach – tree-fellers could be seen. On the soft sand beaches their footprints suggested there were a good number of them as the Intruder's men moved along the beach, covered by the Stens in the two canoes now closer inshore. There was no adequate laying-up area and so the patrol withdrew, having had no sight of the islanders but having smelled their insanitary bodies as the reek of urine wafted from some huts on the night air. Captain Stroud flung a grenade before the marines left – 'this failed to explode (bad maintenance!)' – so he fired a few Sten bursts and waited fifteen minutes in cover. But no Japanese came to investigate. Next morning they would find the noisy spare inflatable, its bottom ripped, left with a tracing from the chart for this island, the duplicated sheet of a standard set of military intelligence questions and some boxes with British markings.

The marines made long passages in submarines to reach such remote islands often 2000 km or more from their base in Ceylon. On 'Carpenter III', for example, three RM lieutenants and seven marines took passage in HMS *Thule* for the 2500-km voyage, passing through the Selat Sunda straits – at some points with only 1000 m between Sumatra and Java – leaving Sumatra to port and looping north of Singapore to a beach on the east coast of Johore about 7 km south of a Japanese camp near Sungei Klesa. On the voyage the marines, as is their usual role aboard ships, worked as lookouts and in other routine sea duties. Going through the straits, *Thule* was submerged sixteen hours a day, which left less oxygen in the air than was usual with her purification system, so at the end of each dive 'most of us felt a little muzzy'. Arriving off the target beach on 29 May, the submarine made a surface recce with night glasses, studying the shoreline some 9 km to the west and the many passing junks. She dived before dawn, a routine with which all embarked marines were now familiar for she had crash-dived several times to avoid aircraft when off the west coast of Java.

The marines now checked their Intruders and the stores

to be landed on this trip: anti-tank rifles, small steam generators to drive battery chargers for SOE radios, grenades, ammunition, toothbrushes and a case of Scotch, over 4 tonnes of supplies. Three inflatables were on the casing soon after *Thule* surfaced at about 2100 hours. They were floated off, the first of nine with outboards and three to be towed. Submarine crews were most efficient by this time in launching boats and often did not let the marines anywhere near a craft till it was afloat, but *Thule*'s crew (as submarines do in the 1980s) helped the marines to float off the dinghies once they had boarded them. These headed for two pinpoints of light set by SOE's Major Hart, an Australian leading a guerrilla unit of Malayan Chinese. In twenty minutes the first marines were ashore on a narrow beach 15 m wide, behind which the dark thick jungle hid Hart's men, who came out to collect the stores and anything else they could lay their hands on – including the marines' Stens and pistols if Hart had not made them leave these. A typical Malay guerrilla, carrying a rifle, two pistols, two knives and with a bandolier over his jungle-green battledress, topped it off with a pork-pie hat in matching green. He gave Corporal Buxton a half-coconut shell full of rum and coffee, perhaps because the corporal had nursed that case of whisky all the way to the beach. Over the radio he told the signaller on the submarine that all was off-loaded, the men to be brought out were ready and there were no Japanese patrols in the area.

A single white Verey light had been seen to the north as the first wave moved shorewards, but guerrilla standing patrols of three or four men placed where they could see any movement on the coast road some kilometres away would have given warning of any Japanese approaching. Nor had the junks sailing up the coast taken any notice of the Intruders. Buxton watched for the green spots of the submarine's RG lamp on his infra-red receiver, and passed this to one of the men waiting to be taken out to her. Had the Intruders been forced to leave in a hurry, they would have put to sea and then used their bongle – as X-craft did on 6

June 1944 – to make sound waves for the submerged sub-marine to home on. As it was, *Thule* came inshore and the marines went out to her. With them came an American B-29 bomber pilot and two of his crew, SOE's Lieutenant Douglas Browning (who, like Spencer Chapman, had worked behind the Japanese lines since 1942) and five survivors from the Singapore garrison. Three were sergeants who had volunteered to stay in the SOE-organized parties 'left behind' on the surrender of Malaya; two privates were the only survivors of 22 who had taken to the jungle at the time of this surrender two and a quarter years earlier. The survivors and marines were landed in Australia, where they had fourteen days of hospitality in Perth the like of which 'was beyond anyone's dreams'.

'385' carried out fourteen operations and in August 1945 Nos. 1 and 3 Troop were aboard a landing ship and No. 2 at Madras, India, preparing for the next landings, which were intended to lead to the recapture of Singapore. For this, Fourteenth Army were to land near Port Dickson during October with the intention of recapturing the British Empire's major Far East base in early 1946.

The landings were intended to be on flat open coastline with XXXIV Corps coming ashore on the Morib beaches 13 km northwest of Port Dickson, and 140 km northwest of Singapore. At least, that was the plan, after Alex Hughes's COPP 3 had made one of the most complete recces of a beach in the Second World War. They were landed on the night of Saturday/Sunday 9/10 June 1945 – how often the weekend is chosen for such raids and recces. (In Europe these coincided with most soldiers', especially garrison soldiers', night for a 'binge' during the Second World War, but among other cultures the night-out in a week does not always come on Saturday.) The four canoes landed in this Operation 'Confidence' came ashore without interference. They began methodically making a survey, first up the beach at each of the four landing points and then out into the waters of the Malacca Straits – or at least far enough from the tide line to find a false beach on a spit of sand, the height of the water above this at both high and low water and the rates at which the tide flowed across it.

On this first night, however, only one other canoe came off the shore to join Hughes (who had the bongle in his canoe): Sub-Lieutenant Hood and Able Seaman Fowler were missing, as were the Canadian Captain Alcock with Corporal Turner. Only after a thorough search of the shoreline did Alex Hughes lead the two surviving canoes to rendezvous with the submarine, where his hopes of finding the others, who might have moved on their infra-red RG kit, were dashed. During the morning, *Seadog* kept the daylight rendezvous, but the missing canoes did not appear. Next night the surviving two canoes went back to complete their survey and to look for their comrades. What Hughes did not know was that, having missed the rendezvous, both canoe teams had got back ashore south of the beach they had surveyed. Alcock and Turner spent sixteen hours that Sunday hiding in a swamp after ditching those items of kit that would show they had been reconnoitring a beach. Their jungle-green battledress blended with the cover, but Turner's rope-soled shoes proved (for all their grip on wet decks) quite unsuitable for marching, in contrast with Alcock's rubber parachute boots, which survived the canoeists' many long marches in the next two months. Hood and Fowler were also hidden-up that Sunday.

Seadog returned to base, her periscope photographs providing vital silhouettes that landing craft and landing ship captains would need to identify beaches. Hughes's teams had also prepared all those close details needed to find landing points to beach 5000-tonne LSTs and the large LCIs that could sail such distances as the 1800 km from Rangoon to Port Dickson to disgorge tanks or infantry over ramps on to the beaches. Such vessels required that a more careful study for runnels and snags be carried out than was necessary for an LCA or the American LCVP.

Such finer points of beach gradients and tide states were of little concern to the Chinese guerrilla band that Alcock and Turner joined some days after finding themselves unable to return to *Seadog*. These ruthless fighters of the Anti-Japanese Civilian Force (AJCF) matched the Japanese in savagery, burning suspected spies on log fires before beheading them. The two canoeists had been with the guerrillas for several days when Hood and Fowler joined them. The four COPPists subsequently spent over two months with this band of blood brothers – there was a reward of 10,000 Straits dollars on each canoeist's head – before returning to COPP 3 after hostilities ceased in mid-August 1945.

The operations by SOG canoeists included seven operations in support of clandestine forces, ten beach reconnaissances and two sabotage raids (mounted by SB Sections). These figures include COPP 9's piece of true 'assault pilotage' the previous April, when they not only made the usual beach recces, but snatched a prisoner from a Japanese OP, the distinction between the subtlety of reconnaissance being blunted for once by the COPPists' hunting instincts.

When the Japanese were negotiating a surrender in mid-August, the Supreme Commander, Allied Pacific Powers, General MacArthur, ordered that all landings should be deferred until the various Japanese commands had signed surrender agreements. The assault battalions of 25 Division did not cross the Morib beaches until 9 September, coming ashore ready for battle even though the Japanese Government's surrender had been signed over two weeks earlier. But the landings met no resistance from the Japanese, and nor did they resist elsewhere in southeast Asia, when local national forces in Indonesia caused the only difficulties for British and Dutch forces landing in these islands.

The demobilization began for some of the swimmer-canoeists who had been preparing in 1945 to recce the beaches of many landing points in Asia, stepping stones to a final assault they expected to guide into Japanese beaches. The SB Squadrons had returned from the Mediterranean to the United Kingdom and were about to embark, re-mustered into the SAS Regiments for the Far East. COPP parties had arrived in India to relieve COPPs 1 and 3. All these parties, along with '385', SRU and the SBS Groups were deployed by SOG ready to take part in recces and as guides for landings scheduled for August, September and October. Two troops of '385', for example, had sailed for Penang Island off the northwest Malayan coast. They landed there on 28 August as part of an occupation force and moved with other Royal Marines to Sabang Island off northern Sumatra before returning to Britain in the *Athlone Castle*, and then became SCOBBS at Fremington, which had been one of several training and experimental bases for Combined Operations on the north Devon coast of Bideford Bay. RMBPD canoeists had been brought to Teignmouth on the south Devon coast from Eastney at the end of June 1944, to join the *Mount Stewart* base.

Mountbatten had signalled from SEAC headquarters, to say that RMBPD would not be needed in the Far East. Hasler, who had trained most of the '385' officers in Ceylon, was later to comment that 'no worthwhile role could be found for them . . . as soon as offensive operations by large forces became possible'. In truth, there was little Japanese shipping of any consequence in southeast Asia by June 1945, for they were reduced to resupplying their island garrisons by landing craft and a few cargo-carrying sub-marines.

Hasler also pointed out that aggressive small-scale raids are 'at a premium' when the main military forces are on the defensive. In southeast Asia he believes SOG was too late on the scene: they would have been invaluable in 1942. At that time there had been the two Royal Marine raiding forces in the Far East, both hastily created, yet they gave a good account of themselves. The operations of Force Viper on the Irrawaddy, commanded by Duncan Johnston, had much of the modern SBS's aggressive boldness, even if these marines of 1942 had little specialized training. A second small force, known as the SS Platoon, was even closer to the

SBS raiders in its role. They were survivors of HMS *Prince of Wales* and formed part of the special service Force Rose in December 1941, carrying out several raids in the first few weeks of 1942 to ambush staff cars and cut road communications behind the Japanese lines on the west Malayan coast. The idea of extending such raids was considered by several Royal Marine officers and by Major (later Brigadier) J. M. ('Mike') Calvert, Royal Engineers, among others. The reason they could not put these ideas into practice lay in the difficulties of coordinating such forces rather than in any lack of volunteers to undertake them – especially in Australia, where four Independent Companies had been trained in the winter of 1940–1.

Even more difficult at that time was persuading Far East commanders of the need for any special forces. Even the idea in August 1941 of leaving parties behind in the Malayan jungle, should the Allies have to retreat during an invasion here, was vetoed 'in case such preparations might unsettle the local population'. Such parties were assembled by SOE with great haste that December, as the Japanese advanced through Malaya. In the European theatre, the tri-service ISTDC was working at Eastney on a range of special techniques and the training needed for them. The Centre's activities had been closed down for some weeks in 1938 during the Munich crisis, but by February 1941 it was concentrating on amphibious techniques. In April 1942 Lord Mountbatten, with his usual keen eye for practical administration, reorganized the Centre: half became the Combined Operations Experimental Centre, concentrating on such experiments as floating armoured vehicles and landing petrol in bulk, among a wide series of developments of which dories and canoes were a part. The other half moved to Combined Operations HQ in London, to coordinate such new ideas with what the planners required. Such developments, always in great secrecy, had taken over three years before they bore a variety of fruits for the victories in Europe; and, although they were never to come to full flower in the Far East, there were healthy offshoots there.

PART TWO

The Navy's SBS

8 The Continuing Wars

With the war over, the British Government had to compromise between the cost of keeping a sizeable trained force for amphibious operations and the need to have this option for what seemed remote possibilities in 1946 – yet within five years swimmer-canoeists would be off the Korean coast. The secrecy surrounding beach reconnaissance was continued to a later date, and mention of the Combined Operations Assault Pilotage Parties did not appear in newspapers and magazines until the late 1950s. By then their fund of knowledge had been passed on to the marines of the Special Boat Sections, three of which in the 1970s formed the Special Boat Squadron. These Sections by 1947 had been formed initially from men of RMBPD, '385' and 'S' COPP, the last-named being the Party of the senior (hence 'S') COPP officer. (His assistant had 'A', the Sappers 'E', and all their craft were maintained by 'M' COPP.) This reorganization in 1946–7 was part of many reshuffles in the rapidly reduced Combined Operations commands in Europe and India. But the School of Combined Operations at Fremington was continued in north Devon, where the British Army had carried out its water wading trials for vehicles. The experimental establishment, COXE (Combined Operations Experimental Establishment) also continued. The RMBPD moved to Appledore in 1946, still under Admiralty control in the sense that all Royal Marines were victualled and paid by the Board of Admiralty as they are today by MOD (Navy). But the establishments in Bideford Bay, which had included Appledore and Instow, would be reduced to a joint services unit at Instow, which in 1979 became the Amphibious Trials and Training Unit, RM (ATTURM).

At Fremington in 1946, the swimmer-canoeists of 'S' COPP and some '385' canoeists who had not been 'demobbed' were formed into a demonstration team, as the School of Combined Operations Beach and Boat Section (SCOBBS). Demonstrations that they put on for the staff colleges and occasionally on visits overseas showed off Britain's 'frogmen' (a term not used by the SBS themselves, if not actively disliked by most of them). There were, therefore, two units of swimmer-canoeists for a time: RMBPD and SCOBBS. Major Pritchard-Gordon, RM, commanded the 'Patrol' Detachment; and Major Antony Rainey, RM, commanded the 'Beach and Boat' Section. Pritchard-Gordon was succeeded by Captain S. G. Hurst, RM, in 1946, who had trained his Section of MSCs in Scotland ready to attack Norwegian shipping. He was followed in 1947 by the stocky boxer Lieutenant (later Lieutenant-Colonel) Peter G. ('Pug') Davis, DSC, who has become a legend in the SBS, but served in landing craft during the Second World War. Colonel Davis had won his DSC landing with six men to search for a patrol of 2 Commando on the well-defended Dalmatian island of Brac in June 1944; he was later one of the first batch of the few 'Hostilities Only' officers after the war to become a Regular.

The Royal Marines, having taken over all Special Boat operations in 1946, moved their canoeists from Appledore and Fremington to Eastney in October 1947. There for a time they called themselves COBBs dropping the 'S' for 'School of', although they would now form part of the Amphibious School, RM. This unit was to contain both the remaining landing craft flotillas, a Landing Craft Obstruction Clearance Unit, an LC Recovery Unit and all that remained of the naval Beach Commandos. In the Second World War, these Beach Commandos had set up their command posts on the shore at Dieppe, in North Africa, in Normandy and the Far East, to control incoming craft and traffic crossing the beach. When everyone else in Combined Operations quit the beach, taking empty craft back to sea or moving inland to the relative cover of some sand dune or cliff, the Beach Commandos stayed on the exposed beach. Their skills had been kept alive in 1946 by an officer and eight marines who were trained by the last of the wartime Beach Commandos.

Throughout the late 1940s the role of the SB Sections, as part of the Small Raids Wing of the Amphibious School, seemed to entail only demonstrations, but the School's chief instructor Major (later General Sir) Norman Tailyour, RM, had the vision to set up the SB Sections for roles covering the beach recces, deep penetration raids and anti-shipping activities, which would be their principal tasks in Europe's defence. Peter Davis took a dozen swimmers to Germany in February 1950 as the RM Demolition Unit – later renamed the more familiar SB Section – with the Rhine Flotilla. Only by rigorous selection and training can a swimmer stand a reasonable chance of surviving such exacting roles. Indeed he must refresh himself on say anti-shipping raids, if he has spent a month in OPs behind enemy lines.

The first purely Royal Marine Special Boat units drew on the Second World War experiences of swimmers, but many marines who served in them in the late 1940s and the 1950s brought with them also the experiences of brush fire wars and counter-terrorism to add to the SBS's fund of knowledge on the tactics for out-of-the-way operations. For the SBS swimmers in the 1950s there were involvements in a number of theatres: canoeists probed the Chinese coast defences in Korea; on the Rhine the Squadron's future role in NATO was crystallizing; and their strategic role was becoming more apparent by the end of the decade. What must also be remembered is the part that swimmer-canoeists played in routine commando operations when not serving with the Squadron. (The title 'Squadron' was not strictly adopted until 1975 and from the 1950s the SB Sections were in the SB Company.) One or two canoeists were probably in the Royal Marines' team that in 1954 advised naval staffs on the defences of bases in Northern Ireland, where swimmers in later years tested these defences. A number were to serve in Oman and on other detached duties from the Squadron, but it was in Korea that they carried out the roles most closely associated with their Second World War counterparts.

In the early 1950s there were beaches in the eastern Mediterranean on which information was required, for after the peace of 1945 much beach intelligence had been filed away if not lost, and governments and alliances had changed in the first years of peace. The task of updating the intelligence in one case, at least, fell to two swimmer-canoeists. They were launched off their target beach on a reasonably calm night, but after going inshore they failed to RV with their two canoe paddlers. The obvious political repercussions of such a mishap might have amounted to an international incident had not the swimmers been well versed in their cover stories. All clandestine operations require some convenient cloak – one used in the Second World War was the claim that the swimmer had been washed off an ML by a sudden wave and obliged to swim ashore. The raider had always to ditch the tools of his trade and would need to explain away his heavy surface swimming suit if he could not leave it below the low-water mark. Off the eastern Mediterranean coast the two swimmers apparently provided adequate explanations for their presence after one had swum many kilometres along the coast away from his target beach.

The political risks of putting canoeists on to other people's beaches, necessitates leaving as hostages to fortune those marines who may be caught. At worst they may pre-empt political initiatives in an international situation, where – should the swimmers be caught – any future military plans are then placed in jeopardy. Thus, no SBS recces were made prior to the Suez landing in November 1956. What must be remembered, however, is that mounting from the United Kingdom an amphibious intervention for which the SBS could have recced some beaches takes weeks rather than days. For when the ships of an assault force have passages of several thousand nautical miles (let alone the 8000 nautical miles to the Falklands) they need a considerable time to bring the landing force to a beachhead. Whatever recces were made in the western hemisphere during the 1950s appear likely to have been constrained by political considerations; but in that decade there were open conflicts in the Far East.

The Malayan Emergency

The Malayan Communists from 1945 aimed at establishing an area that they could dominate and eventually expand to rule all Malaya. These Communists, formerly the Malayan People's Anti-Japanese Army, had fought the Japanese in the Second World War. But on the return of the British, who supported the government of these Federal Malay States, some MPAJA went underground without surrendering the weapons given to them in the war. The tight-knit political cells of the Communist party organized three military forces: the uniformed 1000 Chinese guerrillas of the Malayan Races Liberation Army, the clandestine civilian Min Yuen of individuals indistinguishable from the villagers among whom they lived, and the Lie Ton Ten hit-squads of assassins and saboteurs.

The first SB Section to serve in the Far East with 3 Commando Brigade was not formed until 1952, but in the meantime swimmers served with the Brigade on general duties during their time away from the Special Boat Sections. The term 'general duties' perhaps sounds too prosaic a description of jungle patrols across terrain as varied as the swamps of the Perak coastal plain to the west, the more open rubber plantations of its central plain and the virgin jungle rising eastward to the Cameron Highlands with peaks 2000 m high. Marine commandos were to cross and recross this state in northern Malaya during the two years the Brigade were there from May 1950. This was the first spell of sustained jungle operations for many young regular marines and during the last year or so for some National Service marines too. (At that time, National

Service marines had to have served in the Royal Marine Forces Volunteer Reserve before they joined the Corps; later they continued in part-time service for some two years with the Reserve after completing their eighteen months of full-time service. Some reservists were also trained swimmer-canoeists, who in the 1950s provided Nos. 4 and 5 Sections of the SBS with teams coming from several different training centres as far apart as Bristol and Merseyside.) For many of these marines the Malayan experience included techniques of surveillance and cooperation with local police forces that set a pattern for subsequent operations against terrorists in many countries: joint police-and-marine patrols, searches with the help of dogs, and the use of local intelligence provided in Malaya by Junior Civil Liaison Officers. Working patiently with a JCLO to sift intelligence from gossip, a marine commander could work out a plan of action that would bring what little success was possible in the face of resistance by the locals to give away any information they might have on the terrorists' comings and goings.

SBS canoeists in general service as commandos see action that has particular value to their SBS roles. In Malaya, this experience included techniques of surveillance and cooperation with local police forces. Without their help, a Commando could send out countless patrols and never even reach a valley where terrorists had been, never mind surround one of their camps. Much of the intelligence was provided by the Special Branch police through their informers who on one occasion had reported four or five terrorists living in the scrub jungle, belukar, where thickets, massed creepers, banana trees, bamboo thickets and patches of man-high elephant grass had become secondary jungle in the now uncultivated part of a rubber estate.

Ipoh golf course lay across the river from the terrorists' hide, but on this Sunday before Christmas, 23 December 1951, the festive calendar of the British had little to do with the planning of the raid. Indeed, the JCLOs had explained more than once that the Chinese of Malaya did not have a breakfast in the westerners' sense, nor did they observe the British feast days. What did affect the timing of this raid was the need to get the auxiliary forces into positions where they might block any escape. Some of these were not trained well enough for operations at night, but as the villagers were going to be kept in their compounds later than their usual 0530 start, only a short time must pass before the guerrillas realized no one was working in the fields. Therefore, four sixteen-man jungle squads of police officered by British ex-servicemen and under the command of their superintendent, and a number of auxiliary police, mostly Malays, were to be positioned as stops to block any bandits escaping. These stops were placed along the lines of the river and the road, with a troop of marines and some army troopers (about 110 men in all) to cover the 1500 m of rubber along the north side of the patch.

The bandits' hide had been reported as being 'by a prominent tree' which had been seen on an air photograph. Now, in the growing daylight, half of a troop were sent forward to check it as others cordoned the area. The undergrowth was not too thick in this northeast corner of the patch, the commandos taking only half an hour to reach the tree and report that there were no signs of the enemy. About twenty minutes later their Troop commander received a second radio message – a police squad had found something in their advance to the left of the line, a line, incidentally, now moving forward with growing difficulty as the thickets and bamboo clumps tended to break up the advance in places. The captain went down the line to check what the police had found: a biscuit tin of sweaty gelignite sticks, quickly consigned to the river much to the finders' communal relief. Nearby, a low tunnel entrance, not a metre high, was found going into a patch of elephant grass and leading to a den covered by a few stunted trees' branches which hid it from spotter aircraft.

Two wicker baskets of old clothes, thin blankets and a wad of damp documents with a few personal odds and ends showed this to be a hide. A second tunnel led from the first. Some pig-hunting dogs with the patrol, having the scent from the clothing, panted off down this tunnel to a stream where the scent – as the bandits had planned – was lost in the water. Apart from the panting of the dogs, all was quiet but the pig-hunting dogs being used by the security force were not to be denied. After casting about they flew off towards a thick stand of elephant grass, their owner 'practically airborne behind them'. He managed to stop by a ditch and slipped the dogs which, with the scent now strong, hurled themselves into the tall grass. A bang broke the tension and the old pig-hunter staggered backwards, shot in the arm. The commando Troop swung left and the police jungle squads came up at the double, firing into the tall grass which was soon surrounded. With fire going in from all sides, some of it came unhealthily close to scoring a few 'own goals', as marines would say of accidental shootings of friendly forces.

A guerrilla crawled down one of the prepared tunnels in the grass, the only way he could move without being seen for any other movement set the grass swaying. He reached the edge of the stand behind a few last stalks of camouflage and set the makeshift detonator of a grenade. He was out in the open and had flung the explosive before the surprised superintendent and a marine realized how close the man was. The marine shouted a warning as he dived for the cover of a bank, but the policeman did not hear him for he was trying to stop his men firing indiscriminately into the stand. Luckily the detonator failed to go off and the grenade did not explode. The bandit was still in full view as he took the pin from a second grenade. Fortunately, the marine had emerged from his cover and, firing his Owen smg from the hip, he hit the guerrilla several times. As the man fell, his grenade exploded beside him. One may dislike his cause and methods, but his courage was never in question, nor was that of the other guerrillas now totally surrounded but still in action.

The security circle closed in, each man moving carefully, weapon cocked, senses alive to any sound of a movement among the grass. Wisps of phosphorus smoke lingered, causing several men to cough noisily. The smouldering wet grass and the stench of burnt explosive made this seem more like a Guy Fawkes night than Christmas Eve. They found a girl paralysed – she died soon afterwards – and beside her the dead grenade thrower together with the body of a teenager. This lad was armed with two pistols and was probably the one whose shot had only missed the Troop commander by a shade.

To concentrate the efforts of over 200 men from the security forces for the seemingly minimal result of killing three guerrillas and capturing a fourth may seem disproportionate. Indeed, there is a tendency in guerrilla warfare to saturate the area of opposition, sometimes producing the opposite of the desired effect with informers shunning contact with their policemen friends or guerrillas keeping a low profile. There are times when a few well-trained counter-insurgency teams can be more successful than such large patrols.

The Korean War

In the dark night of Tuesday/Wednesday 12/13 September 1950, six marines and a naval petty officer of Pounds Force battled to get their inflatable off sharp rocks. Their purpose in crossing these reefs was to leave some decoy recce gear on Kongsoon beaches, 22 km southwest of Inchon and thus deceptively far from the intended landing place for the United States 1 Marine Division. American troops of an Army Raider Company had landed on Robb Island, some 900 m off the beach – and were making their presence known, for accurate Korean machine-gun fire killed two of

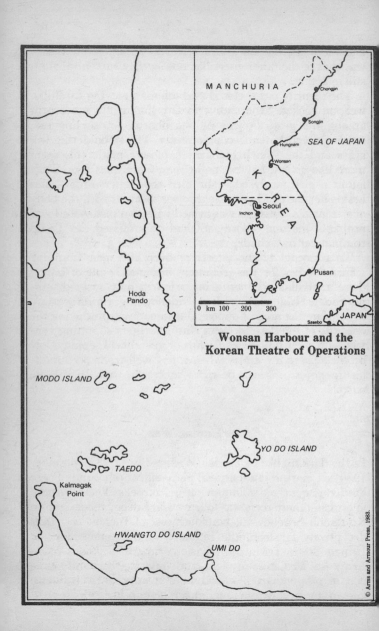

MANCHURIA

Chongjin

Songjin

SEA OF JAPAN

Hungnam

Wonsan

K O R E A

Inchon

Seoul

Pusan

Sasebo

JAPAN

0 km 100 200 300

**Wonsan Harbour and the
Korean Theatre of Operations**

Hoda
Pando

MODO ISLAND

YO DO ISLAND

TAEDO

Kalmagak
Point

HWANGTO DO ISLAND

UMI DO

© Arms and Armour Press, 1983.

them. The small-arms fire directed at Pounds Force party was less accurate, however. The marines traversed 100 m of beach in a realistic survey, while two swimmers went out from the beach to place weighted lines (as used by COPP), suggesting that the survey had included sea-depth measurements off the beach. The British swimmers came out under inaccurate fire, returning with the Raider Company to the USS *Whitesands Bay*. On the Saturday the US Marines stormed ashore at Inchon after a heavy naval bombardment of the beach defences and met little opposition as they advanced 25 km to the outskirts of Seoul. This capital city of South Korea, only 20 km from the country's northwest border with Communist North Korea, was stoutly defended, and in the next few weeks Pounds Force was in action on the border hills with the US Army.

This tiny force of ten volunteers from the British Eastern Fleet, unofficially named after its commander, Lieutenant (later Major-General) E. G. D. Pounds, RM, was a token of Royal Navy support for the UN Fleet Commander who wanted to increase his amphibious raiding forces. The Britons were equipped and armed by the Americans, as was 41 (Independent) Commando, raised five weeks before these landings. The original plan to send No. 1 SBS to Korea with them was cancelled, as several teams were far away on a training exercise in Spitzbergen, so the Commando formed its own canoe teams from swimmer-canoeists and other commandos while the Squadron remained in Europe.

The North Korean border touches the USSR only 150 km south of the naval port of Vladivostok; the Manchurian frontier also gave the Chinese open access to North Korea. As a result military supplies from both the Soviet Union and China came down the east-coast railway, a track laid on the narrow coastal plain between the sea and the ridge of high mountains running down the eastern side of the peninsula. This railway provided the first targets for raids by 41 (Independent) Commando after its period of training in Japan during September. The first raid, in 1950, by four officers and 63 NCOs and marines of 'B' Troop, landed from the submarine USS *Perch* by inflatables, which were towed inshore by the motor boat she carried 'in a cylindrical hangar abaft the conning tower'. The marine commandos had carried out a full rehearsal, working with an American Underwater Demolition Team (the US naval equivalent of the SBS), before the raid was due to go in, on Monday 1 October.

However, when *Perch* made a recce of the beach near the coast railway that night, her skipper saw through the periscope a number of Korean patrol boats off the beach. In all these operations, a worthwhile secondary target had been studied in order to give the raiders the option of landing elsewhere if the first raid was aborted, so on the Tuesday night *Perch* came in again to the second target, having recced it that afternoon. She floated off ten inflatables, launched her light motor boat and submerged, keeping a telephone link with the boat as the submerged submarine towed her and the craft linked to her towards the beach. The risk of mines prevented the submarine being taken into depths shallower than ten fathoms, which meant that her motor boat was cast off a little over 7 km from the shore, towing the raiding craft to within 450 m of the beach. From there the UDT swimmers went in, checked that the coast was clear and signalled in the raiding force. They brought in anti-tank mines, which were set below the railway tracks, and as the force was leaving the beach they had the satisfaction of hearing these detonated by a train. Meanwhile, 'C' and 'D' Troops were aboard two APDs, USS *Bass* and *Wantock*, assault personnel destroyers from which landing craft towed ten-man inflatables to a target area. In the late evening of the Friday the ships launched their assault forces 4 km from the coast, but in the mist and dark the tows could make only 2 knots as they crept inshore to the 'bouncer' line. From there, some 400 m from the beach, the inflatables were paddled forward another 200 m or so to the edge of the surf.

No close recces had been made of the beach and the strength of the surf was an unknown hazard, so single scout boats went forward to the edge of the tumbling waves. The marine lieutenant in one, having been wished a safe swim by others in the boat, went over the side to find the water only waist deep – to his amusement, for he was on a so-called 'false' beach – before plunging into the surf to swim the last 100 m to the shore. There he found no sign of the enemy. The surf was heavy but not impassable, so he signalled in the boats. 'D' Troop's boats at first missed the flickering shrouded light, for the night was misty; but all the craft were soon ashore on the correct beach, one of the APDs' radar having kept them on her screens and radio contact being maintained to guide them on the right course. In the starlight, under the looming mountainside, over 2000 kg of explosives were laid under culverts, bridges and in the walls of a tunnel. These cut the railway most effectively. The raiders made a second landing on the next night, this time only 8 km from Songjin, a sizeable town. They placed a similarly large amount of explosives under bridges and tracks, which set fire to the surrounding paddy fields. The complete success of the raid was marred by the death of a corporal, who was killed by enemy fire as the commandos withdrew, having laid anti-personnel mines in the craters of their demolitions.

The marines that November were in the battle for the Chosin reservoir with the US 1 Marine Division, after which the Commando was regrouped in Japan and brought back up to strength before their next operation. The Chinese, who had stiffened the North Korean resistance at the time of the Chosin battle, now held the northeast coast of the peninsula. They were a tough peasant army, and had crossed into Korea in November 1950. The more of them who could be drawn to defend the coast railway the fewer would be in the main battles further south, so on 7 April 1951 the raids began again. That morning the Commando's assault transport ships were off the coast between Songjin and Hungnam, but the UDT swimmers found fog so thick that the naval bombardment was cut short even though the landing was delayed until daylight; nor could aircraft be launched from two carriers for air support. Nevertheless, in eight hours assault engineers had blasted a series of bore-holes using 'beehive' shaped charges, into each of which 35 kg of TNT was packed to blow out the base of an embankment, leaving craters 5 m deep stretching for 30 m. These would be more difficult to repair than any demolitions of bridges and tracks, and was accomplished without any commando casualties, despite there being two Chinese and Korean divisions 25 km to the north at Songjin. One small enemy patrol had found the beachhead, but only fired at the marines from a long range and to no effect.

Meanwhile, peace talks were in the offing, and for some months after this raid all operations by this United Nations force were curtailed. Then, in July, the marines headed north once more with the intention of raiding as frequently as practical along the northeast coast. The Commando's base of operations was Sasebo in southern Japan (formerly a seaplane base), a day or less by ship from the southern tip of the Korean peninsula and only two days' steaming from the marines' advanced base at Yo Do Island. The 3-km-wide island was 130 km north of the battlefront, its low hills overlooking the anchorage of Wonsan Harbour's smaller islands. In this bay the arms of the headland, Hoda Pando to the north and Kalmagak Point to the south, almost joined to form a land-locked sea some 30 km long and 15 km across, below the high ridge of Kalmaka mountain.

The marines of 'C' Troop, with mortars, tents, two landing craft, two canoes and rations for fourteen days, landed on Yo Do on 1 July 1951 and were joined by other troops later that week. Thereafter troops were given a spell in the forward base and then relieved for rest and re-cuperation at Sasebo. Several islands in the Harbour were held by South Koreans and various clandestine forces also operated from Yo Do.

The Communists periodically shelled the UN-held islands from the mainland or brought mortars to un-occupied islands to bombard the forward outposts, fire which UN ships and aircraft answered; but to be fully effective they needed naval gunfire support observers ashore. Before these could be taken ashore, however, the marines had to make a series of reconnaissances, often in 'unmerciful rain and thick fog-mist'. They usually worked with two canoe teams supported by a landing craft, eight men in all, commanded by a lieutenant, going into the Harbour before laying up with the landing craft hidden in a quiet creek while the canoe teams searched the shoreline. More permanent outposts were set up on Modo Island, where 'B' Troop lived in the island's high hills while making recces of the mainland. Near the end of August they had their first experience of a typhoon, the strong winds blowing down tents, damaging craft, with torrential rain blotting out visibility and forcing craft to lay up on the nearest coast.

Once the recce patrols had reasonable intelligence of the enemy's positions, they took a naval fire support observer to Hwangto Do Island; this team successfully directed a shoot by American destroyers, which fired 200 shells into Communist coast batteries. Teams of marines were also left for several days at a time in observation posts on small islands from where they could radio reports (like the coast-watchers of the Second World War) on movements of troops or ships. During the late summer, however, there were few Communist troops in the area; and when canoe teams visited several fishing villages on the coast they found only women, children and a few old men. They were not guaranteed a quiet welcome, however. One night in September the scouting canoe team for a raid made three attempts to find a suitable landing point for an LCVP near one village. The canoeists' first two landfalls did not seem promising as the rocky shoreline was unsuitable for beach-ing a landing craft; as they came into a third cove they were fired on at close range, 'one bullet parting the hair of the man forward in the canoe'. Fortunately, both were experienced canoeists and in seconds had paddled clear of the beach.

During these months the marines had also to make sure that their own bases were secure, pre-ranging mortars on beaches and laying mines on routes where any Communist landing party might attack. At other times mortars continued to be taken by LCVP to islands within range of the Communists' mainland defences. After lying hidden all day the mortar-men would bombard the coast that night, slipping away before daylight.

By mid-November the marines had outposts on Taedo, 1000 m from Kalmagak Point, and one OP was established from time to time on Umi Do only 300 m from a Communist battery of 76-mm anti-tank guns being used against United Nations ships. To the north, canoe patrols had made six landings on Hoda Pando, usually landing three canoes 50 to 60 m apart. These were not always without incident: on one, a canoe team was killed in a burst of automatic fire, and on another occasion the engine of an LCVP broke down, leaving her drifting off the southern point, where she was washed ashore and five marines made prisoner (a grim experience in this, one of the first wars for centuries where prisoners were subjected to attempts at converting them to their enemy's ideology).

In late September a new tactic in disruptive raiding was tried when 'B' Troop were landed to attack a railway tunnel while canoe teams came ashore north of the main landing. The canoe teams laid an ambush for reinforcements expected to come south from Songjin to attack the tunnel demolition force, which meanwhile got ashore from USS *Wantock* and was fired on, one marine being wounded. Having created the disturbance required, they withdrew, while the canoe teams, having mined the road, heard a vehicle convoy coming south. As they left the beach, they heard several of their mines go off. All the landing teams had safely re-embarked by 0400 hours before sailing south to their island base of Wonsan. A similar raid was mounted four days later, but when the UDT swimmers got ashore south of Songjin they found the North Koreans in strength, so the raid was aborted. Indeed, other raids during October and November met increasing resistance: two canoes leading a raid in on 10 October could not beach as they met heavy fire; a corporal and two marines were wounded when 'B' Troop landed at 2300 hours on 2 December after United Nations ships had bombarded the target beach again south of Songjin; and a second attempt to land 800 m north of the previous night's raids also met strong opposition. But this was the effect that the raiders were after: Communist forces were being drawn from the main front to defend the coast.

In December 1951, 41 (Independent) Commando was withdrawn from Korea, having won fifteen British and fourteen American awards for gallantry and having shown how swimmer-canoeists, even though not a 'genuine' SB Section, could be used to advantage in general commando operations.

The Borneo Confrontation

3 Commando Brigade was based in Malta and the Middle East from the mid-1950s until April 1961 when the commandos (Brigade HQ and 42 Commando, initially) returned to Singapore. With them went No. 2 SB Section, which was to be based in the Far East for the next ten years. The British were intending to keep one commando carrier in Far Eastern waters, with a second west of Suez, but in the event only two such warships were commissioned, *Bulwark* and *Albion*. These were deployed during the 1960s in both theatres, but with only two of these 18,300-tonne carriers there were periods during their refits when only one of the ships was in commission. For the SBS, commando carriers offered the advantages of ready insertion by air, as each vessel carried helicopters as well as landing craft to land her commandos. SB teams rather than the whole of No. 1 Section, which had joined No. 2, were attached to Com-

mando Groups as necessary during these tours in commando carriers in the Far East. Teams also worked with British Army formations when their special skills of deep reconnaissance were needed. In this role they made a number of penetrating raids in Borneo during the period of so-called Confrontation, an undeclared war that opened with a rebellion in the oil state of Brunei.

In August 1962 the Federation of Malay States became Malaysia, with a government that hoped to bring the three northern states of Borneo (Sarawak, a British colony on the northwest coastal plain; Brunei, a British protectorate since 1888; and North Borneo or Sabah, another colony) into the Federation. These states, however, had a southern border with Kalimantan, the Indonesian part of the island of Borneo which is three times the size of the United Kingdom and straddles the equator. The Indonesian president, Sukarno, was bent on extending his rule not only to the Borneo states but also the whole of the Malayan peninsula – an expansion that would have added 7,500,000 people to the 100,000,000 people he already ruled in the wide arc of islands stretching almost 5000 km around the southern coasts of the peninsula. Sukarno had a number of Malayan volunteers trained, ostensibly to fight the last Dutch settlers in New Guinea, but who returned to the Federation as a Fifth Column. In Brunei one of the several coastal races of northern Borneo, the Kedayans, a quiet farming people of Javanese descent, had been treated by tradition as second-class citizens by local Malays. The Kedayans in Brunei and Sarawak were prepared to revolt to keep these states in North Borneo if not in an Indonesian federation, and with Sukarno's support they seized a number of places including Brunei town (modern Bandar Seri Begawa) and the Sarawak town of Limbang. To meet this emergency, an initial force of Gurkhas flew from Singapore in three RAF Beverley transports, and by 2300 hours on Saturday 8 December 1962 two companies had secured the airfield and began clearing Brunei town. Other British units followed, including 3 Commando Brigade with No. 2 SBS, which had

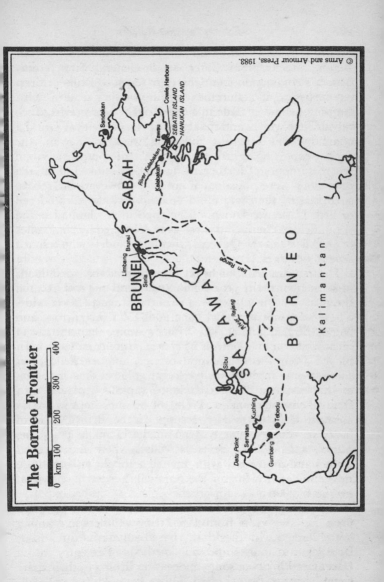

The Borneo Frontier

0 km 100 200 300 400

© Arms and Armour Press, 1983.

SABAH

Sandakan

River Kalabakan
Kalabatan
Tawau
Cowie Harbour
SEBATIK ISLAND
NANUKAN ISLAND

Limbang
Brunei
Seria
BRUNEI

Iran Range

S A R A W A K

River Rejang

Sibu

Kuching
Samatan
Datu Point
Gumbang Tebedu

B O R N E O

Kalimantan

been on exercises off Mombasa in the commando carrier *Albion,* and Captain (later Major-General Sir) Jeremy Moore's commando company were flown to Brunei to rescue hostages, an action for which he won a bar to his MC. Coming ashore at Kuching the Brigade were ordered 'to reconnoitre widely and make your presence felt'. A Gurkha company was sent the following week to Tawau, the timber-exporting centre on the coast in southeast Sabah where rumours of further risings and possible Indonesian incursions were prevalent if not rife. However, the rebels, surprised by the rapid build-up of forces, had surrendered or fled. Little was known of the opposition who had seized the oilfields at Seria and these were recovered by companies of Gurkhas and the Queen's Own Highlanders who rescued several hostages.

During January 1963 heavy rains created the worst floods in Borneo for many years. The River Limbang rose 10 m at the peak, and in places was swollen to nearly 2 km wide. These were not the ideal conditions for river patrols, and No. 2 SBS had a quiet time. Other swimmer-canoeists were meanwhile on long patrols as general-duty commandos deployed from the commando carrier, *Albion*'s helicopters soon proving in these few weeks the value of their mobility, for half-sections of men could be rapidly deployed in a single helicopter and a Troop of 36 men moved in six aircraft. Helicopters also resupplied the British forward bases in country that had no roads, in many places no tracks, and swamps near the coasts where the maze of waterways contrasted with the high jungle on mountain ridges, along which ran the Sarawak border in places at heights of 2000 m.

In January 1963, No. 2 Section was withdrawn to Singapore. In later years from 1965, the swimmers in training there worked with the locally based submarine squadrons from time to time, improving methods of re-entry into a boat at depth, doing some underwater fishing in their spare time.

In 1963 in Borneo British forces had contained the

rebellion, but in April Sukarno launched a long-expected raid by Indonesian forces. This, and others, were driven off, but the British and Malaysian commanders now learnt that there were also possibilities of such raids gaining support from clandestine Communist cells (whether Sukarno wished this or not) who had been training with some of the 8500 shotguns held legally by many Chinese, who had registered these weapons with the police. As a result the police were ordered to recover such weapons, not only from the Chinese shopkeepers and traders, but also from the Iban longhouses. These communal villages-within-villages each held in its bare wooden walls twelve to sixteen families usually above a river bank, where the flood of water on some sites helped to keep the ground clean beneath the hut's slatted floor, used to simplify sanitation. Outside many longhouse doors hung ceremonial shields and the blackened nineteenth-century relics of Iban head-hunting, with occasionally a more recent skull of a soldier from the Second World War – not all of which may have been Japanese heads. The Royal Marines reinforcing the police in recovering shotguns from these homesteads, included patrols from a company led by an SBS officer. His men moved silently deep into the jungle, to come upstream of a river village; after acquiring several native boats they then drifted silently downriver. Landing at the village at dawn, the police team with them was able to collect any firearms before they could be hidden. In all, this company and its police teams collected 300 weapons during a couple of weeks, and took in 60 rebel suspects for interrogation.

The Commandos took their turn with Army battalions in tours of three- and later five-month spells in the jungle, as part of the British forces in Borneo. The landward borders were well covered against incursions by SAS, Gurkha, Marine and Border Scouts patrols, although some raiders did get through to intimidate isolated traders, steal goods and unsettle village communities.

No. 2 SBS came back to Borneo in the early summer to work with 40 Commando on the River Rajang, a fast-flowing water highway sweeping down some 500 km from the Iran Range through Sibu to its estuary on the north coast of Sarawak's Third Division. Here the Section perfected their jungle training, shooting the rapids of the river in their Klepper canoes and learning to distinguish in riverside hides between the harmless 7-cm grasshoppers 'which they brushed aside, while more dangerous insects were treated with respect', particularly the lice carried by river rats, which spread an often fatal fever. They watched out for ambushes from overhanging riverside trees and the black-and-yellow poisonous snakes that could drop from the mangroves into their boat.

One SBS officer piloted an SRN-5 hovercraft, patrolling swamps near the border, where the Anglo-Malaysian command feared that the Indonesians might be running guns through the maze of waterways to the TNKU and to Communist cells. The hovercraft proved effective in crossing all manner of swamp, shallows and open ground and was probably less vulnerable to small-arms fire than helicopters. Its drawback was and is the shipping space that it requires for carriage to an assault beach for conventional operations. In Borneo canoes were used, along with army metal assault boats, inflatables and an assortment of river craft – including native canoes.

In the early autumn, a season as hot and humid in Borneo as any other time of the year, 2 SBS, after a spell in Singapore, moved their recce operations further west where their special skills in small boats would be put to the test. Concern over Indonesian gun-running had extended to Datu Point where the northwestern border of Sarawak reaches the coast. There a company of 1/6 Gurkhas based on Sematan had patrols along the border, after recently taking over from 42 Commando, and the marine commando CO had originally asked for the SBS teams. (It was a request that stemmed in part perhaps because one of his young troop officers had capsized an assault boat when trying to land a patrol.) The SB Section had an experienced captain, originally a National Service officer who became one of several long-service SB Section Commanders. He found the Gurkha company commander somewhat autocratic. The Gurkha major was influenced perhaps by Field Marshal Slim, one of the most respected Gurkha officers, who wrote: 'The idea that certain operations of war were so difficult that only a specially equipped *corps d'élite* could be expected to undertake them' was a nonsense, because wars were won 'by the average quality of the standard unit'. This view he amplified by saying that any action 'in which more than a handful of men were engaged should be regarded as [a] normal operation'. The action on the western Sarawak coast was one for a handful of men in four canoes.

The canoe teams were secretly inserted on to a small island some 5 km off the coast where they made use of a deserted house. From this island, known to the canoeists as Turtle Island, canoes ran into Datu Point at night and established a hidden OP. From there they had a clear view, during the middle of the day, of the jungle-fringed coast running southwest into Indonesian Borneo. Watching and checking what could be seen from the Point nevertheless had its limitations. And, on one occasion at least, the canoes coming in to relieve the men in the OP were mistaken by a patrolling Royal Naval vessel for Indonesians – fortunately with no 'own goals'.

The Indonesian Army had meanwhile taken over the organization of all raids into Sarawak, after a number of attacks by Indonesian Border Terrorists had come to a short and bloody end in ambushes of the Security Forces, while the Indonesian Navy began setting up caches of arms and explosives in the Riau Archipalego, that string of islands south of Singapore. The explosives would be used by the Chinese Communists who had fled to Indonesia after their cells could no longer use local training areas when security patrols intensified that summer: 54 such volunteers as agents, young men and girls, had been caught on the border in early June; but not all the revolutionaries were immature.

The Malaysian prime minister since 1957, Tunku Abdul Rahman, had by now made every endeavour to resolve the Confrontation and had welcomed a visit by United Nations observers to Borneo, but there was one step that his military commanders could not countenance: counter-terrorist actions across the border into Indonesia. The British were thus put in a difficult political position, one that was later resolved by the simple expedient of not informing the Malaysian brigadiers commanding the various military districts after August 1963 of such raids. The Gurkha company to which the SBS were attached received their orders in the normal way from the battalion's CO, who arranged the first cross-border operation along the west coast from Datu Point in late August.

For this operation the canoeists were taken in a minesweeper to a point beyond Indonesian territorial waters, from where they paddled inshore. They came into a beach which had jungle palms close to the shoreline. After first checking that Indonesian patrols were not concealed there, the SCs hid their canoes. At daybreak the canoeists set off on foot for what was the first of several patrols along this coastline, but they found no evidence of regular or irregular forces. They came out that night after thirty hours ashore taking care not to leave indications that might tell the curious that the area had been visited. Within the week, Gurkha patrols were also moving along the coast, being resupplied by the canoeists in night landings. They checked the villages and jungle paths for signs of Indonesian intruders.

The Section had been covering the coastal frontier and beyond for some weeks before they were withdrawn to Singapore, where No. 2 SBS was joined by No. 1 and they were partly amalgamated for ease of administration. They had been training in Singapore when one or two had the almost inevitable parachute injuries of broken ankles or sprained knees that befall men who make many jumps and from which they recovered in weeks rather than months. But once again the need to polish up the detailed training for an immediate role limited the time available to keep their collective hands in at others.

Then, a few days before Christmas 1963, an Indonesian incursion group crossed the border and raided a shop in Serudong on Monday 21 December. The raiders were hard hit, but among those captured were Indonesian marines who claimed to have expected local help from 'people discontented with Malaysia'. Several other parties crossed the border in western Sarawak and over the hills of the central mountains, but met with little success in the face of the highly mobile defence.

1 and 2 SBS had carried out river patrols in several tours in Borneo, during late 1963 and 1964. In October 1964, No. 2 SBS were flown in at thirty six hours' notice to the area of the River Serudong, to help round up Indonesian and Chinese subversives who were finding their way across the border by sea. Six of these had recently been captured by Special Branch police officers after the party had become discouraged in their attempts to recruit and train Communist cells. Although local people were not interested in a bureaucratic ideology, the possibilities for local recuitment of rebels could not be ignored. To counter this threat, the SBS helped to create with 40 Commando what became the Tawau Assault Group. This force was equipped with cabin cruisers, dories and native craft powered by outboards, as well as SBS canoes. The Royal Marines also trained ten coxswains of 3 Royal Malay Regiment to pilot dories in the border waterways. The demarcation between Indonesia and Federal Malaysia (which Sarawak and Sabah had joined in August 1963) was difficult to identify among the backwaters of the River Serudong, which in places ran through thick jungle a kilometre or less from Indonesia, or on Sebatik Island where the border halved the island.

Southwest of Sebatik Island, across a narrow channel, the Indonesian marines had bases on Nanukan Island. Their purpose was to disrupt the hardwood timber trade in Sabah. British intelligence reports in October indicated definite plans by the Indonesians for operations on this

Sibuk Bay coast. A shoreline of mangrove swamps and tidal rivers made it a difficult area to patrol from the district capital of Tawau, a small port with a population of 4300. To the northwest lay Cowie Harbour, an anchorage north of Sebatik Island (with Wallace Bay settlement boasting the only squash court in these parts). Inland from the harbour was the logging centre of Kalabakan, raided the previous December, where large water pools held the felled timber waiting to be rafted out to ships. The trees had come downriver from several logging camps connected by a series of gravel roads through the primary jungle.

Wallace Bay was No. 2 Section's headquarters, from which they patrolled south down the coast in Army assault boats. The distances were too great to paddle, and the Gemini with its outboard was the next best craft to an alloy assault boat, none of which were available. They had also been preparing an OP high in a dead tree near the border. When this came down in a storm, the need for a covert watching point seemed less essential than to deter the Indonesians from using the channel running north into Cowie Harbour. So the Section manned a harbour launch, callsign 'Papa Charlie', which openly watched the passing coasters, junks and local boats.

Indonesian marines kept a similar watch from a bamboo tower on the southwest coast of Sebatik Island, where scrub and jungle came down to the shore. The post had a clear westward view across the waters to other Indonesian bases on Nanukan Island, and provided a coast watch against possible visits by Security Forces coming across the border to infiltrate these training camps. The observation point posed no direct threat to 40 Commando in the Tawau area, but its destruction would undermine Indonesian morale and might make the enemy more defensive rather than offensively minded: for what the Security Forces could do once they might well repeat. In such a war of threat and counterthreat, therefore, the Indonesian post was an obvious target. But before an attack could be launched, a recce would have to be made to determine the state of the ground just beyond the beach, and whether or not barbed wire entanglements and mines were hidden at the jungle's edge. Four SB swimmers were sent to find the answers to such questions one moonless night in November. Their inflatable lurked just out of view of the watchtower while the two swimmers slipped over the side and then swam towards the beach. They reached the beach a little way south of the tower, coming ashore to find no defences in the clump of palms and scrub nearby. They could make out an attap (palm-clad) hut to their right, 70 m from the tower, where the lookouts off watch were sitting round a flickering fire. The swimmers withdrew, having estimated the distance from tower to hut, located the likely impenetrable clumps of scrub and thorn, and found that a small beach southeast of the tower was suitable to land several inflatables.

Their report was studied by 40 Commando who decided to mount a raid in force against the post by fifteen marines led by an SBS lieutenant. They came down the coast in a small motor cruiser, *Bob Sawyer*, on the night of 8 December and launched three inflatables some distance short of the border. These were then paddled south, one staying near the border as covering protection – its GPMG would deter any patrol boats from pursuing the commandos as they withdrew. The other two inflatables covered the 9 km to that sandy beach mentioned in the recce report, with its clump of palms and the hut to the right. The plan was to position two scouts between the OP and the hut to prevent any Indonesians escaping along the path, or – if there were reinforcements sent towards the hut – to prevent them from interfering in what was expected to be a short, sharp fight. The scouts each had an electric torch strapped to his Armalite rifle as an improvised 'night vision aid' but these would not be needed. As the lieutenant's craft beached, it came under inaccurate machine-gun fire – the men in the tower had spotted the movement below them. In the split second that usually decides the outcome of small raids, the lieutenant called to his assault team with their SMGs to 'spread out left and assault forward' as he ran towards the hut. His sergeant, with a GPMG gunner to the right, waded waist-deep along the shore guided by the hutfire. The lieutenant also headed for it, crossing patches of open ground as he raced 70 m towards the hut. In the darkness he misjudged the distance, stumbled, ran on and looked up to find the hut looming before him. His shout of 'Grenades!' sent the sergeant and his gunner ducking for cover under the water, holding their weapons high over their heads as they did so. The lieutenant had lobbed two M26 grenades into the doorway. These had barely exploded before a stream of 9-mm rounds from his SMG raked the palm-leaf shanty. The assault team at last came up (the jungle scrub having been too thick for them to 'spread left') to count three bodies. The patrol's orders were clear: they must not get involved in any prolonged fire-fight. As the element of surprise had been lost very early in the raid, there was now no alternative but to withdraw before the enemy could organize an effective counterattack. Back aboard the Geminis, in no time the raiders had sufficient water under them to open up the throttles of the outboards and make good their escape, just as mortar bombs began to rain down close to the observation post. The only casualty was the lieutenant, with a flesh wound in his clbow, which was probably the cause of his tumble although he did not realize he had been hit until after the skirmish.

SB teams made other recces including several to the islands in the swamps south of Kalabakan. No. 2 Section were back in Singapore by Christmas 1964, leaving the Tawau Assault Group boats manned by naval, marine and 1/10 Gurkha personnel, with Malaysian navy patrol boats and *Monitor*, a big raft carrying an 81-mm/3-inch mortar. At night the guard boat, a frigate still using the call-sign 'Papa Charlie', fired star-shells, and RAF aircraft dropped flares to light the swamp.

The Confrontation in 1965 continued with Indonesian parties crossing the border in bands of 40 to 50, to be met by determined resistance. The Security Forces were reinforced:

2 Para were in action several times that April and May; Australian and New Zealand regiments reached Borneo early in 1965; and the result was that the Indonesians and their Communist supporters resorted to terrorism. Several Chinese loyal to Malaysia were hung near their homes in west Sarawak, eight civilians were shot in one raid on a homestead. These were not the first attempts to terrorize the Chinese and Malays, for many of the explosives and weapons hidden in the Riau islands had been smuggled into the mainland states. Headquarters, Far East Land Forces, in Singapore, had been collating intelligence on these clandestine operations for over a year, when in January 1965 they called on the SBS for reconnaissance and advice. There are strong arguments for saying that all special forces should be controlled from a theatre headquarters, but this was the first time such operations were organized at the theatre level of command during the Indonesian Confrontation. The plan in the Riau Archipelago was to seize the arms caches in raids by men of the Malay Rangers. These Malaysian special forces were trained on commando lines and given training in boat work by Royal Marines. SBS officers helped with the training and found the need for a high-speed small raiding craft. Cheaply built Malay power boats were chosen: they could carry twelve men and, powered by twin 70-hp outboards, would do 20 knots in reasonable sea conditions. (The successor to these improvised raiding craft would be the Rigid Raider, which made many sorties in the Falkland Islands.)

While the Rangers were being put through their paces in training, the SB Sections also practised their techniques for landing by canoe from submarines. Their first recce during the moonless nights early in May 1965 was to Labuan Bilik. The routine followed the pattern of Second World War landings, with the added advantage that submarines could tow in the raiding craft as they had done in Korea, saving the marines the chore of paddling. A periscope recce of the island on 5 May with panoramic photographs showed no sign of Indonesian occupation. The submarine lay well

clear of the island until nightfall, when she floated off a
Gemini and four canoes 8 km from the beach. Linked to the
inflatable, the canoes were then towed inshore by the submarine and beached without mishap. There was no sign of
any enemy activity, and the marines paddled back to RV with
the submarine. But a reconnaissance at the next 'dark
period' found Indonesian patrols on a second island. One of
the three teams that landed on this rocky island found a path
which led to the jungle edge above a cliff. Up to this point
they had been covered by one of the other canoes moving a
little way offshore, but once they disappeared into the jungle
the covering team moved back to the landing beach. The two
canoeists in the third boat swam ashore, climbed quietly over
the rocks and moved inland to higher ground overlooking
some huts. From their vantage point the swimmers could see
men moving about but little else; to go closer risked not only
compromising the recce but (as always in beach reconnaissance) compromising any further raid.

Two canoes came off without difficulty after several hours
ashore, but the two marines who had gone into the jungle
had difficulty launching their canoe, and decided that they
would have to lay up for the day. They disassembled their
canoe and hid it from view before finding themselves a
suitable refuge in which to while away a tropical day. On the
next night a Gemini came into the emergency RV and
collected the canoeists and their canoe. The following night,
making full use of the 'dark' period, a third recce was made
by these canoeists to an island close to the Sumatra coast. A
small river estuary was the target, against which three canoe
teams landed with instructions not to go up the river. They
were looking for the boats used to smuggle arms as well as the
arms themselves, and knowing the ways of the leader of this
recce there is no doubt that he took his canoe as far as was
practical up the estuary.

Thus the cycle of reconnaissance continued, carefully
planned to coordinate recces and raids in a way that added to
the intelligence picture. This information came in part from
the Special Branch, whose knowledge of Indonesian infiltra-

tion on to the mainland was extensive. There had been landings by three parties totalling over 100, who crossed the 30 km of the Malacca Straits on 17 August; but many were captured within 48 hours. An attempt on 1 September to parachute 192 men into the jungle was equally unsuccessful, as most of these were caught within the month. Later landings were similarly contained by the Security Forces. They learnt that, as in Borneo, the raiders had expected local support; and that they had been equally disappointed.

Observers in the lighthouse, Raffles Light, and in patrol boats watched for any suspicious movements across waters, especially from the two Indonesian islands immediately south of Singapore. These were recced late in June, an LCVP taking the canoes inshore from a minesweeper. Two teams approached each island where they made beach surveys and, so far as they were able, checked out the island's occupants. The islands were so close to Singapore that the reflection of the city's lights cast light on to the beaches. In this eerie light the task was more difficult, the team from one canoe having to swim east around a headland after beaching their canoe in order to get a closer look at a hut. They had just crawled on to the beach when they heard a dog bark. Almost immediately a man came out of the hut to quieten the animal. The swimmers froze where they lay on the tide line. Fearing discovery, they decided to return to the canoe. But it was a more difficult swim than they had expected: the current was so strong that they could make no headway, and they were forced to go with it and swim towards Singapore. Meanwhile, the three canoes were paddled back to the minesweeper as planned. The two missing raiders had to swim for several hours until they were 10 km north of the islands before they were picked up by a British ship on patrol off Singapore. By June 1965, with terrorist rather than military action being Sukarno's last hope, one suspects that the Indonesians made little of their finds. When Indonesian parties were caught they probably put their discovery down to informers working for the Special Branch, without attributing those to the SBS – an error others have made.

By the summer of 1965, the centre of the world's attention was switching to Vietnam. In Borneo, there were signs that Indonesian incursions were decreasing; ambushes set up throughout that summer by the Security Forces found fewer Indonesian intruders than for several years. By 1966, the 70,000-strong Security Forces were intercepting Indonesian parties as they crossed the frontier. The Royal Marines fought their last action of the Confrontation in mid-March, pursuing Indonesian commandos south of Biawak. A truce was finally agreed in August. The total casualties of the Commonwealth military forces in this undeclared war, which had lasted over four years, were 114 killed and 181 injured, a fifth of the Indonesian losses, half of whom were prisoners. The SBS had suffered no fatalities, but a number had gone down with virulent diseases such as scrub-typhus with its weakening fevers, kidney failure and possible death of the victim in a coma.

While Nos. 1 and 2 SBS had been fighting among the swamps and forests of Asia, other swimmer-canoeists were in the equally hot but more arid climate of the Arabian peninsula. Some operated in their Section teams; others fought in 45 Commando, away from the Squadron; and others were seconded to the forces of the Sultan of Oman. No. 6 SBS was still based in Europe, sending teams to recce potential landing places for British Forces wherever the country's interests might require this. They may even have recced some African beaches, for in 1967 one of the commando carriers, HMS *Albion*, spent 100 days off the West African coast. Certainly from about this time there began a special relationship between the Squadron and the highest British government authorities, which made the swimmer-canoeists something of a law unto themselves within the Royal Marines, but operations in Borneo had confirmed their professional ability.

The Sand Seas

The mud-walled city of Muscat, which lies by a busy if little known natural harbour on the Gulf of Oman, was ruled in 1957 by a gentleman recluse, the Sultan Said bin Talmur. He lived for long periods away from his capital, Muscat, several weeks' camel drive to the south in the coast town of Salalah in the largely desert province of Dhofar, which had come to be regarded by his Omani tribesmen of the north as their Sultan's personal domain. A sheik governed Dhofar on behalf of the Sultan, the same man being governor from 1932 to 1970, which says much for the stability of this administration.

Increasingly, the rulers of the Arabian peninsula were under pressure from Arab nationalists encouraged by President Nasser of Egypt, and in the next twenty years the Arabian coastal states would be torn by the dissensions of this nationalism, adding to the long-standing disputes between tribes. The rule of the Sultan of Oman was challenged by local tribesmen in 1955; thereafter the cause of the nationalists, at first backed by Egyptian propaganda, Saudi money and Soviet arms, would spread from Yemen on the west coast (which became a military republic in 1962) through the Aden Protectorate and Aden State (a British colony until 1963) to wash against the defences of Dhofar in the 1970s. On the high plateaux north of Aden, the tribesmen formed a National Liberation Front, while the Aden unions supported the Front for the Liberation of Occupied South Yemen. Meanwhile, a group of sheiks formed the Federation of Arab Emirates of the South, and their Federal Government took operational control of the local levies in 1961.

Each night, the gates of the city of Muscat were closed, as they had been for over seven hundred years: but the pressures of western communications and ideas could not be shut out, despite the Sultan doing his best to exclude what he felt were evil influences against his people's religion. He did not allow the import of transistor radios, sunglasses, cameras,

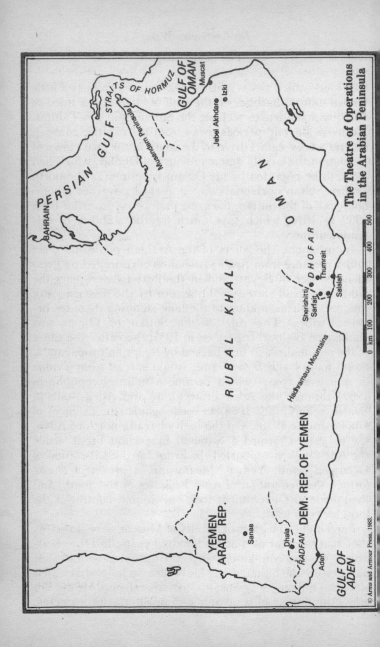

The Theatre of Operations
in the Arabian Peninsula

GULF OF HORMUZ

GULF OF OMAN

Muscat

Izki

Jebel Akhdar

Musandam Peninsula

STRAITS OF HORMUZ

PERSIAN GULF

BAHRAIN

O M A N

RUB AL KHALI

DHOFAR

Sherishitti
Sarfait
Thumrait
Salalah

Hadhramaut Mountains

YEMEN ARAB REP.

DEM. REP. OF YEMEN

Sanaa

Dhala

RADFAN

Aden

GULF OF ADEN

0 km 100 200 300 400 500

© Arms and Armour Press, 1983.

dolls, gas cookers or other western trappings. More drastic was his distrust of education for his 550,000 people – he feared that the expatriate teachers who would be involved in any large-scale education scheme would be inclined to be left wing, a likely challenge to his 'autocratic benevolence'. Not without reason was he concerned for the state's security: in 1955 the Imam Ghabia had seized power in the mountains and, although he had been overthrown in a bloodless coup, two years later he had reappeared to incite the hill tribes. This time he had the backing of Saudi Arabian money, Egyptian propaganda and the help of his brother Talib.

The British had been an ally of the Sultanate since 1798, an alliance of significance in the 1950s because the northern tip of the Musandam Peninsula belongs to the Sultanate. This headland commands the Hormuz Strait, through which half of the free world's oil passed from the Persian Gulf in that decade. The Sultan received military advice from the British, and in December 1957 a lieutenant and six senior NCOs were sent from Royal Marine detachments in the Persian Gulf Frigate Squadron to help train the Sultan's forces. At least, that is what they expected to do. In fact, they were flown from Bahrain to 'a stony camp at Izki and found themselves involved in one of the fiercest battles of the year'. In 1958 a more formal arrangement was made between Said and the British Foreign Office, which created the Sultan's Armed Forces, commanded by senior British officers. The troops were mainly Omanis from the north, well disciplined, cheerful and able to withstand the stifling heat, but with little resistance to the cold and wet of the monsoon-shrouded coastal hills during June to September. Among the British officers and NCOs seconded to SAF were a number of Royal Marines (including swimmer-canoeists) who, after the initial tour of the ships' marines, came from the Commando Brigade on six-month tours.

During 1958, Talib led the tribes on Jebel Akhdar, the high arid plateau of the 3000-m range known as the Green

Mountain, in a revolt against the Sultan. To counter this, British forces, including SAS and marines seconded to the Sultan's army, were brought in, and in little more than a month they had the situation under control and the rebellion petered out.

In 1962 another minor rebellion began in Dhofar, with sniping at SAF vehicles and the blowing up of an oil exploration truck. This last was a small indication of major changes to come in the Sultanate before the final defeat of these rebels, who three years later formed the Dhofar Liberation Front. For another ten years they would fight on, with Communist help from the former Aden Protectorates. These became the 'People's Democratic Republic of Yemen' in 1967. The diplomatic difficulty for the British in the 1960s lay in the practical realities of sheikdoms ruled by hereditary princes, with whom the British were linked by long-standing treaties, but who were rulers without any formal expression of their people's choice as defined by the United Nations. In this feudal situation, British troops, including 45 Commando, which first went to Aden Colony in April 1960, had a difficult task. They fulfilled it with good humour, professionalism and the ability to help the less fortunate that has earned British servicemen the goodwill of poor people around the world. '45' kept two Troops, rotating them at intervals on the North Yemen border to help the Federation Regular Army prevent arms, agents and troublemakers infiltrating into the Protectorate, while other Troops from time to time helped the Security Forces in Aden.

The situation took a turn for the worse in December 1963 after an unsuccessful attempt to assassinate the governor and several federal ministers. Although the FRA battalions cleared the road to Dhala and penetrated the desert strongholds of the Radfan, there were not sufficient of them to hold this vast plateau and the Yemen border at the same time. Therefore the Federation called on the British in March to help the FRA in accordance with the Anglo-Federation treaty. The task fell to 45 Commando. It was a war of ambush and patrol, but the best the marines could do was to contain the tribesmen, who were never completely subdued. SBS swimmer-canoeists, far from their usual environment, played their part in these skirmishes, for their training fitted them particularly well for deep penetration patrols. These were often made by the Commando's Recce Troop, some 60 men trained along SAS lines to lead the Commando in night infiltrations, and who could survive for long periods in the torrid heat of the day in the Radfan valleys by conserving energy and water.

This Troop had its first kills in Wadi Dhubsan, over 20 km from the Aden road, on the east of the high central plateau, when the Recce Troop were left in a deserted village with enough food and water for eight days. They lay low despite the overpowering heat of an Arabian day on the rock-hard ground of the wadi floor. Each night they set ambushes, while some kilometres away to the north on high ground overlooking the village a Rifle Troop had a patrol base to provide additional fire power if needed. In the early hours of 12 July, their third night in the village, Jock's Section moved to the north from the village to a position where five tracks met around a hillock on which stood a ruined mud-walled house. The sentry hidden in the roof saw two tribesmen making every use of cover in what marines described as 'moving tactically down the wadi'. They were at the 'house' before the sentry could alert the Section but, fortunately, did not see the marines. A short time later they returned hand-in-hand and were both killed at 300 m by a couple of clean shots from Jock's Section.

The marines then prepared to be counterattacked, but the two friends had been on a lone walk for their own enjoyment. Nevertheless, when the first man had been killed, his companion with extreme bravery had fired back at the marines despite being wounded. Half the Section moved out of the ruined house to search for the bodies. Jock's broad Scottish accent came over the radio to report the finding of the first body nearly an hour after the contact. Then his men found the second body 'eight zero bravo, ye can count that as tey' confirming by radio the Section's success. This was the first time that rebels' bodies had been recovered in the Radfan, one proving to be a rebel leader and the second man wanted for murder.

There was at least one SBS-type raid down the coast from Aden in operations mounted by Royal Marines to put ashore SAS and other parties. The long southern coastline of Arabia is mostly sheer cliffs where the Hadhramaut mountains, for example, end in 500 m of near-vertical rock above the sea. The few breaks in the cliff face are narrow, towering gulleys with climbable routes to the plateau above, where in one area a dissident Yemeni-trained band of about twenty terrorists had their base. This lair was unapproachable overland, for tribesmen would give warning of any fighting patrol's approach and the Yemeni terrorists would skip away further down the coast; but they had no regular watch on the gulley, as they did not expect anyone to come 'knocking at the back door'.

A Royal Navy landing ship with LCMs and helicopters aboard came along the coast one night to pluck these terrorists from their seclusion. It was a task that called for delicate timing, quick action and iron nerve. The raiding party was drawn from the SAS, the LCM crew being marines and the two helicopters flown by naval pilots. There were political considerations one suspects in this operation, for it was mounted far away from the usual areas in which British forces were keeping the peace. Certainly, the LCM was held on her start line until the last possible minute before being given the 'Go' signal, and she hit the beach just at first light. The helicopters disgorged their assault parties and the terrorists were seized before they had any chance to take up their weapons. Back aboard the warship the terrorists were interrogated in the calmer atmosphere of the ship's offices. They were later passed to civilian authorities for trial, convicted of terrorism and shot.

During 1964, various British regiments had undercover teams working in Arab dress. A man on this duty had to be able to draw a pistol from the folds of his futah robe quickly enough to surprise a terrorist on a chance encounter. These teams searched for well-trained assassins, who by any standards were competent marksmen, with intelligence and a ruthless passion for their cause. One patrol of uniformed marines from 45 Commando found during a cordon-and-search operation that they were not the only avid readers of their Corps magazine. They had put a ring of men around the mud-walled shanties with their hot corrugated 'tin' roofs in one back alley, before methodically searching each room. In one they found a copy of the latest *Globe and Laurel* open at the page narrating the Commando's activities in Aden some six weeks earlier. The Arab readers had vanished, but their choice of literature indicated their understanding of the principle of 'knowing your enemy' (a principle they followed through in making their main targets the Special Branch officers working undercover). 45 Commando, along with units of other regiments, formed small Special Branch Sections of their own; in '45's' case two teams of four men working mostly by night in civilian clothes. They would drive in a disguised Land-Rover or a smart civilian car, their hair longer than usual, shoes not too shiny and in general appearing not to be military, as they pulled up by some club or loitered as if deciding where to have a night out. They would gain entry to the selected night spot, appearing as tourists, perhaps; or were they men from the local refinery having a roisterous look at the pleasures of the East? The restaurant owner did not care until suddenly these diners stood up, armed and ready, while some suspect at the next table but two was disarmed before he realized that this was a raid. The work brought out once again those lessons learnt in Malaya: the value of close cooperation between police and the military in anti-terrorist operations.

British officers were attached to Federation sheiks' courts and the Princes' councils of war. Known as Political Officers, these British representatives could advise the local rulers on tactics. Later the Political Officer could assess the result of particular military operations in terms of its effect on the balances of local power. In less formal ways, the British troops too were among the most successful of political emissaries. One marine lieutenant on his routine patrols had a naval medic with him who administered simple remedies to sick children. Although the patrol never followed the same route twice, or visited villages at predictable times, they came to be frequently met by 'a local sick parade of ailing children, pregnant mums and infirm old men' – not what they were expecting on the first few occasions. By the time they had built this rapport with the tribes, however, the campaign was nearing its finale.

On the eastern coast of the Arabian peninsula, meantime, the Sultan of Oman's forces continued their steady resistance to outside intervention and local dissidents. These now came mainly from Dhofar, where the southwestern border was settled in 1965 after lengthy negotiations with the Governor of Aden. But it remained an unmarked and largely unrecognized boundary in both physical and legal senses. Tribesmen crossed it at will, and although Sarfait was acknowledged by all to be in the Sultan's province, the coastal village of Hauf was in the Aden Protectorate. The Sultan's Armed Forces continued to have the benefit of British officers and senior NCOs seconded to them, but the employment of officers and NCOs of various nationalities on contracts was increasing. Such contract personnel were men of military experience many of whom had resigned from the British forces; they accepted specific terms of service for the Sultan. They were not, of course, subject to British military law: they could be given a reprimand, fired or dismissed, but while in Oman were subject to the Sultanate's laws. A varied and interesting crowd, many were extremely good; some – escaping domestic crisis at home, perhaps – were not. Among one of the best contract officers was Captain Hamish Emslie, MC, RM, one of the Corps 'characters' and a fine leader. He had won his MC in Malaya, a Mention in Despatches during the Suez crisis and had been an 'SBS officer of considerable renown'. His unconventional leadership seldom followed accepted military routines, but achieved the loyalty of his men, particularly when he commanded X Troop of 45 Commando in the late 1950s. He was commanding a company of SAF in Dhofar in May 1966 when he was killed, leading his men from the front as was his custom. The operations of SAF at this time were largely directed towards protecting the oil drillers working on the edge of the Rubal Khali, the empty quarter of trackless desert across which no one had ventured except the occasional explorer. Here in 1967 the drillers struck oil, with lasting effects on the economy and importance of the Sultanate.

That same year the British also quit Aden. In the final months of the agonized birth of the Republic of South Yemen, the NLF fought FLOSY. The Federation Regular Army, renamed the 'Southern Arabian Army', deserted the sheiks and declared its support for the NLF, with whom the British Government negotiated a final handover of authority. In the last couple of months of these negotiations, the orders to 45 Commando were so repeatedly changed that while patrols on the streets had one set of instructions on when to open fire, their colonel was briefing his company commanders on a second set, just before he was called to Brigade HQ for a third. 45 Commando left Aden by air on the night of 28/29 November, 42 Commando by helicopter to their commando carrier next morning.

South Yemen was now left to determine its own future with neighbouring Oman. Understandably, having seen the British leave, the impoverished Yemenis cast their eyes eastward at the potential oil wealth of Oman. Fostering revolution in Dhofar was a first step to achieving this prize, and it was not a difficult one to take. The polyglot peoples of the province lived mostly in coastal villages and were Kathiri tribesmen. In the mountains lived the nomadic herdsmen who fed their cattle on dried fish in the arid months of March to May, never wandering outside their tribal areas. But one tribe, the Mahra, were a warlike people who knew no boundaries, for their goat and camel herds frequently crossed the border. From their number came a notable soldier of fortune named Barakat, who had fought for the British in Aden; for a good deal of money and arms he was prepared to continue a frontier war for the Sultan. With over 100 warriors and their families in the high hills of southern Dhofar, he carried out a series of raids against Yemeni forces. A wily, clever rogue he later succeeded in getting himself off the Yemenis' hit list and returned with his men to the South Yemen side of the border.

Said's only son, Qaboos, had been trained at Sandhurst. In 1970 'with assistance from individuals and sources which may never be known' he engineered an almost bloodless coup. He then set about introducing an enlightened and progressive programme to improve the lot of his peoples, which did something to take the steam out of propaganda from DLF's successors, the People's Front for the Liberation of the Arabian Gulf. Their bullies had driven the SAF forces from the mountains, tossed any resistant tribesmen off cliffs or tortured them into acceptance of Communism by burning out an eye or roasting their genitals. Qaboos's reforms gave men reasons to resist such terror, and not surprisingly there was great rejoicing when he came to power. (His father retired to the Dorchester Hotel in London, where he died two years later.) Among a number of actions in which swimmer-canoeists became involved, either as officers on loan or on contract, were deep penetration patrols and company operations as the mountains were gradually repossessed by the SAF.

Sometimes they fought in the hammering heat of the coastal plain, more often in ambush in the high mountains or in the clammy cold of the monsoon cloud when troops on the ground could not get air support. Sarfait, above the border escarpment, was seized in a *coup de main* by helicopter-borne elements of the Omani Regiment in 1972. The lodgement could not be extended along the Darra ridge, 20 km to the sea, but this isolated battalion stronghold denied the Communists a camel route, although SAF battalions holding it had to be supplied by air. Two hundred warriors, looking for a spectacular victory, attacked in July 1973 the coast village of Mirbat, east of Salalah and over 200 km from the border. Their combat groups – as Tony Geraghty describes so vividly in *Who Dares Wins* – attacked an SAS team of ten, which drove the warriors back up the hill. The Communist forces received a bloody blow from which they never recovered. Two SAS soldiers were killed together with two SAF defenders.

By 1974 a 53-km fence of Dannert wire protected by mines had been laid in a continuous stretch up near-precipices, across rock barriers and through the jungle scrub. Picketed and patrolled, this 'Horndean' line, 45 km west of Salalah, was never crossed by the Communists' camel trains. But further west, below the enclave at Sarfait, their supply route passed across the so-called Capstan plateau which, although below the Sarfait escarpment, could only be reached from the enclave by crossing a broad wadi and scaling a vertical rock wall 200 m high to reach the camel route. On the afternoon of 15 February 1975 an RM captain in a penetration raid typical of SBS desert operations had led a seven-man patrol down into the steep valley, across its floor and begun to work his way up the precipice. By 1730 they had climbed to a point halfway up the rock wall where a gulley ran back and up to the summit. The captain left five men there and clambered up the remaining 100 m with his Omani sergeant-major to recce a cave near the top of the climb. He intended to cache food and water here for future patrols who would operate on the Capstan plateau. So far all had gone well, for the patrol was the first to scale the cliff, but just as Captain Dick stepped carefully across bare rock to avoid mines, his sergeant-major triggered one off.

It is possible that the sergeant-major had a moment's inattention – costing him his left foot and more – but the Communists may have been using a type of camouflaged mine. SOE had mines which looked like cowpats, camel dung or elephant droppings, depending on the climate in which they were laid. Whatever the cause, Dick's patrol was in difficulty. The patrol's medical orderly and a lance-corporal scrambled up to help, the corporal triggering a second mine which badly injured both of them. Fortunately, the enemy had not heard the explosions or, if they had, decided not to interfere as two Strikemasters had appeared to cover the patrol. Dick had radio contact with the Desert Regiment's HQ which sent in a ten-man patrol who by the time it was dark had stretchers and ropes a third of the way up the precipice. Dick had climbed down to meet them and act as their guide. They reached the gulley another 100 m up the face without mishap, but a third patrol in going further towards the cave set off another mine. In the dark it was difficult to distinguish firm rock from any soft ground around it, and this probably led to the third mishap, which seriously wounded one soldier and destroyed the medical kit of a doctor with these reinforcements.

The operation was turning into a disaster, but one man was lowered to the first ledge above the wadi floor – the route lay diagonally up the cliff from the ledge 'Point 3', to the gulley mouth 'Point 2' and up to the cave at 'Point 1'. He was lifted out by helicopter at 2345 hours, but died on the way to Salalah. A contract officer, Captain Keith Ride, moved up to do what he could for the three other wounded, despite the difficulty of climbing the steep route less than a couple of metres wide running up from Point 2. Torches had been brought and a stretcher party, risking more mines, carried the wounded down from '1' to '2', where the sergeant-major died. His body was carefully laid aside and all the available ropes used to lower the other two wounded men. It was a difficult operation in difficult conditions, with the risk of attack uppermost in the minds of those not on the cliff face. There, they were too busy with their ropes and stretchers to think of such consequences. But the CO of the regiment flew in more sections and the Brigade Reserve was stood to. These actions were coordinated by radio, relayed from one of the Sultan's Defender aircraft, whose pilot flew over the scene for nine hours in a lonely but vital vigil. At

0500 hours the wounded reached Point 3 and were 'casevacced'. An hour later the Strikemasters were back and covered the survivors' withdrawal from the wadi floor back up to Sarfait. Captain Dick wanted to bring out the sergeant-major's body, but this would have added two hours to the recovery operation, putting all the force at risk for an hour or more in daylight on the cliff, inviting warrior sharpshooters to exact an even higher toll. The Capstan plateau was later reached by a recce patrol of eighteen men on the night of 23/24 May.

Gradually, the tide of war and of loyalties in the mountains turned in the Sultan's favour. The drilling of deep (1000-m) water wells, the introduction of schools, the cattle owners receiving stock to improve the local breed – all won over the tribesmen's support. A tarmac road from Salalah into the mountains linking the provincial capital with Thumrait, reduced a five-hour car journey over tracks to an hour's fast run. From Thumrait, 70 km in from the coast, a road ran to northern Oman. After that year's monsoon when the lushest of the vegetation had died back in mid-October, the SAF regiments broke across the Wadi Sarfait and secured the Capstan plateau and others mopped up the Communists around Sherishitti further west. Here Hunter aircraft dropped 1000-lb bombs and were attacked by SAM-7 missiles, before the enemy dispersed and no doubt filtered back to Yemen. Other mopping-up operations left only 50 or so active dissidents in the Dhofar mountains by Christmas. Shells were still fired into the SAF regiments' positions around Sarfait in the first few months of 1976, until the Saudi Arabian government helped to bring about a final cease-fire. Then, the desert war over, the last of the Royal Marine officers on loan to SAF completed their two-year tours.

9 Triphibian Training

The canoe loitering under a willow on a quiet Hampshire river lay motionless in the lee of the bank. The local land-owner, infuriated by the intrusion on his trout stream, bellowed his anger:

'I'm Colonel Salmon. Who the hell are you?'

'Sergeant Pike, Royal Marines', came the honest answer, mistaken instantly for a cheeky reply and later reported by the farmer to the Officer Commanding the SB Section on this exercise. Yet Pike was as undisturbed by this flurry of words as he was by explosions of a more lethal kind, continuing on his way in due time to complete the exercise by 'blowing' a bridge. This was but one of a series of exercises, including in 1951 one with the British Army's 3 Division, who were planning an advance through Pangbourne, Berkshire. General Templer had been at the SB briefing of 'Pug' Davis and six men who were given their target but had to find their own billet as the 'enemy' for this exercise. This billet by luck turned out to be the farm of a retired naval officer. With his help, the swimmers went into the Thames unseen, reached the bridge and chalked up that cheeky 'Chad' symbol – two hands, a nose and the bald head with eyes, over a wall – familiar to the 1940s generation for 'Wot! No Second Front?' before the landings in Normandy. Below the SB 'Chad' was the simple slogan: 'Wot! No Bridge?' – as devastating in its way to 3 Division as if the swimmers had used PE instead of chalk. The exercise umpires closed the bridge to the Division's trucks, but somehow this fact did not reach the HQ. The military traffic jam built up, causing the general much displeasure but amusement when he met the naval farmer to learn of the visitors' activities. How was it done? The swimmers prefer not to say, but perhaps six labourers in a field, like a 'priest' in the Aegean, could be understandably mistaken by sentries for harmless folk. On this exercise there were none of the safety precautions associated with swimming and diving in the 1980s; Peter Davis just 'walked up the river bank'. One suspects that he looked for all the world like a Berkshire native, while making sure that none of his men got into difficulties.

The years 1946 to 1951 were a period of transition for the SBS, after the strenuous years of action. They put on demonstrations and ran at Eastney a most lively routine, but carried out their canoeing and diving with that independence of manner which is a characteristic of the SBS in modern times. Nevertheless, Major Tailyour, the Chief Instructor at the Amphibious School, must have watched with approval as his junior officers plotted and planned, devising their schemes to test the canoeists, even if they did this in comparative secrecy and comfort by a roaring coal fire in their 'cabins'. (Marines, with the habit of generations who have served at sea, refer to their bedrooms in an officers' mess as 'cabins'. In the same way, they talk of 'runs ashore' when speaking of a night out from their barracks, or use the naval term 'heads' for lavatories, although it must be nearly a century since any marine or seaman climbed out on the head of the forepeak to perform his bodily functions.) Tailyour, whose career was more Army-orientated than many marine officers of that time, had organized in 1948 the first realistic post-war SBS exercise. In this, four canoes were to land from a submarine and blow up an imaginary radar installation in the Mountains of Mourne, 'which sweep down to the sea' in Northern Ireland. The boats were launched in rough weather, causing such delays that the pairs of swimmer-canoeists had to make their way to the mountain top in daylight, for the target was a full day's march from their rendezvous on the coast. Peter Davis was caught, so to speak, at teatime by a Royal Ulster Constabulary patrol car. The RUC had been warned of the 'raid', and each canoeist carried a special identity card, which in Davis's case also gave him access to a high tea from a farmer's wife at the hamlet where he waited for an hour – any man 'caught' was honour-bound to wait one hour before moving on towards the rendezvous.

There were greater risks in these exercises and in demonstrations than some old hands would have you believe. In part this was because in the years immediately after the Second World War there was an element of anti-climax, which could make people careless in exercises when they knew no one would be shooting to kill. Although nothing was left to chance in a demonstration put on one Saturday morning by the SBS off Eastney beach in 1947, all appeared realistic enough to the young marine recruits watching from the shore. Three canoes paddled in, one a three-seater, after a swimmer had landed to see that the coast was clear. An inflatable was then hauled to the beach by line, and out stepped an agent resplendent in civilian blazer and slacks to go about his secret business. In the final part of the exercise a lively and ever cheerful naval petty officer who had served in COPPs swam in but did not reach the beach. The demonstration was immediately cancelled because the petty officer could not be found. An enquiry at first suggested that there had been some 'fault in his equipment' but this was doubted by the SBS as the inside of his suit was dry. They had swum considerable distances without difficulty, and a team (which incidentally included Corporal Gilchrist, formerly of the SRU) had been demonstrating this in Sweden. Tests carried out then proved that even if full of water, a swimmer's suit had enough buoyancy to keep him afloat. Further studies then showed that the COPPist had suffered a heart failure on his sudden immersion in cold water after several weeks without a swim. Thereafter, swimmers at Eastney went for a dip every morning before breakfast, a chilling brief discomfort in the Solent during winter but, surprisingly, one to which you can become accustomed and, more importantly, to which your body becomes attuned.

All this did not particularly impress the Royal Marines' staff at Eastney, who were a formidable hierarchy of Second World War veterans, most of them former gunners in big ships, more used to the exacting drills of 14-inch gun turrets than the rough and tumble off a beach. In their blue uniforms and glossy peaked caps, they viewed with disdain even commandos in smart khaki battledress and correctly worn green berets, not jauntily worn high on the forehead as Lassen had worn his SAS beret. Not surprisingly therefore, the senior drill instructor voiced loudly his displeasure at one man in a white sweater, grey denim trousers and gym shoes, only to find that he was an SBS senior NCO of the instructor's rank. Had the SB sergeant been wearing a beret, it would have been a blue one, for the SBS swimmers had not all completed the commando course at Achnacarry or Bickleigh, and at that time only men serving in 3 Commando Brigade were allowed to wear the Commando green beret.

The Swimmer-Canoeist

In the 1980s all SBS are recruited from the Commandos, trained, as are all Royal Marines except the Band Service, in a series of courses lasting over thirty weeks. The recruit, one of the few selected from many volunteers, learns to handle himself and his weapons to such good effect that marines in the Falkland Islands could march carrying loads of 54 kg or more across bogs, rock runs and up mountains, fight major battles and reach Port Stanley by a route of 140 km from their landing point. Their general training in some respects differs from that of the Army Commandos of 1940, who became the first of Britain's military canoeists. These creators of the Commando tradition lived in billets for which they were paid a daily allowance of 6/8d (34p). There were none of those off-duty restrictions one used to find in a barracks, the commando presenting himself when and where required, which for some in 1942 might be on a 1000-m mountain to attend a pay parade. The training programmes devised by the unit's officer included weapon training most mornings in a week, map and compass work in the afternoons, a once-a-week march of over 30 km or a cross-country run, with a full Commando unit exercise every third week. All was aimed – as training is today – at creating men capable of independent action. Nevertheless since the formation of the first Commando Basic Training Centre at Achnacarry in February 1942, this training has been on a more formal footing. In much the same way, the recruiting of all special forces moved from an informal approach in the early 1940s to scientific (if that is not too clinical a word) methods of selection by 1945.

Stan Weatherall, one of the first canoeists, volunteered for the SBS literally in a field; here there was no pressure to join, as his Troop filed by a chair on which an officer quietly took the name of individuals volunteering for the second Special Boat Section to be formed. The first had gone to the Middle East with Roger Courtney by this time. Other recruits were introduced to the SBS, as was Bruce Ogden-Smith, through first joining SSRF at his brother's suggestion. But selection for the SBS in 1941–2 often owed a good deal to 'friends of friends'. Sometimes it was a chance reunion: Ian Patterson became an SB squadron commander after just such an encounter with George Jellicoe, an old skiing companion, over vermouths in the officers' club on Kos in 1943. There were several similar introductions: only through Nigel Clogstoun-Willmott's personal knowledge of other officers in the navigators' branch of the Royal Navy was he able to contact several potential COPP leaders. They required, however, not only the personal qualities needed to keep a cool head in boiling surf, but also had to be skilled in assessing what problems might face a subsequent landing force on the beach being recced. From the navigators' branch came men like Lieutenant Neville McHarg, RN (later OC COPP 4) and Lieutenant Norman

Teacher, RN (later drowned off Sicily) despite the competing demands for navigators in all theatres of operation in the summer of 1942. Lord Mountbatten, therefore, had to use his considerable influence to obtain their release from deep sea duties to join the Combined Operations Assault Pilotage Parties. 'Blondie' Hasler had somewhat different selection problems, but was supported with equal enthusiasm by Admiral Lord Mountbatten, himself no stranger to small boats. Once, when Chief of Combined Operations, he had taken a Welman down to 10 m in Brent reservoir at Hendon, North London, when the water pressure burst a window. The admiral had some difficulty in shedding the boat's keel to surface in this emergency. The result was that when he arrived at the prime minister's country home, his suit was still wet. Winston Churchill upbraided him, for he did not think admirals' lives should be risked in hazardous experiments – to which Mountbatten replied that the men in his command would expect their leader to share such risks.

The modern SBS have lost none of their nimbleness. A swan, lifted so swiftly and surely from the waters near one 'local' that it did not have time to flap a wing, survived, for rationing as RMBPD knew it when they 'captured' hens, is thankfully a thing of the past in the 1980s. But the SBS use more general forms of cover. No longer do they pretend to be what they are not (although they may well pass off some of their reported activities as being SAS operations). Nor do they give demonstrations in school swimming baths as they did in the late 1940s, since none should be identified by name or face in case his life is needlessly put at risk in a clandestine operation. This elite of elites, therefore, is lost in a sea of 8000 faces serving in the Royal Marines. One or two may turn up for a party by unconventional means, free-falling out of the night sky, as all are parachutists, or leave a jollification, perhaps, with a clean dive from a river steamer.

If their recreations are not far removed from those of the ration-snatching canoeists of 1942, their recruitment certainly is. Volunteers, all serving marine commandos, are given a series of suitability tests. Are they physically fitter than the general run of commandos, who are fully fit by most standards? Are they mentally suited to the claustrophobia of underwater swimming? Have they that infinite patience needed to lie all day undetected in a hide? They already have that individuality that makes a commando; but the SBS, being closer in their modern roles to COPP canoeists than to Lassen's raiders, ask: is the volunteer intelligent enough to learn those points of astral navigation and of electronic devices he will need? It goes without saying that the man must be able, on his own, to press home a limpet-mine attack or blow a bridge many kilometres if necessary from a friendly shoreline.

Even having passed these tests, the would-be Swimmer-Canoeist with the Specialist Qualification (SQ) of an SC3, has some thirteen weeks of an exacting course to pass before he receives his first swimmer's SQ badge. This covers small boat and canoe handling, underwater swimming with various mixtures of gases in a modern free diver's equipment. He will learn about reconnaissance of beaches, measuring runnels and studying what does and does not make a suitable beach exit. He will become a competent photographer, learning how to carry out effective demolitions, which are today more deadly than even the Second World War thermite bomb. He will understand how to arm his limpet-mines for anti-shipping or bridge attacks. Finally, he will have an elementary knowledge of radio and similar signals or communications devices and of first aid. The last is important: a wounded man left in a hide in enemy territory is as revealing as his canoe.

No figures are available in the 1980s of the numbers who drop out through their own dislike of prolonged underwater swimming, or through failing to match up in their 'weekly reports' (or equivalent) to what is required of them. A good number of well-motivated and efficient marines do, however, fail the course, a measure of its rigours being that failure is not held against them, although their personal disappointment is great. The successful who are potential leaders will go on in later years to the SC2's course for junior NCOs and the SC1 course for seniors and Section officers. Along the way, individuals may take further specialist courses in demolition, photography, signals and first aid.

The trained swimmer-canoeist will join a small organization with probably no more than 120 serving in the SB Squadron at any one time, its structure still following a long-established pattern of two (three in the 1970s) active Sections and a cadre for training and experimental work. There was also in the 1980s Nos. 4 and 5 SBS (Reserve) of canoeists who can be mobilized independently of the rest of the Royal Marine Reserve in what are called 'times of tension'.

Over the years, qualified swimmer-canoeists completed their two-year tours and moved back to general duties in the Corps. For, as mentioned elsewhere, the Royal Marines had no intention of allowing a small coterie of specialists to become more mysterious than was necessary for their operational security. This also had the sensible effect of spreading a wide understanding within the Corps of the abilities of swimmer-canoeists. By the 1980s, there were several major-generals who had served for one or more periods with the SBS during their careers; no doubt one day the much respected senior RM officer, the commandant general, will have had SB training. All have been Commando trained, and in recent years they have included a senior signals officer and men with landing craft experience from the Second World War.

The influence of the SBS in the Corps is no greater, however, than that of other specialist branches, including their reconnaissance brothers the Mountain Leaders (MLs), who fulfil roles that are just as demanding in the high snows as those of the SBS in the ocean depths. Indeed, these groups of experts vie in friendly rivalry when sent on less exacting missions, for both are parachute trained.

About one in ten Royal Marines are qualified parachutists, and SC volunteers are para-trained after their SC3's course. Parachuting in the Corps goes back further than many serving marines may realize. In 1917 Lieutenant-Colonel Thomas H. Orde-Lees, RMLI, made some pioneer drops by parachute at a time when the possibility of escape from aircraft was hotly debated – pilots in the Royal Flying Corps at that time were not issued with parachutes. In fact, parachutes had existed since the 1790s, albeit in rather dangerous versions, but since 1815 had been used by showmen who dropped at first from hot-air balloons. Yet by 1913 *Flight* magazine saw little future in a parachute as a safety device, while the RFC Command felt that pilots might leave their aircraft unnecessarily with a parachute that could land them safely. The dogmatic Orde-Lees was not popular with them, nor with his fellow members of an expedition in the Antarctic in 1914 who had selected him as the first victim should they have to resort to cannibalism. Fortunately they were rescued and Orde-Lees made many jumps, including one from only 50 m off Tower Bridge, his parachute being 'attached' to drop him gently into the Thames. He preferred these 'attached' parachutes to the free-fall type using a ripcord, but in 1925 the Irvine free-fall version was issued to the RAF.

In the next decade another Royal Marine, Lieutenant-Colonel R. G. Parks-Smith, with others made a number of experimental drops with a view to landing paratroops. The Germans had demonstrated a form of this using a static line which, attached to the aircraft, pulled out the parachute as the trooper dropped clear of the plane. Parks-Smith was killed on the beaches of Dieppe in 1942, by which time the static line was the accepted method of opening parachutes in a mass drop. Hasler's men used them, dropping into water – 'a super DZ, without obstacles and ideal for an RV with a ship or submarine'. The only special care needed was an extra-rapid release from the harness. The first such quick-release had been provided in 1930 for the Fleet Air Arm, with a central fitting 'turned 90 degrees to disengage its four attachment points simultaneously so that the pilot could get free in water'. Experiences in the Second World War had shown that many men could successfully be taught to 'drop' even if they did not understand the mechanics of a quick-release box. Improvisation was the key word in 1941: they dropped from a small wooden plank across a hole in the fuselage of an aircraft, the static lines fixed to what often appeared rather insecure fittings – like the alloy chair frame in one Flying Fortress from which the SB Squadron canoeist Rifleman Lynch dropped into Albania in 1944, going out through the belly turret.

Yet that instant when the body hung for a fraction of a second, as the jumper straightened up on his perch, arms to his side, before plummeting through the hole, would always hold terror for some. The rattle of his static line, suddenly taut before trailing slackly from the hole, might have unnerved those following. But they jumped, feet together into the void, buffeted by wind till in a magic moment all was quiet and they floated down. The practised jumper can pinpoint his descent, steering with hands above his head by pressure on the webbing of his harness, while he extracts his legs from the harness during the ninety seconds of a fall from 200 m, ready to release himself as he drops into the water. Accidents have occurred; one Reservist NCO coming out of his harness 150 m up, to fall to his death. Such accidents are sometimes difficult to explain: but the air, like the sea, is always dangerous if you do not follow the established drills.

Jumps have become routine for the modern parachutist, dropping in training from 60 m with the static line of his conventional parachute firmly secured in a helicopter or the vast interior of a Hercules. Others from 2.5 km or higher with high-performance parachutes ('Unit' 'chutes) can delay the opening of their parachute, taking care not to tumble in a confusion of arms and legs, watching the altimeter till they pull their ripcords at, say, 200 m. Still together and in diving gear they can land and vanish under the sea. On the way down through the air they virtually fly, as sports parachutists do, but they need to take great care to avoid collision with other parachutists – a reason for not using Unit-type parachutes in mass drops.

Evolution of the Canoe

The canoe, however, has become the traditional means by which SBS swimmers approach their targets, since Roger Courtney's demonstrations in a Folbot in 1940. COPP parties in their seamanlike manner improved the Folbot's stability, for in 6 Commando's view it was 'prone to turn turtle'. The seamen added an inflated collar around the cockpit coaming, making the boat more stable by countering any initial heel; this version was sometimes described incorrectly as a 'Rob Roy' canoe. There was no way the beam might be increased, as this canoe was already 5 cm too wide to pass through some torpedo-loading hatches on submarines. In one Mark, the centre ribs were adjustable, enabling an assembled canoe to be squeezed through the hatch before being stretched back to its full beam. The more solidly built Cockle II was designed with a narrow enough beam to pass through the hatches of a T-class submarine despite the Mark II's solid deck. The Mark III** was a logical development from the Mark II, when for many operations collapsible canoes were no longer necessary. The III** had a one-eighth-inch (3-mm) moulded and waterproofed plywood hull stiffened by an inside lining of 'rubberproofed stockingette', to make it watertight even if the wooden hull was fractured. The greatest innovation was the use of outriggers, which could be extended 10.5 cm either side of the hull, lie alongside it or be carried inboard until required. There seems to be some doubt if these added much to the canoe's stability except when under sail. However, these were the canoes used by the SB Squadrons in the Mediterranean.

Sailing canoes in a more elegant catamaran form have been raced on the Thames since before the Second World

War and, knowing Colonel Hasler's practical uses for sail, one can see his adaptation of this for canoes. Marines in Ceylon used to race their loose-footed lugsail canoes in regattas, with the sails made of camouflaged parachute silk. There was even a hinged keel you could strap to a Folbot, raising it by means of trip lines flat against the bottom of the canoe before you beached.

Although the Mark III was not collapsible, it comprised three sections, each sealed by watertight bulkheads. The bow and stern contained table tennis balls for buoyancy described as 'ping pong balls in bags containing 48', with storage lockers for gear. The canoe could lift a heavy load of two men with over 225 kg of stores, and still draw only about 20 cm. But now one moves further from the simple sport canoe to more complex craft, for in the Mark VI the bow section was replaced by one with more sheer and flare (not unlike the upsweep of a liner's bow). This prevented the canoe burrowing into any sea that was running when it was under power, as its 4-hp two-stroke engine could drive it at 7 knots in calm water, compared with the 3.5 knots (5 knots under tow) which paddlers in a Mark II could achieve. The engine could keep going for 150 km at a cruising speed of 5.6 knots on its '14 pints of 2-stroke mix (½ pint oil to 1 gallon of petrol) in shaped tanks each side of the driver's legs'. He sat in the aft position, the man forward steering the canoe by rudder lines, but there were some difficulties at first with this engine despite its retracting gear. The engine and three-inch propeller was one unit, and the lot could be raised at the turn of a wheel, lifting the propeller above the keel before beaching. A Mark VIII version, 6 m long, with outriggers extending up to 25 cm from the hull, had an engine with a water-cooled silencer and a second silencer 'slipped on by hand' when required for a silent approach. The engine could also be easily jettisoned in an emergency, but like the Mark IX it was never used operationally. The 'IX' was the last of the wartime wooden-hulled canoes, proving extremely wet even in a gentle lop, with so much spray that the canoeists wore their diving masks or eyeshields. Its petrol-mix tank held only enough fuel for 10 nautical miles (18.5 km); topping this up was difficult because once the engine was stopped – as it had to be in all but a flat calm – for refuelling from reserve tanks, it was difficult to restart even when hot. But the Mark IX sailed well on its lateen sail and was one of the craft raced in Ceylon.

It was a different line of development, with alloy hulls, outriggers and fitted with a variety of power units, that led to the MSC and a fast, stable canoe. The SBS in 1945 ran at least one of these 'tin' canoes fitted with Bren and Vickers K machine guns on the Irrawaddy, where it proved ideal before the river current became too strong for hit-and-run attacks on Japanese outposts. The art was in the quiet night paddle against the current in the slack water under the lee of a bank, then opening up both engine and guns as a Japanese post came into range around a bend. The gun could fire several hundred rounds before the canoe spun on her keel to power away to safety, the current near midstream adding to her speed.

Canoe developments in the decades after the 1940s produced the fibreglass kayak one-man canoe, but while this turned out to be fun for surf riding, it was too small for operations. But, by the mid-1950s the Klepper Company in Germany were producing a robust five-metre boat, and it is a military adaptation of this that marines use in the 1980s. Its beam gives it more stability than the Cockle types, but its great advantage is the way the loose skin can be laid over its frame; its buoyancy bags are then inflated, giving the skin the tautness seen in the pictures of Malaya and Borneo. The Royal Marines who have manned virtually all the Royal Navy's assault landing craft since 1943, also have at their disposal in the 1980s a number of craft that can serve as intermediate carriers. The 'Rigid Raiders', for example, with their 35-hp high-performance outboards can if necessary deliver a canoe and its team into the target area, or even land them in certain conditions. Other methods are continuously under review, and one can imagine a variety of intermediate carriers based on the principle of the shallow-draught inshore lifeboat with its twin 140-hp outboards. These are noisy at speed, but outboards ride up on hitting a shoal to prevent damage to propellers, making a high-speed withdrawal a practical proposition across shallows impassable to conventional boats.

A swimmer-canoeist can, as we have seen, parachute to a DZ at sea and may also 'drop' with the outboard, one of his companions in the 'stick' bringing in an inflatable and the other two of the team dropping with the combat stores. There are probably even more sophisticated ways of doing this type of airborne infiltration today, but twenty years ago the team quickly inflated their boat, hitched on its engine, loaded the stores and were on their way to a target beach before an enemy would realize that they might be in the area. Needless to say, aircraft can provide suitable cover by dropping bombs later in the raid or by flying over the area on successive nights, so that the local garrison find nothing unusual in the flight on the night when the team drops in. The standard inflatable of the 1980s is the Gemini, like its forerunner, the Intruder, a craft for many purposes. This makes it no less useful for swimmer-canoeists, who are adept at using standard equipment (or 'pieces of kit' as they would say) for all manner of non-standard purposes. Experiments, apocryphally, were tried in 1945 with canoeists in pods dropped by parachute – not unlike the way in which extra fuel tanks could be jettisoned – from the wing-tips of naval fighter-bombers. 'Away starboard watch of marines, away port watch of marines', as one test pilot delighted in describing his 'jettisoning' of the swimmers in their capsules.

Swimming and Diving

The delights of underwater swimming are enjoyed by many SB swimmers in underwater fishing and exploration, as a natural recreation from their military calling. Yet whenever swimmers are diving there are dangers, even if the relaxed weightlessness gives the diver that feeling of exhilaration which enables him or her to bound tens of metres in a stride or glide through the multi-coloured grottoes of a coral reef. SBS equipment has enabled the military swimmer to do much more than swim at depth, its development over the years paralleling some of the most sophisticated civilian gear available in the 1980s, but risks remain. In the 1950s, with television series like *Sea Hunt* (in which Lloyd Bridges played an intrepid and often lone underwater swimmer), the sport appeared simple enough for any bather to enjoy. Few viewers realized that to take fifteen minutes of underwater film took a day and a half, and the problems became sadly apparent in the number of fatal accidents, especially in America, where quantities of surplus US Navy diving kit were sold to people with little or no idea of the risks of using it. Yet in the ten years to 1961, free diving came of age. Lloyd Bridges was seen being towed through the water by an underwater craft as handy as a motorcycle, if not as fast.

The Royal Navy's 'hard-hat' divers, including marines in the Second World War, had many years of experience with the problems of deeper diving. Their heavy equipment, with its air hose and pumps, limited underwater work to a confined area, although often at considerable depths. The navies of the world had used self-contained breathing sets in shallow water since the 1880s, the first practical oxygen recycling unit having been produced by the Siebe Gorman Diving Company in England in 1878. There had been a unit invented over fifty years before then, but it was limited by the back cylinder's strength, which could only be pressurized to 30 atmospheres, as against the 200 of modern commercial gas cylinders. Air and gas pressures are the problem, for a balloon of air on the surface will be compressed to half its size at a depth of only ten metres, and to a quarter its size at thirty. Such a squeeze has two consequences: the air in the diver's lungs is always compressed to the pressure of the surrounding water, as the walls of his chest contract like a balloon; and his body tissue and bloodstream absorb greater proportions of gases as he breathes them under increased pressures.

There are natural divers who have attuned their bodies to cope with these stresses, holding their breath as they dive for sponges, pearls or, like the Ama Japanese women, to collect the nutrient-rich agar-agar seaweed. It was the bamboo-frame goggles of the Ama divers that gave impetus to underwater swimming as a practical means of fishing in the depression of the 1930s. Californian beach boys dived for the abalone, a large shellfish that has to be prised from its home, as only half the body is covered by a shell and the muscles of the other half clamp this delicacy to the rock. These divers' methods suggested a purpose for the Sea Reconnaissance Unit (SRU) of the Second World War, but the impoverished fishermen dived with no more than their goggles and pry-bar. Even then they found that the air inside their goggles could be squeezed at depths of 10 m to make their eyes look 'as if they had been hit by two baseballs'. To counter this unpleasant effect, face masks were developed that totally enclosed the diver's eyes and nose; the diver's breathing pressurized the head set, which also gave better vision than goggles. By 1960, modern masks were being fitted with pressure compensators for deep diving but this was limited by other factors.

Shallow diving, on the other hand, has been feasible with unsophisticated equipment for many years, as Royal Marine Engineers in 1944 found in Ceylon. There they dived on a wreck while wearing a modified respirator (gas mask) attached to an air line. Working in less than 15 m of water, they salvaged a valuable (to them) cargo of beer. Naval clearance divers, whose work on clearing harbour mines, repairing ships and defusing unexploded bombs on a sea bed is as dangerous as it is useful, often have to work below the 15-m mark. Their underwater work on ships is particularly useful in peacetime, as this saves the expensive business of putting a vessel into dry dock for minor repairs. Royal Engineer divers may also work at depth setting the foundations for piers or for river bridges and clearing underwater explosives. Until the RMBPD used their motorized submersible canoes towards the end of the Second World War, they had only needed to dive in the shallows off a beach. For this, Dunlop in 1943 produced an underwater breathing set working on similar principles to the Davis Submerged Escape Apparatus, but with two oxygen bottles. These enabled the swimmer to dive for approximately forty minutes at shallow depths. The set was self-contained and did not emit the tell-tale air bubbles that could reveal a diver's presence. Also, the amount of oxygen was 'on demand', the diver recharging the breathing bag by hand when he needed more oxygen because of some extra physical exertion. During the 1960s, however, when swimmers' exits and re-entry of submarines became a more general practice, they had to work at more dangerous depths. Here, the pressures having contracted, the diver's lungs will rupture tissues in them if he surfaces without exhaling as he rises, even when his tank of air is exhausted. Such injuries from an air embolism may easily be avoided; but more dangerous are the nitrogen bubbles absorbed under the pressure of depth into the tissue, bloodstream and joints of a diver. These bubbles have to be allowed to disperse slowly: hence the decompression chambers of modern diving. By surfacing slowly at 7.5 m a second, they will disperse naturally after dives to 30 m, always provided the time at depth is limited. Two hours at 15 m is no problem, but a dive must be limited to fifteen minutes at 45 m. Surfacing too quickly or diving for longer periods in any twelve hours causes the nitrogen bubbles to produce the painful 'bends', which can disable a diver for life.

A number of developments in the 1950s carried forward the free-diving experiments of the Second World War. These were mainly concerned with the mixture of gases a diver might safely breathe at depth, for the normal air we breathe, about 79 per cent nitrogen and 21 per cent oxygen, also contains a little carbon dioxide (CO_2). In the pressures at 35 m this natural mixture comes to include a higher proportion of CO_2, the effects of which, as the

RMBPD found, could be lethal. These Second World War swimmers had been able to spend up to two hours underwater breathing pure oxygen, but at depths below 10 m this absorbs twice as fast as normal into the bloodstream, causing convulsions and sudden blackouts. These cancel out the advantages of the smaller tanks a swimmer needs to carry when diving on pure oxygen than when breathing compressed air. The SBS and others experimented with a mixture of three times the normal oxygen levels in air and half the nitrogen, which at 30 m provided a safe mix in less bulky tanks. It still limited the time available for working at depth, but it was an improvement on the earlier compromises.

Modern free diving has come a long way further and deeper than was conceivable in 1943 when the first aqualungs were being used in the United States. Yet the dangers remain and before looking at these more closely, the pioneer work illustrates the fundamental problems faced by divers. The SRU went to the USMC's Camp Pendleton in California where the US Navy's Underwater Demolition Teams were training. These and their successors, the American Seal Teams, have liaised closely with SBS over the years; but early in 1943 the presence of white sharks too often limited the time the swimmers could practice, and the relatively cold water prevented a man paddling much over 15 km on his board. They therefore moved their training to Nassau in the Bahamas, but even so their troubles were not over.

Other troubles came at that time with the protosorb that filtered out the carbon dioxide exhaled by a swimmer, preventing a build-up of this gas in the breathing system. It also passed the used air or oxygen out of the helmet in a tell-tale string of bubbles, a dangerous indication to sentries that swimmers were under a harbour jetty or alongside a ship. Modern systems do not leave such trails.

The MSC or 'Sleeping Beauty' had first been tested in an experimental tank used by the Navy to test hull models, and later in Horsea lake, both near Portsmouth. Its pilots, unfamiliar with the effects of carbon dioxide poisoning, had one fatal accident, while in Scotland COPPists training in X-craft experienced hallucinations from the build-up of CO_2. An MSC pilot was in the Hasler tank one evening, carrying out static tests with the craft in about 3 m of water. He was on the bottom some time before Jock Stewart, commanding RMBPD as a major after Hasler's departure for southeast Asia, realized that the twenty-year-old pilot was not moving. He was brought quickly to the surface but failed to respond to an hour's artificial respiration. There was still oxygen left in the diver's second bottle: the young officer had obviously not recognized the symptoms of carbon dioxide poisoning and had failed to switch over to this second supply. There were obvious problems for a man alone in a dive: for safety, divers usually work in pairs so that if one suddenly appears to be unduly carefree – a preliminary sign of CO_2 poisoning – his companion can guide him to the surface. In an MSC the pilot had to learn to recognize the first symptoms of breathing or *re*breathing the waste gases. After this death, the pilots paraded in breathing sets with the protosorb removed: as they marched up and down, under the watchful eye of the Detachment's doctor, men who were particularly susceptible to blackouts could be spotted, while others quickly learnt the degree of tolerance that they had in absorbing CO_2.

In X-craft the five crew on a training run were always conscious of their breathing. Despite the air purifiers extracting the CO_2, or at least sizeable quantities of it, the proportion of oxygen in the air they breathed gradually decreased. A man might then imagine in some fantasy that he could open the craft's hatch, although she was 10 m down in Loch Striven. All the crew found that their heads began to ache, an early symptom of CO_2 poisoning; concentration was difficult; and making the simplest calculations in writing notes from a recce could be exasperatingly difficult, when the chinagraph figures on a slate were difficult to read (not surprisingly perhaps, when such notes had been made while the swimmer was on a beach at night). The COPPists had no fatalities in training with X-craft, but two Americans being trained in the winter of 1944–5 to use MSCs were drowned through not wearing life jackets. Hasler had always insisted that his MSC pilots be trained in stages, swimming first underwater in the calm of Horsea lake before doing so at sea in daylight, and they had to become competent in free diving at night before taking out an MSC. Yet they had always to wear an inflatable life jacket when taking the craft to sea. This Reliant jacket took up virtually no room when deflated under a swimmer's suit, its front and back flotation being given by 'three or four breaths to give the necessary buoyancy', far quicker than with the usual screw-down valve of those years. The secret of this jacket was a rubber non-return valve in the inflation tube, so that there was no need for the fumbling of cold fingers to close a screw valve.

Safety precautions understandably limited accidents to few, but the most carefully staged training cannot prevent panic, which is one reason why swimmer-canoeists are carefully selected as much for their coolness in a tight corner as for their guts to break out of it. Back in 1944 only one swimmer died through an error of judgement: entangled in his safety line, he snatched off his face mask before he could be brought to the surface. In 1946 not all RM swimmer-canoeists were trained divers, but by 1951 all SC ratings were free divers, their training being supervised by a diving instructor with a trained stand-by diver ready to go to any recruit's help if he needed it. The bobbing of the float on his safety line would show he was in trouble. When one National Service officer was 'down' in a lake near Poole, the sudden disappearance of his float caused the supervisor to send Amphibax, alerting the rescue services. A good swimmer and Navy rugby player, the young man had not needed the usual underwater swimming tests, but in the murky waters of this clay pit he had swum round getting the safety cord to his float entwined around his legs and arms. The rescue divers had great difficulty, as the mud had been stirred into a fog that reduced visibility to centimetres rather than a metre or two, and the young man was drowned. Such accidents in recent years have virtually been eliminated by radical changes in training, which in many ways has reverted to those step-by-step stages of Hasler's training, with the added advantage of training divers in the 30-m-high tower of water used for training submariners to escape from a boat stuck on the bottom. Its bays at regular intervals enable instructors in their breathing sets to monitor each trainee's progress up the tower. The trained SC rate, however, must sit periodically on the bottom of this tower for the requisite period to keep his diving qualification up-to-date; but he does not subject himself to this boring chore without first having a medical check.

His suit for such tests and in operations is far removed from even the best Second World War equipment. Since the early 1970s he has worn a military version of the one-piece dry suit used by sports divers. One of the drawbacks of suits for both surface swimmers and divers in the 1940s was the relative ease with which they could be torn. By 1944, COPPists wore a rubberized suit with a watertight hood fitting around the face, its zip-up front over a loose-fitting apron made watertight by clamps. The whole one-piece contraption took up to an hour to put on when in the confines of an X-craft. Despite every care, and although it was reinforced at the knees and elbows, the suit could still be ripped if caught on barbed wire or any other sharp object. Nigel Clogstoun-Willmott, the most experienced COPP officer, tore his suit on an exercise in 1944. It filled, and he was only kept afloat on the dark waters of a Scottish loch by the efforts of Geoff Galway. At first he could not inflate his chief's life jacket and had to fire two emergency flares. These fizzled out, one burning Galway's sleeve as they bobbed about trying to float on their backs. Luckily, the X-craft from which they had dived surfaced nearby just as Clogstoun-Willmott was losing consciousness. He was taken aboard and after the craft submerged was revived – almost too enthusiastically. The craft's inspection lamp on its wandering lead was pushed under the lieutenant-commander's suit to prevent him losing too much body heat, until the strong smell of singeing rubber made Galway realize that he might have overdone the cure.

Other suits were designed for surface swimming only, as those used in Postage Able, with rubberized Grenfell fabric in one piece, it weighed over 6 kg, but with a watertight fit at the neck and wrists. The lighter 3.6-kg paddler's suit gave him some protection from spray, but it was not waterproof. It had an inflatable stole and kapok belt for buoyancy. The four pockets, according to official recommendation, were to carry in the left pair: a brandy flask (the essential first requirement?); a pad and slate to write on; pencils; torch; and a weighted line for taking depth soundings from the canoe. A spare weight and line were in one of his right pair of pockets with his emergency rations of chocolate in a waterproof container and a knife with a spike. Needless to say, in the thoroughness of these designs all pockets had an eyelet drain hole and single-buttoned flap. Mention has been made of the two-part tropical suit, which was not waterproof but weighed only 2.25 kg. Whether or not a swimmer wore fins with his suit depended on the stage he had reached in his training, Hasler's men having first to master swimming underwater without fins.

The diver at depth also faces the hazards of pressure on his suit. This had been no problem for RMBPD swimmers, who used so-called 'dry' suits with a layer of air as insulation against cold, but diving below 15 m in a dry suit brought new difficulties. These could be pressurized by forcing air into the hood, with its rubber seal around the mask; however, even a pinhole leak in a dry suit at depth would permit so much water to flood in under pressure that the diver's warm clothing became wet and he rapidly lost body heat. Another problem at depth was that the air in the suit tended to be squeezed into the upper shoulders and mask. Then the so-called 'wet' suit, originally developed for American naval divers of the Underwater Demolition Teams in the Second World War, became the more practical wear for swimmer-canoeists. The material of this suit contained air pockets in its cellular structure for heat insulation, the skin-tight suit over the naked body forming in effect 'a blanket of dry air' separating the swimmer from the water. A pinprick only destroyed the insulation in the immediate area of the leak, with little loss of body heat; the pressures at depth made the insulation thinner, but did not cause the bruising from rumpled clothing under a dry suit.

Movement underwater was considerably aided by fins – or 'flippers', as civilians know them. However, the fins worn by sports divers are considerably smaller than the powerful Swim Fins Mark II that had been worn by British naval divers including the RMBPD since 1943. Both sorts traced their origins back to the palm fronds that South Sea islanders strapped to their feet to increase their speed of swimming. A swimmer who has used fins finds his ability to lift weights through water is greatly increased, as are the distances he can cover without fatigue. They leave his arms free – for carrying a limpet-mine, for example.

Whatever training a diver has, one of the ever-present dangers of the deep is the shark. The British used a slow-dissolving fish-scarer tablet in southeast Asia in 1944–5 that expelled copper acetate with a dye added, as experiments have shown that fish are less likely to attack a black patch. These tablets were carried in a moulded plastic container on a diver's belt. There are, however, no reports to suggest that they were any more or less effective than man's normal immunity to the predators, which do not normally attack swimmers unless they have a wound from which blood is flowing. One exception to that may be the Great White species of shark. It was these carnivorous monsters whose presence, when the SRU were training in California with American Underwater Demolition Teams, limited the time they could train in these waters. Most sharks prefer to attack their victims from behind, and there are many tales of swimmers turning to face an attack, causing the shark to veer away. What they can do is pick up the sound of a struggle from great distances. Sound travels nearly five times as fast in water as in air, and this can bring an unexpected shoal of sharks before a diver can surface with a speared fish. Octopuses on the other hand can be hauled to the surface, even though the larger of their eight arms can measure more than five metres. Whales are harmless apart from the killer whale, but these have never been reported to take a diver. Since they live off porpoises, seals and even larger mammals, they could attack divers, but if one did so it would be more likely in murky water through mistaking its victim for a seal. Giant barracuda, with razor teeth capable of biting through shark skin, have attacked divers in the Caribbean, apparently snapping at the bright glint of a knife or, possibly injured, attacking as the best form of self-defence. Moray eels, for long regarded as particularly ferocious, turned out to be aggressive only if attacked – then they can bite a finger to the bone. Most dangerous of all is the sea snake, for one drop of venom can kill three people.

Far greater hazards to the military diver come from his human enemies: the anti-personnel depth charge, the mined beach obstacle, even wire hawsers hauled under a ship's bottom when her crew suspect limpeteers may be attacking her. Whether or not Lieutenant-Commander 'Buster' Crabb, RN, was caught by such means in 1956, there are many curious features of his dive when two Russian warships were anchored in British waters. The SBS could certainly have inspected these underwater hull forms and may have done so, but their techniques would have left no indication of their presence. Such underwater work with cameras in pressure-proofed cases in the 1950s, or perhaps by electronic means twenty years later, would not require the diver to swim all that close to the ship provided he could find her in clear enough water.

The Future

In the 1980s the would-be intruder on an enemy shore has to contend not only with devices set to entrap him, but also

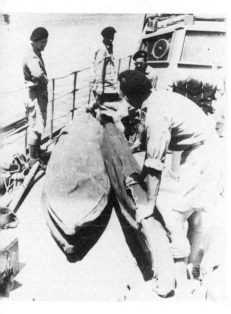

Three Mark II** canoes collapsed and in canvas covers being stowed on the deck of an ML before the raid on Leros, June 1944.

A Motor Submersible Canoe (MSC) of the type taken by Australians of 'X' Group on a raid against Singapore in 1944.

A swimmer launches himself from a canoe, a delicate job requiring both agility and a sense of balance.

Raiding teams prepare to float off a submarine in Gemini inflatables as she submerges during an exercise.

A swimmer comes ashore to recce an unknown beach in the 1950s.

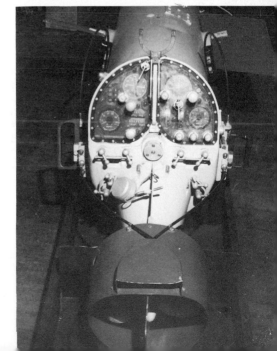

This purpose-built underwater unit towed swimmers inshore during the 1960s.

Early designs of underwater swimmers' suits and their breathing sets adapted in May 1943 from Davis Submerged Escape Apparatus.

A swimmer-canoeist about to drop from his parachute harness during a water jump exercise.

a number of factors that have made the average garrison
sentry into a crack shot. He may, for example, be armed
with a rifle aimed by means of an electronic sight: this gives
him a red dot in its telescope, which moves as he aims at a
swimmer 100 m off, ensuring that the fall of shot is within
an 8-cm circle of his point of aim. He could hardly miss by
day or night, for darkness no longer cloaks the raider.
Sections of soldiers in most modern armies carry at least
one image-intensifier, turning night into a blue-lit day. Or
he may have – as the raider may have – a thermal imager,
which in crude terms gives a heat picture of the beach and
all that moves on it. That fighting patrol moving along the
shoreline will also have its battlefield radar, the operator
scanning the ground up to 1500 m ahead of the point man.
The scanner strapped to his chest gives a high-pitched
whine in his headphones at any movement, the whine
changing in intensity according to the direction in which
the intruder is moving.

So the rules of the game today are radically different from
those of the Second World War. When the swimmer comes
ashore, he avoids the obvious sentry posts and the pattern
of patrols, for they gave themselves away on the previous
night when the pulse waves of their radar scan were picked
up by the raiders' detection equipment. But the swimmer
has other hazards besides the wire and the mines – more
difficult to detect than those with a metal case – as he moves
towards his target. On all likely routes (and on some unlikely ones leading to an airstrip, perhaps) there may be
unmanned electronic ambushes. In these, small sensors are
buried or concealed in undergrowth, each connected by a
metre of cable to a delicate trembler that reacts to all but
the lightest footfall. These can not only detect a vehicle
passing along a road but identify the type as well. Should
the swimmer feel he can tread softly enough not to disturb
these seismic transducers of the detector, it also has some
infra-red elements that will note his passing. Either way,
the detector signals its warning to a command post up to 7
km away. The device has many varieties and could even be

used in some shallow waters to ambush the swimmer before he gets ashore.

He nevertheless avoids these ambushes, for they cannot be laid everywhere, although once set up the CLASSIC type (C Type Local Area Sensor System) just described will be active for a year with the right batteries. He now has to enter the target airfield, where the dispersed aircraft may be protected by portable microwave fences. Cross their energy field and a silent signal will flash in the guardroom or a screech siren will alert the whole garrison. Having made his sortie, nevertheless, the swimmer must come out: again he has to pass through minefields, plastic-cased mines no doubt, not as easily detected as the canisters of jumping anti-personnel mines with their trip-wires of the 1940s. Indeed, on his way to the rendezvous he may find himself in a newly laid Astrolite 'field', sprayed from aircraft on his most likely route to a beach. This high-explosive liquid soaks into the top few centimetres of soil, and may be set off by a sentry controlling it from a distance or by the intruder stepping on one of the detonators laid in it. The very ground would then explode beneath his feet. (No details are available of the precise way in which Astrolite liquid explosive is triggered off: it is said to be undetectable except by chemical sensors or possibly by dogs trained to recognize its scent.) Fortunately, its effective life is reportedly only four days, which means that this field does not have to be cleared like conventional mines.

Our swimmer on such a raid probably carries an Ingram MAC II, measuring 22.2 cm, about the length of the jacket sleeve covering your forearm, when the butt is folded along its short barrel. Weighing only 1.6 kg, the weight of a five-hundred-page novel, it can nevertheless fire 20 rounds in a *second*, more 9-mm bullets than in the small magazine. Fitted with a suppressor to silence the noise and flash of a single aimed round, it is accurate up to 50 m. If the swimmer wants an SMG with greater range, he may take a Heckler & Koch MP5 firing 9-mm rounds with an effective range of 200 m, at nearly ten rounds a second. The difference between these modern SMGs and the Stens and Thompsons is that instead of the bolt having to move back to allow a bullet into the chamber, it is wrapped around the barrel. This principle, first used in the prolific Israeli Uzi, not only enables the weapon to be shorter but, by keeping the weight of the bolt nearer the muzzle, overcomes that tendency of earlier SMGs to climb as they were fired, resulting in all shots after the first two or three in a burst flying above the head of the target. On some recces where a weight of fire power is needed at short range for clearing a building (the Villa Punta, for example) a pump-action shotgun is ideal. There are 12-bore combat types being tested that fire 200 rounds a minute with a lethal spread of heavy shot at up to 150 m.

The anti-shipping raids of the 1980s require a more delicate technique, but the successors to the buoyant and magnetic limpet-mines of the 1940s are still on the secret list. The old faithful used by Hasler on 'Frankton', with its six magnets and 1.2 kg of plastic explosive, is listed by some authorities as being still in service as the 'rigid limpet assault mine'. (The Russians have a plastic-cased limpet-mine weighing over 3 kg, with an unusual mechanical time fuse: its strong spring is restrained by a wire that takes time to cut through a lead strip, the temperature and thickness of strip used giving a delay of between five minutes and over a month. Its charge of 'TNT with high aluminium content and RDX booster' can probably blow a 3-m hole in heavy steel plate, but it appears cumbersome compared with similar modern weapons.)

Incendiary devices have become more compact than the 1-lb thermite bomb with its chemical mix, and grenades like the 80WP can start all the blaze a raider might need in most circumstances, with its incendiary blast of persistently burning phosphorus splashing everything within 15 m of its explosion. This convenient incendiary also gives thirty seconds of heavy white smoke, behind which an intruder may escape to cover. When used in the open it is one of the broad group of defensively used grenades that spray lethal fire or fragments while the thrower takes cover. In assault grenades you want a high-blast effect to stun your enemy without any risk to yourself from the wounding fragments of your own bomb. The most effective of these is the XFS with its two-second fuse. All the hard metal of its mechanism parts from the cardboard carton of its explosive as the grenade is in the air. (Those who remember the whizz of a lead ball from the plastic '69' blast grenade will appreciate this safety feature.) The thrower is in no danger, but a couple of metres from the stun grenade's explosion there is a flash as bright as fifty billion candles and a noise fifty times as loud as the backfire of a motorcycle! If prisoners are to be taken alive or their hostages not wounded, this is the grenade to use.

Little appears on the subject of mortars in the history of the SB Squadrons; these 'never played any great part in the training in the Mediterranean'. This is not surprising, when the weight of a 3-inch mortar and the twenty bombs a skilled team would fire in a minute weighed over 145 kg – the Squadrons wanted more than a minute's 'stonk' from a canoe-load of combat stores. In the 1960s, however, new types of grenade launchers, the poor man's mortar, came into general use. Some, like their Second World War ancestors, fitted on a rifle or SMG. None of these seems to offer particular advantages to the SBS, but they may well find uses for the Jet Shot, a Belgian grenade launcher with some novel features. Silent, without any flash, the launcher fires a grenade using a high-pressure charge. This forces a piston against a rod, which leaves the barrel with the bomb, but as the piston and charge are in a container (each bomb comes with its charge in a container) the source of its flight cannot be seen, although it can be detected by radar.

On a beach recce the modern yachtsman's electronics are of greater help to the SBS than much of the conventional soldier's radar and detection devices. The 'pocket' echo sounder with its waterproofed taped graph, the satellite navigation checks pinpointing positions on a beach or a mountain hillside, are but two aids that the COPPists would have exploited to the full. However, after a time of tension, should the tanks start rolling down Norway's northern motorway (the E6 running from the Finnish border to Oslo, 1500 km to the south) the navigation or communication satellites seem unlikely to survive the preliminary ambushes in space. It is then that the SC1 will need his astronavigation, his simple sand-testing auger and most probably some devastatingly simple means of stopping tanks which had not been publicized.

All radio communications at such times have their drawbacks, for not only may they be jammed but an eavesdropper can make good use of the pattern of signals from a particular source, even though he cannot decode them. Radios on the modern battlefield therefore can hop electronically from one frequency to another, the transmitter and receiver changing in unison one hundred times or more a second. This may not avoid the transmitter being D/F-ed, however, because direction-finders work over wide frequency bands. Therefore a high-speed brief transmission has to be made of a pre-recorded message, going out in a quick 'squirt' of sound, too short for the D/F antennae to locate its source.

How the SB canoeist will reach his target in a future war is not known in any detail. We will see how he landed in the Falkland Islands from Sea King and Wessex helicopters, but these cabs take fares only a relatively short distance and are not risked in actively hostile areas. The Lynx maybe offers a better service, able to land ten fully equipped men over 325 km from the ship it flew off. Alternatively the SB Section may come from the sea, their intermediate carriers, no doubt, launched from a submarine. The COPP swimmers were the grandfathers of this technique, via a submerged X-craft's airlock. Its heavy watertight doors always trickled some water, making 'dry' a relative term for this wet-and-dry compartment lit by a pressure-tight torch. In its meagre beam the small space could be seen to be chock-a-block with the pumping gear to fill and empty it, the non-return lavatory below the hatch lever, and a gash bucket. During the Second World War, leaving and re-entering submarines by divers was not a general practice, but with the advent of nuclear submarines divers would need to go out for some maintenance routines during long periods while the boat was submerged. This led to a more general acceptance of divers re-entering a submerged boat, which the SBS began practising as a matter of routine from the early 1960s.

Nuclear boats are even a more vital asset in Britain's defence forces than were the S- and T-class boats in the Second World War. The raid for which the big boats might be used is in consequence going to be even more vital than the destruction of the aircraft that might have bombed a Malta convoy. Nevertheless, one Valiant class, HMS *Conqueror*, sports the 'Jolly Roger' embellished with a dagger of a raiding operation on her fin conning tower (whether by SBS or SAS has never been disclosed); it is painted alongside the symbol for the Argentine cruiser she sank on 2 May 1982. More frequent carriers of the SBS are the O- and P-class patrol submarines. Their crews are particularly slick at launching canoes after bringing them on deck, rafting them up in pairs or threes before floating off the loaded craft with their swimmer-canoeists. The marines of the SBS in the last thirty years have the same respect for submariners as did their predecessors.

In the 1980s the tall fin-tower of a submarine is – as we saw off Borneo – a big enough reflector to make a 'splash' on any coastal radar scan. Yet in the Falklands as in the waters of Phuket Island almost forty years earlier, submarines came in and kept their rendezvous at times far past the critical hour for leaving a coast still in darkness, putting their crews at extra risk of air attack when dawn came.

Underwater communications are now at the stage where, once outside a submarine, the swimmers could still communicate with her skipper. These can be used at much greater depths – up to 1000 m – than an SB swimmer is likely to go, with a small transmitter receiver on the diver's back-pack and a similar device trailed from the submarine. These provide two-way conversations in a frequency on 40–44kHz waveband. Designed for use in various types of diving, the radio corrects the 'Donald Duck' speech of a man breathing an oxygen-helium mix.

Swimmer-canoeists may not dive to great depths operationally, but their training fits them for such work when they retire from the Corps. A number were in the teams working for Ocean Survey International recovering bullion from the *Lusitania*; others work on or under the North Sea oil rigs.

Contacts in civilian life are matched by international links between Royal Marine swimmer-canoeists and their counterparts in the special forces of other nations. The Americans, since the roundabout contacts of RMBPD through SRU to the UDT, have made more direct exchanges. Colonel Peter Davis, a captain at the time, made the first SBS official visit to the United States swimmers in March 1960, spending two weeks with the UD Teams in the Virgin Islands, where he made exits and re-entries to submarines at depth. He also made a jump – his first in a free-fall parachute – from the helicopter of a USMC Force Reconnaissance Company. 'Being so busy to check I did not get my rigging lines twisted, I forgot to count', he recalls: nevertheless not much over ten seconds must have passed before he pulled the D-ring and was 'swinging to my toes'. Not long afterwards the officers commanding both the UD Team and the Company spent some time with the SB Sections at Poole. Peter Davis and others made further exchange visits: to the French Nageurs de Combat, diving off Toulon, and to the swimmers of the Australian SAS, to name but two. SBS ranks also serve with British Army units, as do many marines at different periods in their careers. Several have served with the Parachute Regiment and with the SAS Regiments, one SB officer commanding an SAS Squadron in the early 1960s.

In days when the SB Squadron's roles were less exacting than they are today, a number of countries sent teams to the Squadron's courses, Australia and Israel among them. But probably these exchanges have been discontinued to avoid political misunderstandings, for the Squadron keep their plans and techniques to themselves, properly so in the changing patterns of world alliances. Whether any Argentines were SB-trained has never been made known, but certainly some of their officers attended commando courses.

When the authorities needed help with such difficult tasks as searching the *QE 2* for a terrorist bomb in mid-Atlantic, a team was parachuted from a Hercules into the sea near the great liner with her 2000 passengers and crew. The team included a Royal Ordnance captain who had not parachuted into water before, an RM lieutenant and corporal, and a sergeant from the SAS. The NCOs dropped first in the late evening of 18 May 1972. The sea was choppy, the wind gusting to 20 knots, and the overcast sky necessitated a safe but lower height than they might have preferred for the drop – they came out of the aircraft some way below the 300-m height needed to give time for a reserve parachute to open if the main 'chute fails. The NCOs, each with over 45 kg of bomb disposal stores on a short line from his waist, hit the sea and made ready for the liner's cutter to pick them up. Meanwhile in the Hercules the Army captain was feeling the effects of four and a half hours in flight. The lieutenant reassured him and, as time was running short (the terrorist had telephoned a late evening deadline for his bomb to explode), the marine helped his charge through the aircraft door. They came out nearly together, 'not the best way to start a descent'. As they went out, a waterproofed bag of stores was snatched from the line at the lieutenant's waist, yet this rope had a breaking strain of 680 kg.

In the water, under the lee of *QE2*, the cutter took ten minutes to gather them in while the marine kept his fellow officer afloat. Once aboard the liner, they searched the suspect cargo but no bombs were found. All the team subsequently received the Queen's Commendation for Bravery. Another bomb search at sea seven years later on the *Oriana* had a team led by the same RM lieutenant airborne for a similar operation, but the drop was cancelled by the ship's captain while the aircraft was still over the ship.

There have been a variety of amusing and adventurous pursuits suggested as SBS recreations. But, in reality, the foremost of these must be sailing, including single-handed trans-atlantic voyages and quiet afternoons on the River Exe with the family. One is known for the persistence with which he plays his guitar to enliven early morning hours in the bar. But most tend to be thinking men – whatever MLs may say – able to pass for ordinary people, despite their extraordinary talents.

10 The European Dimension

Northern Ireland

Two marines left Ballsbridge on a raw January evening to begin their patrol, leading down Leeson Street. They walked steadily, avoiding the brisk step of marching men, for these men were in civilian clothes. Skirting St Stephen's Green, they passed the cathedral. No longer could you buy a glass of porter from the grog shop in the vaults as the marines had done fourteen years earlier in 1868: such abuses of Christian charity had all been tidied away. The marines paused a while to admire the building. They were in no hurry, for they had four hours in which to cross the city. At Heylesbury Street they saw, but did not acknowledge, the other strollers in heavy overcoats and rounded bowler hats, fellow marines dressed as they were. They also had their coats loosely belted, not buttoned as one might expect; but each man carried a heavy naval .45-inch revolver in its holster discreetly hidden beneath the loose folds of his coat. They were big men, these marines, but their muffled appearance and the casualness of their ways attracted no attention from passers-by.

They were crossing Carlisle Bridge in the dusk when they saw a knot of bullyboys on the corner of Phisborough Road, three louts in old caps and long tattered jackets. The marines subconsciously quickened their pace. At first glance to the bullyboy, who swung a stick from his shoulder, they might be any two friends on some late afternoon errand: a second glance made the bully more wary, for at twenty paces this stick swinger thought better than to accost the friends for the price of a night's lodging. An accomplice tugged his sleeve and all the 'ruffians' vanished up a sidestreet. The marines did not follow them, but went on up the hill, before a cry and the sounds of a fight ahead caused them to lengthen their strides. Moving quickly but not running into the gloom of soot-laden fog lit only by lights from house windows, they came upon a scuffle, two men standing over a prostrate figure on the ground. The footpads were too intent on rifling their victim's pockets to notice the marines before brawny arms swung each assailant off his feet. In the brief struggle that followed, the oaths of the footpads in an invective of hate might have surprised any onlooker, yet the marines hardly made a sound. The prisoners were handcuffed, the victim stood on his feet and all five trooped off to the police station. There the marines reported to one of their officers and were sent back on patrol. They had been firm without being violent, for they were under orders to use no more force than was absolutely necessary, a point the officer checked in a quick inspection of the prisoners, shabby, pale young men, the broad belts of their trousers now removed as they stood in the charge room. He had made a dozen such inspections since Christmas, but once word had gone around that there were marine patrols on the streets, there had been fewer arrests, for the street attacks on innocent citizens of Dublin had become less frequent.

The officer and the two marines were from the Plain Clothes Detachment of 300 hand-picked men who had been sent in December 1882 to reinforce the Dublin police. Three officers of the Detachment organized patrols in such a way that no pair of marines had to retrace their steps in following a carefully set route across the city. Each route crisscrossed others, intersecting other patrols at specific points and times, the places of these intersections being changed each day. Knowing these points, however, the duty officer could assemble 250 men in half an hour without anyone noticing, as orders were passed from patrol to patrol. The scheme had proved most successful as the *Irish Times* pointed out: 'The unseen presence proved a terror to the implacable "Invincible" or the ruffian corner boy who invariably chose the time for his attack when the helmet of the uniformed constable was not in view.' The first large-scale use of marines on plain-clothes security duties brought a lessening of the tensions after the secret society of assassins calling themselves the 'Invincibles' had murdered the chief secretary of Ireland and others in May 1882. Before returning to Chatham, Kent, in 1883, the Detachment put a cordon round the houses of several 'Invincibles', whom the police then arrested. They were tried, convicted and sent to England under the guard of the Detachment, who sailed away that summer as secretly as they had arrived the previous December.

This episode was only one of several in the marines' association with Ireland since 1690 (if not before). On occasions they had proved – and not only in Ireland – politically more acceptable for security duties because local people tend to think that marines will withdraw to their ships, while army garrisons maintain more permanent an occupation. Be that as it may, the Chiefs of Staff in 1940 held two Royal Marine brigades in readiness for operations in Ireland, should the Germans land there. This is the reason why their Corps, despite the wishes of its senior officers, was not allowed to carry out commando raids and Army Commandos were formed instead. In the troubles of 1956, when IRA parties were blowing up electricity transformers and other installations, a Troop of 42 Commando patrolled to the border with Eire, their commander, an explosives expert, defusing the 'odd' bomb. From that time to this, marines have taken their turn with other British units in helping the police maintain the peace in Northern Ireland, much as they had done in the nineteenth century, when the Plain Clothes Department was commended by the Dublin press for 'their tact, keen observation and constant attention. . . . No section of the marines committed any excess, in the way of interfering with the just liberties of any class of the people.'

No details have been disclosed in the press on the SBS's role in Northern Ireland, apart from a passing reference or two to the use of 'water-borne patrols' and occasional implications that they have teams in the Province. Where the task of the modern marine (in common with other British forces of the 1980s) differs from that of their counterparts of the last century, is in the more sophisticated nature of the terrorism they are fighting.

Northern Ireland is an area of 14,121 sq. km with a population of over 1.5 million, roughly one-third of whom live in Belfast. The town suburbs, such as the Turf Lodge Estate less than a couple of kilometres from the centre of Belfast, have neat modern semi-detached houses 'where a burning bus is as incongruous as it would be in a housing estate in Manchester or Birmingham'. The countryside of the Sperrin Mountains of Londonderry or the hills of Tyrone have that rounded shape of the southern uplands of Scotland, and tourists in their cabin cruisers on a backwater of Lough Neagh could well imagine they were crusing on the Norfolk Broads. In the south of the Province lies County Armagh, one of the 'remotest' corners of the British Isles, where many of the locals are staunchly Republican. Here open hillsides and farmland provide more room for the Security Forces to manoeuvre than is possible in the council estates and other built-up areas.

The 320 km of border with Eire was the scene of IRA disturbances from 1956 to 1962, where a maze of unofficial border crossings along country lanes and farm tracks proved difficult to seal by the conventional means of road craters, giant concrete blocks (some weighing over a tonne) and other static devices. These were more than an inconvenience to farmers with adjoining fields on both sides of the border; and no doubt the local smugglers, with their lorry loads of pigs, butter or sugar beet seeking illegal subsidies from the north or south, helped the IRA to clear any obvious road blocks. Other means had to be found to monitor these byways.

On 28 September 1969, the first commandos to go to Ireland in the present emergency were '41'. As the Spearhead Battalion of the British Strategic Reserve, they were ready to move anywhere in the world at 72 hours' notice and their tactical headquarters, with one company, were ready to move at even shorter notice, 24 hours. They were on Divis Street in Belfast containing riots in the next few days, and in the next few months were to withstand more than brick-bats. Petrol bombs were thrown at them, pieces of window glass were flirted at their shins, and all manner of abuse from both 'Protestant' Loyalists and 'Catholic' Republicans fell about their ears. Yet the marines had no protective clothing, no flameproof Makrolon shields or face-visors. In this and later tours they discovered such foibles of the Irish as the actions brought by bullyboys claiming in court compensation for alleged ill-treatment, yet refusing to recognize such courts when they themselves were the accused. Information identifying just who were the activists on a Commando's patch was difficult to come by in 1969, but the marines' experience of working with police forces in Malaya, Cyprus, Borneo and Aden stood them in good stead.

The Protestant extremists had become almost inactive by 1976, but in the early years of the present emergency they were a violently disruptive force. In 1969, 'D' Squadron of the SAS had been in the Province for a few weeks, parading openly in uniform and laying a wreath on the grave of Colonel Paddy Mayne near Newtownards. They had been deployed quite openly to prevent any repetition of the Protestant gun-running of 1914. This had been a seaborne piece of smuggling which, if successfully repeated by either faction in Northern Ireland, would make nonsense of the careful patrolling of the land border. Marines, including some SBS, became involved in these amphibious operations, and by 1976 were operating from Londonderry an overt patrol on the River Foyle. Their principal concern was gun-running by the Provisional IRA across the open waters of Lough Foyle, 10 km wide and twice as long. Here the border crosses the lake before following the course of the river to the south. The marines had a detailed knowledge of this waterway. More, they knew poaching was rife that August when the season's fishing was poor, the local fishery having taken only 3000 salmon as against 7000 the previous May-to-August season. If the reader is wondering why the marines (or this book) should be concerned about local fishing, the explanation lies in the type of general information needed to set security intelligence against a realistic background for semi-clandestine operations. Had Anders Lassen and his recce patrol not claimed to be fishermen on Lake Comacchio, where there was *no* fishing in 1945, the sentries who challenged them would have been less suspicious.

In 1977 the river patrol was taken over by the UDR, who since 1972 had used Dell Quay dories (the civilian version of Rigid Raider Craft built by the same firm) on Lough Neagh, the large inland lake west of Belfast. Working in pairs, one covering a boat with a GPMG, while men from the second dory searched her, they checked cabin cruisers, fishing boats and barges to intercept illegal movements of arms. They had a similar patrol on Lough Carlingford, whose southern shores are in Eire's territorial waters, running 17 km in from the sea to Warrenpoint, where in 1977 a new container terminal had been built to service ships on weekly sailings to Garston and Preston in Lancashire and every second week to Rotterdam in Holland. To protect these sailings and to watch for arms smugglers over the shallows of this estuary of the Newry, one of two 82-tonne Fleet Tenders was always on patrol. She carried a marine detachment with 'specially trained Royal Marine helmsmen' for two Rigid Raider Craft and a Gemini inflatable in order to land the army or marine section of troops living aboard. (The marines, as part of the ship's company, were aboard for six-month commissions.)

The soldiers found that even routine patrols at 30 knots in the RRCs 'can be exciting' but on the night of Saturday/Sunday 19/20 March 1977 the tender HMS *Vigilant* picked up the echo of a small craft on her radar heading for the Ulster shore, but the boat was too small to give an echo when under the lee of the dockside clutter. Then an hour later the operator picked her up again as she ran into Eire territorial waters. Her crew probably expected her small size to enable her to escape radar detection. Two Rigid Raiders moved quietly, as they would do five years later in the Falklands, to drift silently on the channel edge in the lee of two moored ships. Later the echoes on *Vigilant*'s radar gave warning that another – or possibly the same – small boat was leaving the southern part of the lough.

Once this intruder, a white speedboat with a powerful outboard, was in the channel she was challenged by the nearest RM craft. Both craft had also opened up their powerful engines to come close to the intruder; but she was gathering way, to speed into the comparative safety of Warrenpoint docks, dodging behind a coastal container ship sailing out on the high tide. The boat did not get far. Refusing to stop – heave-to seems inappropriate for a speedboat – when a rifle shot was fired across her bows, the marine rifleman put a bullet into her outboard. As the leading RM craft reached the disabled boat, they came under fire from at least three gunmen on the Eire bank. 'We fired back' the patrol leader later said 'but kept the five men we had arrested held at gunpoint'. When the firing had stopped he made them row their boat into Warrenpoint docks, the first IRA bombers caught at sea. They had already landed two or more men on their first crossing and these five men, aged between eighteen and twenty-three, had two loaded pistols, a hand grenade and 4.5 kg of gelignite with which they had intended to sabotage the container terminal.

In the early days of the present emergency, British troops adopted an open 'hearts-and-minds' policy, foot patrols receiving cups of tea from the most unlikely quarters, and the marines' good humour and tact won many friends just as they had in more distant lands. (Of Borneo, for example, one assault engineer wrote: 'We engineered much, but assaulted nobody.') As in the Radfan, they helped the local children, taking some of the most deprived for days in the countryside. But the British services dropped its overt hearts-and-minds campaign in the 1970s (although individuals are not discouraged from simple kindness). One suspects, although the reasoning is by no means clear, that the British forces were apt to gain the confidence of the local people at the expense of a neighbourhood's relationship with the police, as they do anywhere, for they are not concerned with motoring offences or other minor misdemeanours. Yet, after taking the leading role in anti-terrorist activities in Northern Ireland until 1977, the British forces handed back the prime responsibility 'for the discipline of the community' to the police.

The activities of the Security Forces in Armagh are regarded by the IRA as more of a danger to their interests than the routine foot patrols of the forces in the cities: one authority on the Provisional IRA's organization expressed the view that, of the 350 or so hard-core terrorists, the most efficient are deliberately sent by the PIRA command to South Armagh. Even here in the 1950s there was not much support for the IRA – the 'Officials' or the 'Red' IRA as it became – until, by the 1970s, the Provisionals or 'Green' IRA began to enjoy wider support and therefore had the use of safe houses denied them in earlier disturbances. When five of them opened fire on Belleck police station on St Patrick's Day 1971, they were wearing long black coats that passed for uniforms, and must have been obvious to any local witness as the dress of an IRA soldier. Two of the five were hit by fire from the police station, but both were firing from across the border, only one of the raiders having crossed it for this attack. The attacks became more complex as the years passed: 90 kg of explosive in a culvert detonated by wires from across the border; radio-controlled explosions; and booby-traps to kill any Ammunition Technical Officer trying to disarm a landmine.

Apart from their weaponry and bolt-holes across the border in Eire, the Provisionals had a local knowledge that could confound all but the best British troops, and occasionally caught them napping. One such incident in

November 1975 led to three men of the Royal Regiment of Fusiliers being shot dead in their OP and a fourth being seriously wounded by IRA gunmen. Questions were asked in the House of Commons as to why the British services 'had not been given orders to clean up South Armagh'. From such events stemmed the dispatch of more British troops to the Province, but the British government wanted to impress on the Northern Ireland Unionists that some more dramatic steps were being taken and announced in Parliament that the SAS were to be sent to Northern Ireland. A minor rumpus was caused in the national press when the advance guard was revealed to be only eleven men but their regiment's reputation is such that people expected what they soon saw demonstrated: these soldiers' special abilities in surveillance were remarkable, for 'the IRA were led to believe that the SAS would wait in hiding 36 days rather than 36 hours'. At times their four-man teams would wear the uniform of the British regiment patrolling the area in which SAS was operating; at other times they wore civilian clothes and occasionally their distinctive beret with its winged-dagger cap badge. The SBS who are stationed from time to time in Ireland are, however, indistinguishable from other marine commandos.

Many SBS serving outside the Squadron have been in the Province from time to time with Commando units, but to remain invisible they do not publicize the fact. Nor has their role in collecting intelligence by observation ever been described in detail, but their ability to remain undetected while operating in an area is certainly of the level of 36 days and probably longer. Being experienced in the ways of countering modern surveillance themselves, they have no difficulty in playing the opposite role. They are expert in distinguishing one echo or blip on a ground radar screen from another; adept at distinguishing the passing of two men along a mountain track from a grazing horse or wandering sheep.

40 Commando completed their tour with the capture of a twenty-two-year-old car driver who later admitted several

murders. He had been driving a gang of hijackers around the area when he was 'bounced' by a helicopter swoop. Subsequently he was sentenced to seven periods of life imprisonment for the murder of five Orangemen and two soldiers of the Ulster Defence Regiment. He was one of eighteen hard-core terrorists whom the commandos had seized on this tour. His capture indicated a considerable improvement in intelligence. '40' were, incidentally, the first unit for some years to complete a tour in South Armagh without suffering a fatality (which says much for their professional approach to security duties). The Security Forces' pressure on Provisional IRA leaders in South Armagh was taking effect. In the continuing struggle for peace in Northern Ireland, the unseen surveillance by both SBS and SAS, the relentless work of the Royal Ulster Constabulary and the restraint shown by British troops on the tedious business of foot patrols, had all contributed to reducing to 75 the number of people killed by terrorist factions by 1980, the lowest for any year since 1970.

Meanwhile, this decade had seen a major change in the SBS's role in so far as their work involved NATO, for 3 Commando Brigade became fully committed to the northern flank. In 1979 they first deployed there as a fully integrated brigade in Norway with a Royal Artillery regiment and Royal Engineer Squadron under command. A very different role for 1 and 4 Commando Brigades which had been withdrawn from Germany in 1946 after their spearhead roles in the Second World War.

The Coasts and Rivers of Europe

The fit young man thoughtfully drinking a pint by the verandah windows of the 'Still and West' pub seemed absorbed in the yachts passing up the harbour. He might have been any day-tripper, for he did not look a whit different from the other dozen or so young men relaxing in the comfort of a Sunday drinking session. Yet his attention to the detail on the far side of the harbour would suggest to anyone 'in the know' that he had an important date in Gosport. Indeed, he knew more than he might care to admit about the Gosport 'side' and the Naval Air Station beyond the town at Leigh-on-Solent. One of his friends was at this moment passing the airfield aboard a Southdown bus to get a better view of the target in preparation for next Tuesday's (?) 'operation' by the Small Raids Wing. Then the air station's staff would be on the alert for intruders as swimmer-canoeists tested the airfield's defences.

That day began with two 'sailors' passing themselves off as station staff. They walked into the operations room on the pretext that they had been sent to collect an old filing cabinet. The sailors' cover story caused some confusion and while telephone calls were being made to determine which cabinet was to be removed, as bold as brass the 'sailors' began rolling up a wall map. (In a real operation they would have photographed it, but this was only an exercise.) The duty officer started to protest, but then realized who these intruders were – too late to stop them dropping a couple of teargas grenades. The exercise was prevented from getting completely out of hand by the appearance of a naval sub-lieutenant. It was unclear whether or not he was an umpire for the exercise, but he required the duty petty officer to salute him for – as he explained at length – they had not met before that morning. By this time the 'sailors' had vanished. The sub-lieutenant went on to explain the object of the exercise, but did not elaborate his role in the proceedings before walking off towards the wardroom, no doubt for coffee at stand-easy.

The seamen sentries at the perimeter wire had been questioning the value of security exercises. They argued that in a real-life situation one would shoot an intruder, not fool about asking him questions. Just then a corpulent three-badge petty officer appeared, looking as if his twelve years in the 'Andrew' had been spent in many a ship's canteen. He jovially sent the 'hands' off for an early dinner, having plausibly explained that there had been some confusion over the timing of their reliefs. Well, in December 1951 no one expected infiltration attempts by 'intruders'. These mysterious beings only appeared in war films and on the radio. Dick Barton, Special Agent, and his assistant, 'Snowy', featured nightly in some such daring enterprise, but this was not something anyone 'did for real'. The portly petty officer mentioned above was last met in this book in a canoe of the RMBPD at Leros in the Mediterranean. By December 1951 he had not gone to seed, for his plumpness was padding. Now, he and three 'sailors' guarded the wire. They let in their OC, who promptly went to the wardroom and held up the assembled drinkers. Two 'dockyard drainage inspectors' also enlivened the seamen's lunch with teargas. The sub-lieutenant had meanwhile vanished back to Eastney and his proper RM uniform.

That night, after the guard on the wire had been returned to the station's seamen, several of the sailors were spirited away, allowing more teargas bombs to be lobbed into the barrack huts. The young National Service seamen must have viewed these events more seriously than did the cheerful marines, who made light of it all. Their NCOs had seen service in the Pacific, in northwest Europe and the Mediterranean, for the Small Raids Wing was formed largely from the original Royal Marine canoe units. Since the formation of the SRW, they had carried out similar exercises to the one described, to test the defences of naval bases. The marines' task has become increasingly difficult over the years, as sentries the world over have become more alert to the presence of would-be saboteurs. Even in 1952 the swimmer-canoeists did not always get away with their deceptions: in their attack on the Naval Air Station HMS *Condor* at Arbroath, now the home of 45 Commando, the defenders captured the swimmers' staff car and with it all the raiders' plans. Their only success was the capture of the station's bus with two rather perturbed Wren passengers. The bus driver thought the whole episode a great lark and, at pistol-point, drove the bus into the camp.

Such fun and games have a more serious purpose, as they not only test the naval defences, but sharpen the SBS operators in roles they might undertake in any future hostilities in Europe. This use by SBS of the term 'operator' instead of 'swimmer-canoeist' during the 1950s has, perhaps, a touch more of Dick Barton-type theatricality than the hard-nosed approach of the branch in the 1980s. Be that as it may, in the 1950s the organization was just emerging from its post-Second World War transition phase. This change swept through not only the SBS but all of the Allied services, cutting the British and US armies of 1945 from an estimated four million plus to less than a million by 1946. Between the late 1940s and the mid-1950s the Special Boat Section was organized under a variety of titles which, for simplicity in this narrative, are called the Special Boat Squadron as the unit or branch of the Corps with a number of SB Sections and an SB Training Cadre. Swimmer-canoeists, as we have seen, do not spend all their service in the branch, but are to be found throughout the Corps. In the late 1940s these SCs were formed into each Commando's diving teams; three of the 'old hands', for example, being described – no doubt to their annoyance – as frogmen of 40 Commando, although at that time not all SCs were also divers. Their courses, however, began to take on the pattern of the present-day SC1, SC2 and SC3 in 1950. The syllabus for the first SC2's course was approved that June.

In the 1950s the SB Training Cadre ran a basic course, sometimes described as a 'canoe acquaint' course, and up to five courses each year for SC qualifications. Judging by the few figures published at the time, the failure rate was as high as 60 per cent. The numbers on each course were small. There were only fifteen potential SC3s in January 1958, yet the course was split into two halves in order to give that individual attention to each man's training that perfects the SC's skills. Even then, only eight of the volunteers were passed. On other occasions as few as four men have qualified from the ten or so who started. The more advanced SC2 and SC1 courses of the 1950s had a low failure rate, but only three or four men went on each of these senior courses.

During this decade, Italians, Israelis, Australians and Belgians trained with the SB Cadre, as mentioned earlier. On one course, there were two Italian lieutenants and a petty officer wearing several medal decorations for bravery: some weeks passed before their hosts realized just how many Allied ships these three swimmers had sunk during the Second World War. Such exchanges were two-way; two former SBS senior NCOs served with the Australian Army in 1956, helping to form No. 1 Commando Company there. The routine of training at Portsmouth did not radically change in these years, but the swimmers' roles were broadening from beach recces to include greater emphasis on long-distance swimming by the mid-1950s and even longer canoe passages.

In 1948 two SCs had paddled a canoe around Malta while serving there with 40 Commando. Their time of 11 hours and 40 minutes for the passage of over 75 km could not be bettered by a second attempt in 1954, when heavy seas filled the canoe several times in the first five hours and the paddlers repeatedly had to bring their craft ashore and drain it. Despite these difficulties, the crew got round in 14 hours and 20 minutes. In the intervening six years the Squadron had established an enviable reputation in the annual Devizes to Westminster canoe race. Two of the SBS canoes entered in 1950 came second and fourth; their service Mark II canoes weighing 50 kg to the 15 kg of the canoe clubs' boats. The leading SB canoe was faster than the Richmond Canoe Club craft by an hour over the first 170 km. They failed, however, to catch the ebb tide from Teddington Lock, an unavoidable hazard in this race when the canoes are started at intervals of a couple of minutes. The SB canoe which came fourth had an undetected leak that filled the boat and put them behind their schedule for the first 80 km. But they were only just beaten into fourth place and would be back again the following year to compete.

By 1960 the SB canoes had won the Devizes race six times, although SAS held the record with a time of 23 hours 01 minutes for the 200 km (124 miles) and 77 locks. In 1961 Sergeant G. ('Gillie') R. Howe, DCM, and Marine C. E. ('Ted') Tandy were the SBS's leading canoe entry. They had trained hard for the race, which Howe had won in 1956 and 1958 and never been lower placed than fifth in the previous six races. 'Ted' Tandy had been in the 1960 race, but failed to finish when his canoe was damaged. Racing together in 1961, they stood a reasonable chance of a place; although in 'Gillie' Howe's own words: wasn't he getting a bit old for this? He had other doubts too about his own stamina, for during the three months of pre-race training he had shed over 10 kg, while 'Ted' Tandy had lost only 6 kg. There were also problems with the canoe: it might not be strong enough after the removal of some frames and the keel slip (cover) to make it lighter; 15 cm had been cut from the bow and then fibreglassed to give a stouter if lighter hull; the alloy rudder had snapped once in training; and the broad-bladed paddles were new on the morning of the race. The canoeists had set themselves a tough schedule of 25 hours if the weather was bad, 23 hours 30 minutes for normal conditions and 22 hours 15 minutes – over three-quarters of an hour inside the record – if the weather was good.

The weather report was favourable: 'surface wind speed 8–10 knots, weather cloudy and dull, temperatures in the low 50s'. At least it was not going to snow as it had for most of the race one year. By starting at 0915, 'Gillie' Howe expected to catch the ebb tide at Teddington. His entry was taken with some disparagement by the starter. Did 'Gillie' not know that there would be 100 canoes ahead of him? Why not start later? 'Gillie' dismissed such teasing. Even if these boats cluttered the course, the tide was the key and a later start might miss the best of the ebb. Next morning, their support team of two marines filled the Hasler bottles (named after the founder of RMBPD who has invented many practical pieces of kit), prepared breakfast and made coffee for the vacuum flasks. This, and 4.5 litres of glucose-laced Ribena and orange juice, would have to last them for the race. They greased 'the parts of the body that usually get chafed and skinned', stowed their dry clothing in polythene bags in the stern, and loaded the canoe on to the truck for the short run to the start.

There, everything is hustle and bustle. The men in front of the marines trip and drop their canoe on 'ours'. The shortened bow could have been damaged but withstands the shock. The other canoe has a 5-cm hole in the bottom, which the marines' back-up team repair in ten minutes for they are experts at such patchwork. They draw Howe's entry number, No. 21, from the starter and the entry papers are carefully stowed in a waterproof package. Howe and Tandy then busy themselves with final checks. Everything – rudder lines, stowage, etc. – has already been checked, but there are last-minute decisions, such as should the spray cover be taken after all, just in case it is rough on the tideway?

The starter interrupts the train of thought: 'OK "21", I am starting you at 0914.' He checks their kit sheet and with 30 seconds to go hands it back with the lock passes. At 10 seconds they each grip their double paddles firmly . . . '3, 2, 1, Go!' The voices and cheers of the back-up team die away as the bow cuts through the green weed and slime of the canal. At 800 m they pass the first canoe ahead of them. 'First blood', Tandy grunts, his steady rhythmic paddling following 'Gillie's' firm strokes. Eighty minutes from the start, they make their first portage. Six other canoe teams are struggling to get their boats past this lock. The marines come smartly to the bank, 50 m short of the landing. In a well-practised drill they are out of the boat, swing it on to their right shoulders and double for 200 m to launch the canoe downstream and clear of the others. At 2 hours 28 minutes they come to the first 'secret' checkpoint where, to their surprise, the OC SBS is one of the checkers. They have been making good time, covering 18.5 km through the slack water of the canal, but now there are more canoes ahead, with portages every 100 m in some cases and others 3 km apart. A shout of 'coming through on your left, please' is repeated by 'Gillie' for each canoe as the marines overtake them, and the vanquished sportingly move aside. Reaching about the fiftieth canoe in the Savernake Tunnel, 'Gillie' begins to wonder if there could have been 100 ahead of them at the start. The dark tunnel is only 4 m wide. Halfway through, 'Ted' shouts his customary warning to a canoe in front. Its paddlers seem to have moved to the right. There is a clash of paddles in the dark – 'a horrible crunch, we are caught off balance'. For one terrible moment they hang on edge, but a lightningly quick recovery stroke brings the canoe on even keel and they power on, having come through 500 m of chancy darkness.

Near Kintbury locks 'some kind person has left out a bucket of water and glasses, as they have done every year' and the marines each drink a refreshing tumblerful. Except for a couple of oranges eaten while they paddled in turn, so far their only refreshment has been a piece of chocolate or glucose sweet as they ran round carrying the canoe past the lock. Near Newbury they pass the first SAS canoe ahead of time. At Newbury lock the speed of their portage catches the lady official by surprise and she almost falls into the river. Coming out of the Newbury stretch of water, a canoe ahead blocks the landing. 'Ted's' sharp kick of the rudder jars the hull on a grinding rock, and star cracks appear in the floor between 'Gillie's' legs. Gingerly, they get out, trying not to increase the damage. They expect to lose half an hour in repairs, but luck is with them and the fibreglass is not holed. They are on their way, the current here speeding by an extra 5 knots when they can take advantage of it.

Half a Hasler bottle of juice each gives them a 'lift'. The marines' competitive spirit is further spurred by the sight of two red paratroop berets ahead. The two officers from 1 Para are not to be passed easily, but once '21' have sprinted by, half an hour of relentless chasing fails to hold the marines. Their next conquest is an SAS folding canoe –

later to be first in its class – with a former marine now a trooper in 22 SAS. Nine hours 27 minutes to Reading and a change into evening wear, with urgent calls from their back-up team: 'Come on, faster. You're wasting time.' But once past Reading the course lies entirely in the Thames and there are only twenty locks to go, although there are still plenty of hazards, for the water in the river is higher than on their practice runs.

Launching the boat below Hambledon lock into a strong current with back eddies, 'Ted' has just got aboard when an extra-heavy wave nearly pulls the boat over. His shout of 'Let go' sends it toppling on the wave crest, his recovery paddle stroke failing to keep the canoe upright. But as he goes under, he keeps a firm grip on his paddle, for they would never have found it again in the gathering dusk. 'Gillie' realizes that their only chance is to swim the canoe to an island in the river. 'Ted' tries to do this, pushing the canoe towards the Surrey bank, but the boiling current is too strong for him. Then, with that quickness of purpose that earned him decorations for gallantry in far more dangerous places than the River Thames, 'Gillie' takes a firm grip of his paddle and dives into the river. He swims to the bow and with 'Ted' pushing the stern they swim in a circle, back eddies pulling them towards the weir. The canoe circles again and again, but each time they kick hard to swim her further into midstream. Fortunately, 'Gillie' knows about these waters from a former SBS canoeist who used it to practise wild water slalom.

The water is freezing, and if the swimmers are in it too long their hot muscles will spasm in cramps, which is reason enough for 'Pinky', the leader of the back-up team, to urge them on to greater efforts. His voice can just be heard above the roar of the weir as the canoeists reach the revetted bank round the island, which is far too slippery to climb and drops into deep water. There they manage to hang on to tree roots, treading water as they empty the boat. Getting back into the canoe is even more difficult, but with his paddle resting across the stern of the canoe and the

bank, 'Ted' edges himself over the stern. The violent rock-
ing of the canoe almost throws him back into the water, but
he steadies her and 'Gillie' heaves himself aboard. The cry
of 'get her moving fast, you've lost fourteen minutes' is
hardly necessary, but 'Pinky' still bellows his encouragement. The canoeists are so cold by this time that
they risk a further delay to drink some coffee, but keep
paddling in turn.

The delay on the island has enabled other canoes to catch
up. The 1 Para boat has passed '21', and as the marines run
round Chertsey lock they find the paras having a drink from
their flasks. Then the marines race on, towards the vague
outlines of mooring buoys. 'Gillie' sees one of these at the
last moment, kicking the rudder hard over and the canoe
just scrapes past it to a 'wow' from 'Ted'. At Molesey lock,
'Pinky' darts out to meet them. His encouragement is now
more cheerful: 'Only one more lock.' But now the cold and
the exertion is beginning to take its toll. 'Gillie' has touches
of cramp in his legs, and 'Ted' takes over as No. 1 for the
last 27 km. They are both glad there will be no more
portage, for in the last couple of hours, as they stiffened up,
they have experienced more and more difficulty in balanc-
ing the canoe whenever they had to step ashore. They have
fleeting impressions: of 'Pinky' shouting to them as they
pass under Putney Bridge; tantalizing dreams of pints of
frothing ale to slake their by now considerable thirst as they
pass Mortlake Brewery. They pass a police launch and flash
a torch at its crew who immediately slow down and move
from midstream to reduce the wash of the launch. 'Pinky'
appears on every bridge. The 'putt-putt-putt' of his 2-stroke
motorcycle can be heard along the Middlesex bank, as
'Pinky' races from one bridge to the next to be ready with
more encouragement.

'Get that tub moving' from Battersea Bridge warns of the
sprint expected over the last 4 km, and the aching arms take
a firm grip as numb fingers respond to hidden reserves of
strength. The tide is boring out at 4 knots by this time,
coming up to 0500 hours on a chilly morning. The paddlers

make a final sprint for Westminster Bridge, passing under the Surrey arch and turning to starboard for the finish. The river is not to be trifled with, however, and an eddy round the bridge pier sends the canoe on to her beam. . . . Their recovery strokes are not as quick as they had been 20 hours and 48 minutes ago, but they are quick enough, and they stay upright to cross the finishing line broadside on in the next minute. Sergeant Howe and Marine Tandy have broken the record by 3 hours and 12 minutes.

The 1961 Devizes race has brought us ahead of our story, for in 1950 when the SBS were first committed to the mainland of Europe, there began an eight-year commitment on the Rhine. The first SCs to go out with Colonel Peter Davis were known as the RM Demolition Unit of the Rhine Flotilla (forerunner of the Rhine Squadron), but to all intents and purposes they were No. 2 SB Section, their title from 1951. No. 1 SBS became the operational Section based in the United Kingdom with the SB Training Cadre, although men from all Sections would be interchanged over the years. Those with No. 2, as with marines in all the Corps' units overseas, were posted to the Section for a tour of eighteen months or occasionally for two years. By this means of so-called 'trickle drafting', a unit could be abroad indefinitely with its personnel changing over the years. Service in Germany, however, has long been regarded as a 'home' posting in the British services: 'Gillie' Howe, for example, entered the Devizes race in three successive years while serving in Germany.

The job of the Rhine Squadron, to which 2 and 3 SBS were attached, was to patrol this great waterway, using landing craft to ferry tanks 'back across the river should a strategic withdrawal ever make this necessary'. The swimmers would destroy any boats that might be left on an enemy's side of the river and in places use barges to block tributaries of the Rhine. At least, this has been put forward as a theory of the late 1950s. In practice, while the SBS could demolish riverside installations without difficulty, the barges were large vessels of several thousand tonnes that could not be scuttled with a few kilogrammes of explosive. No doubt the marines had more subtle plans. 'Dick Barton' Davis, as Colonel Peter was affectionately known to his unit, was – and is – a man of ingenuity. His men worked with the Rhine Squadron at Krefeld, 20 km from Duisburg, the only industrial city on both the Rhine and the Ruhr, with the largest inland harbour in Europe in the 1950s. LCAs with several German torpedo recovery and other craft carried the demolition teams on training exercises from Duisburg up the broad reaches of the river away from the industrial Ruhr valley to the upper Rhine beyond Mainz. It was a laboriously slow plug against the river's 6-knot current at some narrows, past vineyards rising on steep hillsides and medieval castles on islands dotted along the 700 km of this river, which is navigable for most of its length.

Manning the Rhine Squadron became a Royal Marine commitment in 1953, with marine officers commanding LCTs, the large tank-carrying landing craft with their crews living aboard. For No. 2 SBS the action centred on swimming and those snatch pick-ups at speed: an LCA running at 11 knots would pass close to a river bank, in slack water, a 'catcher' poised over the gunnel to link an arm with the swimmer, pulling him clear of the water in one neat lift. This trick was not recommended to the uninitiated unless the swimmer wanted to run the risk of having his shoulder dislocated. Not all SBS activities, even in 1950, were confined to the river, and that summer they took part in 'Broadsword', one of their first major exercises with the British Army of the Rhine. After working up for the exercise, the SBS were joined by the marine-manned ML 2912, which was used as a control vessel for assault landing craft. One report has described Peter Davis's pilotage – if that is the right word – of this launch from Rotterdam 'when he always appeared to be looking back down river, the "wrong" way' to get his bearings, because he had not previously sailed up river but had sailed down it. Colonel

Peter's swimmers were joined by 1 SBS from Eastney, Hampshire, with the intention of dropping some canoeists by parachute and sending others in underwater. In the event, however, they swam or marched for long patrols as no aircraft were available. Their convoy of five vehicles drove to Hamelin where Lieutenant Davis was briefed by senior army officers. The Sections were then prepared for three penetration patrols into 'enemy'-held territory.

Exercise 'Runaground', the annual amphibious assault over the shingle of Eastney beach, has often been the scene of some military 'firsts'. Here in 1949 the Brigade Commander, or possibly a marine standing in for him, landed by helicopter from HMS *Suvla*, a Mark 3 Landing Ship Tank, in the first operational-type helicopter flight from a British LST. During the 1950s, helicopters became an accepted way of landing all marines, parallel with their assault craft. Their first drop in public with an inflatable dinghy was at 'Runaground III' in 1952. Two sticks (as a 'drop' of parachutists is called) each of three SCs landed in the water from a Hastings aircraft, to inflate the dinghy and load the combat stores parachuted in with them. During the same exercise, a battalion of Gloucesters was put ashore by Royal Marine landing craft, after a pair of two-man canoes had been launched from a motor cutter to 'survey' Eastney beach. The SBS also brought in a surf boat, for which three coxswains had been trained to use the long steering oar. On this occasion they used the craft to take off a supposed prisoner-of-war from the beach area. This annual exercise attracted over 1000 spectators with such displays, but in 1980 when several hundred so-called water descents were made by parachute from a helicopter on a single Saturday, passers-by hardly paused in their stroll along Eastney promenade. Today, such activities perhaps seem commonplace, but they were very novel in the 1950s. Exercise 'Runaground' was for many years the highlight of Eastney Barracks' public events. The last one was held in the late 1950s.

There were numerous other exercises in Europe. 1 SBS worked with 22 SAS in Denmark in 1953, for example, 'destroying' the massive road-and-rail Storston Bridge when the umpires accepted a few chalk marks for the tonnes of explosive that would be needed to bring down such a structure in wartime. On other occasions the SBS worked with the successors of the D-Day 1944 X-craft, *Shrimp* and *Minnow*. They were also frequently landed from HMS *Ickford*, one of the small anti-submarine warfare ships used in the approaches to a defended port. Parachuting was becoming increasingly popular as a sport at this time, but for training the facilities were usually limited to a few practice jumps from helicopters. However, more parachute training was possible for men of 3 Commando Brigade in Malta, after several SCs were trained as parachute instructors. At this time, the Royal Marines were committed to defend NATO's southern flank. There the weather was kinder and made the parachute appear a feasible means of going to war, something the Squadron had come to doubt in the UK when the wind was often too strong for practice jumps. In the sunshine of the Mediterranean the SB Sections from the UK and Germany enjoyed their recces of Greek and Sicilian beaches on exercises such as 'Weldfast' in 1953, the first major deployment in this area of British and American forces since the Second World War.

Parachute drops in the late 1950s included one with outboards for inflatables; a sergeant jumping with one in a weapon container in 1957 to what was then the new water DZ of Studland Bay near Poole. Familiar to many marines of the combined operations close fire support craft of the mid-1940s, the Bay had been a field firing range for the landing craft based on HMS *Turtle*, a stone frigate at Hamworthy on the outskirts of Poole. The buildings were deserted from 1946 until 1952 when the first marines moved back there and the Beach Wing of the Amphibious School began clearing the broad slipway (the hard) and inshore waters. These underwater swimmers included men trained to clear beach obstacles – the LCOCUs of the Second

World War – but in 1953 this work was taken over by Royal Naval Clearance Divers. Teams of these divers and SB Sections later went to the Mediterranean on several occasions; 1 SBS spent two months there in 1956. On one such visit to Portugal in the previous year, several teams of swimmers helped in the making of the film *Cockleshell Heroes*, which was loosely based on Hasler's epic raid of 1942.

Since 1954 the Squadron had been established at Poole where the Training Cadre and No. 1 SBS moved on 1 December from Eastney. No. 2 moved back to the UK in 1958 after eight years in Germany, celebrating their return by taking only eleven hours' paddling time in a passage from Portsmouth to Poole with only six hours of breaks. They would not be home long, for in March 1960 they left for the Far East, still reminiscing about their days in Germany: Unit Patrol Races in the BAOR Ski championships – highest placed UK teams in 1958; the days of resisting interrogation after being caught on evasion exercises; the breaking of the cross-Channel canoe record twice in 1951 and 1953; and working by the swirling 16-knot currents in breaches of the Dutch dykes when helping flood victims. None seems to remember the local delicacy of Duisburg, Dutch mussels in a piquant sauce, but they have endless tales of Four Lakes camp, the former German fighter airfield, 40 km from the comfort of Krefeld where they still had their German headquarters in 1952. At least by the lakes they were away from the all-pervading smell of lilac from the soap factory by this main base among the industries of the Ruhr. Near the lakes they had practised their demolitions, canoed, played football and spent many a cold night in those deep hides they build. Some were so difficult to spot that once, when away on a desert exercise, an RAF corporal fell through the sand dune roof, to the surprise both of himself and the SBS operators. On the more serious side, many of their sharpest memories were of parachute drops.

'On Thursday we made a balloon jump before breakfast', one officer has commented, 'and in the morning gave a demonstration of SBS swimming techniques . . . in the afternoon we emplaned in a C119.' The first man, an instructor, dropped from this American aircraft, drifted so rapidly in the 15-knot breeze that the cloth panels marking the intended landing point at Schaffen had to be moved. The aircraft stooged about for an hour before the SB 'hands' were allowed to jump. On Friday morning they dropped again from an aircraft at 400 m. In the afternoon several of them jumped with chest packs in a test of the emergency 'chutes, which they do not normally use. Four jumps in two days constituted a breach of the regulations of this Belgian parachute school which, in 1955, normally only allowed a man to jump once a day. Fortunately, the green-bereted instructors from the Belgian Commandos were prepared to help all they could in the training; and extended their hospitality to the visitors by entertaining them in their homes in Diest.

By the mid-1960s free-falling was the name of the game. By this method a man dropped from several thousand metres can travel a considerable distance across the sky before he opens his 'chute. Appearing as a tiny blob in the background of a radar's clutter, he is unlikely to be detected even when his parachute opens, for at less than 200 m he is below the range of many radar screens. The parachutist must take care as he pulls his ripcord that he does not lose control of his position in flight and tumble through the air just when he needs to get control of his canopy. The air flow through the cutaway panels of the canopy is controlled by rigging lines, to land the parachutist within centimetres of his chosen dropping point. He will already be wearing his breathing mask, which has allowed him to fall from, say, 5000 m. On hitting the water, he may dive to 30 m before the defences can be alerted.

Another interesting playground of the SBS is the Arctic wastes of north Norway. For three weeks every autumn since the early 1950s in preparation for Norway they had as a matter of routine trained in Scotland, where they learnt to live off snails and equally unpalatable sources of vitamins,

the food that they might sometime have to eat to avoid
capture when evading an enemy's patrols after an operation. Their evasion exercises were from the early 1960s
always spiced with that unpleasant hammering men must
learn to withstand if caught and interrogated.

The SBS had also trained with the cliff climbers (today
called Mountain Leaders), but by 1954 both groups of
specialists were trained for work in Norway. Diving under
the ice was still not a practical proposition for free swimmers,
so other infiltration methods had to be used when the
Squadron took part in the Norwegian Army's NATO exercise that autumn. In 1956 the canoeists dressed as fishermen and worked from Norwegian fishing boats. In this
disguise they landed behind the Norwegian defence lines and
during three days created considerable mayhem, leaving
chalk notations of bombs here, there and everywhere. Over
the years, however, they perfected techniques – first explored
in 1960 by Canadian divers making use of the thermal layer
of comparatively warm water below the ice – by which free
divers in heated suits could survive under ice, albeit in
discomfort, for the suit does not heat all the body. Tailored
neoprene suits and gloves had been a first step in 1962.

Mention has been made of the swimmers' likely raiding role
on the north Norway 'motorway', but in looking at their more
glamorous roles we must not forget that they are marines
not Secret Service MI6 agents. As marines, they have their
share of parades and drill, although at times the drill squad
of swimmers must be mainly drawn from the Training
Cadre rather than the operational units, for although
haircuts may only take minutes, military bearing can take a
period or two of drill to reacquire. This, after a little
practice, swimmer-canoeists can do like any other marine,
and they have their memories of 'the hottest June Sunday in
yonks, when we once paraded for church at Krefeld'. In
their Corps' tercentenary parade of 1964, when units
marched through London with bayonets fixed, drums
beating and the colours unfurled, as is their ancient

privilege, canoeists marched with other commandos dressed in their ceremonial blue uniforms, with their distinctive white helmets. In another parade to mark this special year for the Corps, six canoeists marched with paddle-boards and a Kestrel canoe.

Throughout the second half of the present century there have been canoeists with the Royal Marines Reserves, although their numbers have tended to wax and wane with the enthusiasm of individuals for this esoteric calling. Many of the first reservists to join Nos. 4 and 5 Sections in 1950 were former regulars from the SBS, although at that time these Sections had different names and indeed the Merseyside reservists did not include any SC rates when some of the Liverpudlians first trained as canoeists that year. Reservists have canoed in Lapland, on the Rhine, in Malta and elsewhere during their military exercises in the 1950s and 1960s, but in more recent decades their training – like that for all reservists – has been integrated with the regular commandos' training. The Lapland expedition was typical of an SB private venture, in the sense that the canoeists were in neutral territory, having hauled their canoes from Narvik, 50 km through the mountains, to cross the Swedish border and begin a voyage of 400 km down wild rivers and across lakes to reach the Gulf of Bothnia, the broad arm of the Baltic Sea between Sweden and Russia. The three teams in two-man canoes found the feeding excellent on fat trout they caught, on occasions without even baiting the hooks trailed in high mountain streams. Their journey went well until quite openly they paddled down the River Kalix into Boden, 30 km from the sea, where they were arrested. They did not have to undergo that violent interrogation associated with breaking a canoeist caught by an enemy, but the Swedish authorities needed three days to satisfy themselves that on this occasion the SBS operators were not taking notes in a forbidden area. As an extra precaution, they also refused to allow the canoeists to paddle the final stretch of their trip to the sea.

11 Actions in the South Atlantic
The Falklands Conflict, 1982

In the cold dark of a late evening on 22 April 1982, a helicopter hovered low over one of the few patches of level ground in the Sørling valley. It had flown from HMS *Antrim* in a brief period of good weather, a rare occasion in South Georgia during winter. Yet this 'narrow window' in the weather would prove deceptive even as the Wessex helicopter prepared to land men of No. 2 Special Boat Section at a landing zone on the island's rugged terrain some 200 m above the waters of Hound Bay. An SBS corporal slid rather than climbed down the short rope from the aircraft to hit the ground in the darkness. He was clear of the rotor's downdraught before he realized how strongly the wind tugged at the hood of his Arctic jacket. Swinging his Armalite rifle from across his shoulders and sensing the rise in the ground rather than seeing it, he led the other three of his team 30 paces to the west of the LZ before they took up firing positions. The first men out of the aircraft, they covered the rest of the Section while radios, ammunition and other combat stores were lowered or dropped from the helicopter along with their precious Gemini inflatables.

In little over a couple of minutes the dark shape of the helicopter vanished back into the night. The teams then began to move on a compass bearing down from the relatively sheltered landing point on to the open floor of the valley's north end. In the dark the going was treacherous as they crossed boulder-strewn heath, watching for the point where they would strike westward over a spur to reach Cumberland Bay. The lieutenant commanding the Section had seen the route only briefly when he had flown over it the previous day. Now, from the ground and in the dark, he had difficulty finding the crag feature that had been so clear on the map, and below which lay their best route to the bay. Each man carried some 30 kg of ammunition, food and spare clothing as they manhandled the Geminis folded in great bags each of 180 kg and a four-man lift. Corporal Will Derby's team* felt the full force of the northwest wind in their faces as they breasted the crest of the spur. Breathing heavily from their efforts, the cold air caught their chests. Fit as they were, they were nevertheless glad after eight hours to reach the level ground just above the point where they would launch the inflatables, some 5 km from the LZ.

On South Georgia, No. 2 SBS were to reconnoitre the Argentine defences at Grytviken and to achieve this without being seen, as in April the Argentines had little or no detailed knowledge of British intentions. The secret British landings on the islands had begun the previous day (22 April) when the Mountain Troop of 22 SAS Regiment's 'D' Squadron were landed on Fortuna Glacier, some 50 km to the west of the SBS landing. The Special Air Service troopers chose a route across the glacier ice, ignoring the well-intentioned advice of those with local knowledge and others with considerable experience of such conditions. In the event, a blizzard caught them exposed on the glacier, and by dawn they were in danger of losing limbs from frostbite. As driving snow swirled into the snow banks on the ground, the horizon was lost in a 'whiteout', making flying nearly impossible. Two Wessex HU.5s flown off the RFA tanker *Tidespring* crashed while trying to land on the glacier, but with incredible skill Lieutenant-Commander Ian Stanley, RN, landed the Wessex HAS.3 from *Antrim* to lift out the SAS Troop and the crews of the crashed helos.

The SBS team were all too aware of the hazards of cold-weather warfare, for they had trained in northern Norway with 3 Commando Brigade Royal Marines. In the South

---

*Will Derby, like his ancestor in an earlier history, is a pseudonym, for no names can be recorded of the unseen and unknown Royal Marines of the Navy's Special Boat Squadron. Nevertheless, this reconstruction of events in the South Atlantic is indicative of the part played by these swimmer-canoeists in the recovery of South Georgia and later of the Falklands.

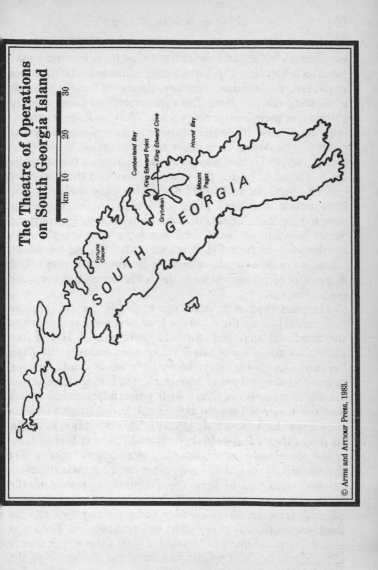

The Theatre of Operations
on South Georgia Island

0   km   10   20   30

Fortune Glacier

Cumberland Bay
King Edward Point
King Edward Cove
Grytviken

Hound Bay

Mount Paget ▲

SOUTH GEORGIA

© Arms and Armour Press, 1983.

Atlantic, however, the weather patterns are different, lacking the sudden rise in temperature that turns ice into slush: on South Georgia the biting cold persisted. As the men unpacked the Geminis, therefore, they soon lost the warmth of their march, the sweat from this strenuous effort turning chill inside their windproof jackets. With his fingers becoming numb now his outer mittens were off, the corporal checked the connections from the boat 'skin' to the foot-pump and the Gemini was inflated. Launching it was not as easy. The wind hurled the bow this way and that, as gusts eddied round the rocks that had given some shelter on the little beach they were using, and rocks under the water snagged the hull. These difficulties left no option but for the teams to wade out with the boats before loading them. A combination of Arctic jackets and body-clinging swimsuits (some types of which have built-in heating elements) afford a measure of protection from the cold, but do not keep one warm all over.

The plan appears to have been to paddle (or did they use outboards?) along the coast for four hours to bring them to the headland that juts out into Cumberland Bay. From there they could see across 5 km of open water to the King Edward Cove with Grytviken visible at its head, nestling below the steep slopes of Mount Paget. The settlement was visible to trained observers with powerful binoculars, and had the marines brought one of the special night viewers they might have been able to continue observation at night. As it was their hand-held thermal imagers gave them a view of the shoreline even though they were 500 m from it. Yet the niceties of such technology were far from their thoughts as they struggled to keep the Geminis on course in the freshening northwest wind. This brought chunks of sharp-edged glacier ice across the bay, to bump and bore against the Geminis despite every effort to fend them off. The ice at first delayed the marines but then forced them to put ashore some distance short of the headland, as the skins of the Geminis had been punctured. Patching was possible, but repeated delays meant that dawn would break before they could hide themselves and the boats near the headland. There would be no chance to establish an observation post, without compromising the whole operation. Reluctantly, at first light, the lieutenant sent a radio flash to the Royal Marine major aboard *Antrim* and the teams were ordered to lay up, hidden throughout the day, in readiness to be brought off that night. They were to spend a cold uncomfortable day as the teams took it in turns to lie almost motionless for two hours among the rocks above their hideout, watching for 'Argie' patrols. None came. Nor were they overflown by enemy aircraft. Years of training in the patience required to win out 'by guile not strength' – the SBS motto – had given the men the uncanny knack of lying motionless yet relaxed for hours on end without too many muscle cramps. When night came, after eight hours, the men could at last stand up and move about. The two sentries kept low profiles nevertheless, for modern warfare special viewers can reveal a man almost as clearly in the night as by day – a point which would be brought home to many troops in later fighting on the Falklands.

Carefully, the SB Section cleared away all trace of their hide before making their way back to a picking-up point out of radar range of King Edward Cove, the helicopter homing on to their radio beacon without difficulty. All the men of the Section would in future have their own memories of St George's Day, 1982, a day celebrated in the Royal Marines' calendar of memorable dates for the exploits of the 4th Battalion, which landed on the mole at Zeebrugge that day in 1918.

If this operation starts on a frustrating note, it is only to emphasize the reality of SBS operations which, on this occasion, had hung on an ice edge. Other marines and SAS troopers were landed next day, after the Argentine Navy had made an attempt to reinforce the island and during which their submarine *Santa Fé* had been severely damaged by British helicopter attacks. During the resulting confusion ashore, a quick-reaction force of 75 marines and soldiers were landed from *Antrim* under the cover of naval gunfire.

No. 2 Section SBS and a Troop of SAS were to be landed as riflemen to the west of King Edward Point, a kilometre from Grytviken, but the Argentine garrison surrendered before this landing could take place.

For the SBS teams there would be further actions in the South Atlantic, but while they were repairing their kit others prepared to carry out recces on the Falkland Islands, 1300 km west-northwest of South Georgia. The special forces, both the Royal Navy's SBS and the Army's SAS, were to provide these teams, sometimes working in small groups, even sections, but more often just as single four-man teams. All were to be under the command of a senior officer embarked in the Task Force flagship, the carrier HMS *Hermes* (although by some accounts there was a tendency for the SAS to retain close contact over their coded, satellite-linked radios with their headquarters in Hereford, England, regardless of their immediate commanders aboard ship). These ships, that St George's Day, were still a long way from the islands. The force that went to South Georgia had left the main fleet ten days earlier, a decision conveyed to the enemy paradoxically that Friday in a BBC interview suggesting that the recapture of South Georgia would be 'an elegant application of pressure'. Before this could be done sensibly, some information was desperately needed, intelligence on which beaches were defended, where the enemy held his tactical reserves and what coast defences, guns and land-based Exocet missiles had been set up. It was to find such information that the secret recces of South Georgia had been launched from *Antrim*; and such intelligence was woefully lacking for the pending liberation of the Falklands.

No detailed photographs could be taken of the islands' defences after the Argentine invasion as the only British airfield was 6300 km away on Ascension Island – as far from the islands as London is from New York. (The first from the air pictures, taken from an improvised camera position in a Harrier's wing, did not reach the land forces until the evening on which they moved against Stanley's outer defences on 11 June.) Therefore, the special forces would have to glean this information on the ground, finding, more importantly, where the Argentines did *not* have coast defences as well as where these were, for the enemy could not defend every metre of the 24,000 km of coast around East and West Falkland. The planning staff of 3 Commando Brigade, Royal Marines, led by Brigadier J. H. A. Thompson, OBE, had made an intelligent guess as to where the enemy commanders would place their defences. Thompson's deduction later proved remarkably accurate, for he had rightly assumed that the Argentinian commanders would be influenced by American methods. The SBS teams were needed ashore as quickly as possible to confirm or to correct this assumption and secretly to recce the likely landing beaches. These had been reduced to some thirty points suitable for landing craft, on the basis of personal studies made by a Royal Marine major while cruising around the islands in 1978.

The British had declared a 'Total Exclusion Zone' around the islands from mid-April; when the Fleet entered that Zone on 1 May *Hermes*'s helicopters were 300 km, three flying hours from the north coast. Nine of these aircraft were Sea King HC.4s – able to lift nineteen men or more if the commandos were only lightly equipped – from Naval Air Squadron 846, and three were the smaller-capacity Wessex HU.5s from 845 Squadron. There were, in all, a dozen aircraft designed to carry commandos, while the remaining Sea King and Wessex helicopters were fitted with sonar gear and other equipment for anti-submarine warfare (ASW), leaving no space for 'cargo personnel'. However, at a later stage in the operation (codenamed 'Corporate') some of these ASW helicopters were partially stripped of gear so that troops or stores could be carried.

For covert operations there are several ways in which SBS may be landed or, to use the military term, 'infiltrated': parachuted in, or landed from helicopters, by small boats or from submarines. This last method has its difficulties, especially in the comparatively shallow waters around the Falklands where submarines are more easily detected from the air, and it seems likely that the only special forces operation reportedly undertaken from a submarine was against targets not on the islands. Parachuting in was certainly possible – the new commander of 2 Para parachuted to join his unit – but larger-scale use of such techniques would have been needlessly complex in view of the available helicopters. At first thought, this may seem a noisy approach to secret landings; but in fact the cover of other aircraft noise, the wind and remoteness of LZs from likely Argentinian strongpoints, made the use of helicopters an acceptable risk. There were also, once the land forces were ashore, opportunities to insert special forces by fast raiding craft based on the beachhead. But, before the landing of the main force, the remoteness of the SBS landing points made them comparatively safe from enemy interference. Many must have been in the mountains, a rough stretch of country perhaps not high by European standards (Mount Kent being the highest peak at 450 m), but a wilderness of bog, rock runs and crags where no 'normal' folk would venture. The men of the SBS are hardly 'normal', however, as their best friends frequently tell them in a different context.

The SBS had to patrol from these remote LZs often for days at a time or at least for several nights, lying low in the daytime. Their information would answer vital questions for Brigadier Thompson, to ensure that his men landed with the minimum of losses, and for the Commodore of Amphibious Warfare, Michael C. Clapp, whose ships would take the men inshore at the risk of Exocet and other coast defence attacks. Both senior officers and staffs worked closely together, the commodore and the brigadier sharing a cabin aboard the LPD HMS *Fearless*, as they planned the liberation of the islands. Broadly, their scheme was to land sufficiently far from the main Argentinian defences at Stanley to get ashore unopposed, establishing a beachhead from which an advance would bring them across the northwest approaches to Port Stanley.

But which beaches were undefended?

Aboard *Hermes* the staff of Rear-Admiral J. F. ('Sandy') Woodward included the Royal Marine colonel who coordinated all special forces operations. A small planning team under his direction, with support from London, devised the various reconnaissance and other raids that would not only help to answer the brigadier's questions but also provide protection teams for the Royal Artillery officers and their radio operators landed to control naval gunfire support and the Forward Air Controllers who guided Harrier aircraft strikes against ground targets. At a later stage the SBS would help to create diversions, position landing lights to guide in assault waves and make deep penetration recces far into Argentine-occupied territory.

The planning of an SBS raid, like any military operation, involves a clear understanding of its precise purpose: there is no point in teams wandering about with vague intentions of taking a look at some village settlement or following a route on the spur of the moment. Specific questions need to be asked and answered. Is there an Argentine OP on the Picos or on Smylies Rocks or Coutts Hill? (All these are hill features in the northwest of East Falkland.) Other questions might involve the numbers of enemy seen fleetingly on Two Sisters Mountain by a Harrier on reconnaissance, although in the Falklands the Argentines camouflaged their movements reasonably well from prowling aircraft. There was, therefore, all the more need for 'eyeball recces', with SBS teams initially patrolling down to the beaches from the hills in overland approaches rather than the swimmer-canoeists' more usual routes in from the sea.

Where these recces might take the teams included the possible landing beaches for a main assault at Port Howard and Fox Bay in West Falkland. On East Falkland, going northwest around the coast from Port Stanley, are: Volunteer Lagoon, for a quick campaign against nominal resistance; Salvador Water, always provided its narrow entrance could first be captured; and various points in San Carlos Water. Landings on the southern shores of East Falkland between Goose Green and Stanley were likely to

meet resistance from the main Argentine defences of Port
Stanley, where 8400 Argentines had their artillery,
minefields and other defences arrayed to meet an attack
from the southwest. The southern half of the island, the
open and relatively flat grasslands and bogs of Lafonia,
could be sealed off by a few Argentines holding high ground
north of the Goose Green isthmus, for this is only a few
hundred metres wide in places.

The SBS teams had prepared themselves for a variety of
roles, but while the Battle Group of warships was over 300
km from the islands the only practical way to insert the
teams was by helicopter. The weather in late April, however, was too rough on some days and too foggy on others
for helicopters to fly off HMS *Hermes*, but on the last day of
the month a Sea King was able to take off. The pilot with
his night vision helmet (Passive Night Goggles) could make
out the carrier's deck, her bridge on its island to starboard
of the flight deck and the lattice steel tower of her radar
mast. The round trip to East Falkland would take some
three hours, and he must be back aboard *Hermes* before
daylight next morning, Saturday 1 May. His return flight
would also coincide with the first air bombing of the Port
Stanley runway by an aircraft from Ascension Island.

For the four-man SBS team, the flight would be like
many others they had made on exercises, but the Argentine
air threat (not taken at this time too seriously in some
quarters) would be real enough, as the Battle Group were to
learn a few days later. Although the islands were on the
limit of the Argentine fighters' range from the mainland, an
unarmed helicopter could be 'splashed' by one of their
fighters from Port Stanley. Dispersed around its runway,
the only hard-surfaced (sealed) airstrip in the islands, were
aircraft that included A-4P Skyhawks with 20-mm cannon
and air-to-surface rockets. In the early hours of 1 May these
would be hit by 21 bombs each of 1000 lb dropped from a
single RAF Vulcan B.2, flying on the first of the 'Black
Buck' raids, the longest bombing missions in the history of
air warfare. Fortunately, the Argentine fighter aircraft were

not equipped with radar for night flying, which gave the Royal Navy helicopters some ten hours in which they could operate in relative safety – although flying helicopters at night even with PNG has many natural hazards.

On this Friday night, the Sea King that had taken off from *Hermes* flew low to avoid the Argentine radar screen off the island's north coast, skirted round Fanning Head where high ground might have provided a good radar sight commanding the sound, and flew south. With Cat Island, a blob of rock a kilometre west of Wreck Point, to confirm his position no doubt, he turned eastward to climb towards the flat ground 270 m up on this headland. From this plateau, the hillside falls steeply to the eastern shore, giving a clear view of Ajax Bay and San Carlos Water beyond.

The marine corporal of the helicopter's crew checked the team's kit for the last time, ready to lower it to them as soon as the pilot reached the point a little over halfway up the gentle western slope to the plateau. There it hovered for seconds rather than minutes. Out went the team followed by their simple kit – 'telescopes, binoculars and night sights, personal arms and food, but nothing spectacular' to quote the sergeant leading the team. They hauled this gear over the plateau, and before dawn that Saturday were gone to ground, literally. The sods that they cut before digging the hides were carefully placed on strips of chicken wire; then they scraped out the soil to a depth of half a metre, scattering the earth thinly over a wide area to make sure their digging would not be apparent. By dawn they had pulled their chicken-wire cover over the scrapes and were virtually invisible, for the sods and some hessian strips on the wire proved good camouflage. On that first Saturday they must have wondered just how good it would prove, for they were apparently only a little more than a kilometre from the shore of Ajax Bay, no distance at all for Argentine foot patrols.

The telescope view across San Carlos Water showed that the grass airstrip on the flat little promontory below the Settlement was not in regular use. Nor – almost immediately below them – was there any unusual activity around the Ajax

Bay Refrigeration Plant with its small jetty. (This mutton factory would later be the centre of the Commando Brigade's maintenance area, the site across which many thousands of tonnes of stores would be carried on improvised roads.) At night the team probably split up into two pairs, leaving the security – if that is not too solid a word – of their chicken-wire covers to go down to the factory and make detailed notes on the state of the jetty, on the fitness of the ground over which roadways of steel mesh must be laid, and to check on the berthing points suitable for landing craft. They must have made some checks into the water off these berthing points – a chilly wade even in their diving suits – but no detailed beach surveys were necessary, for the marines over the years of their garrison duties had collected a good deal of information. Had they not done so, then SBS teams would have made the type of beach surveys pioneered by Combined Operations Assault Pilotage Parties in the Second World War. In the 1980s there were different surveys to be made, for the planned beachhead would include landing zones for helicopters and be protected by anti-aircraft missiles fired preferably from high ground by Rapier launchers. The sites picked for these on Wreck Point needed inspection, if not surveying, by the SBS team, and they crossed the headland north and south of their OP base, making a round trip of 12 km on some nights.

Movement at night in the Falklands was often limited by the rock runs and bogs to little more than 250 m in an hour; above Ajax Bay the going may have been a little easier, but not much. One suspects, therefore, that some recces took a couple of days or more, the routine being to move back over the plateau (which is not as flat as it appears on the map) and march along, say, the 200-m contour at a steady gait. Such movement was hidden from any enemy night observation sentries around San Carlos Water but overlooked from the sea and in the north from Fanning Head. Trudging through a winter's night, in driving rain, two men need all their wits and a retentive memory to follow a compass bearing, for the tell-tale flash of a torch at night can be seen

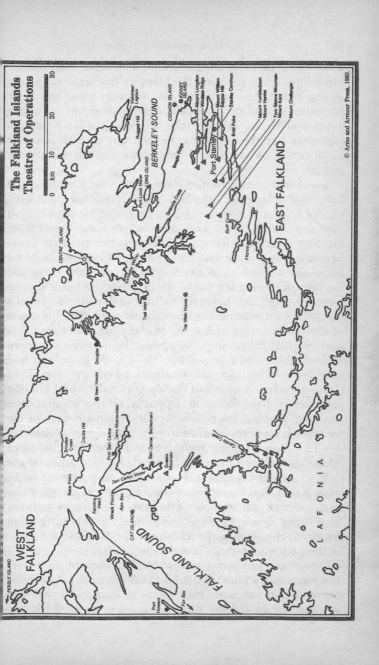

The Falkland Islands
Theatre of Operations

0 km 10 20 30

© Arms and Armour Press, 1983.

PEBBLE ISLAND

WEST FALKLAND

Port Howard
Fox Bay

FALKLAND SOUND

Race Point
Fanning Head
Wreck Point
Ajax Bay
CAT ISLAND
San Carlos Water
Sussex Mountain

Coutts Hill
Port San Carlos
Cerro Montevideo
San Carlos Settlement

● New House

Smylie's Coast

CENTRE ISLAND

San Carlos Water

Douglas

Teal Inlet

Salvador Water

Port Louis Water
LONG ISLAND

Rugged Hill

Volunteer
Lagoon

BERKELEY SOUND

COCHON ISLAND
KIDNEY ISLAND

Estancia Creek

Brenda Ridge

Mount Longdon
Wireless Ridge
Port Stanley
Mount William
Sapper Hill
Stanley Common

Bold Point

Mount Tumbledown
Mount Harriet
Two Sisters Mountain
Mount Kent
Mount Challenger

Bluff Cove

Fitzroy

Top Malo House

LAFONIA

Camilla Creek

Goose Green
Darwin

EAST FALKLAND

a thousand or more metres away. You have to cloak the torch light while checking the map, its case sodden by rain as you study those contrary contours now going uphill on paper, while you are physically moving downhill . . . or are we not at the right spot? On returning to the hide, the change of clothing from a wet to relatively dry vest from the small cache of kit near the scrapes must have been welcome indeed.

There had been activities elsewhere on the islands on the first Sunday that the Ajax Bay team were ashore, but they cannot have seen much activity apart from air patrols high over the islands. They had been ashore some time before the first Argentine helicopter flew over them. Later, one flew in a sweep along Falkland Sound, looking no doubt for submarines rather than any special forces' hide. However, the pilot, following the line of the headland, appears to have lost his way and hovered metres above the sergeant's scrape. The downdraught from the rotors ruffled the cover of the chicken wire and then, as the plane hung over this spot, the turfs began to break up and the hessian strips were torn off. All – and it was a big 'all' – could have been laid bare, for had this SBS team or any of the other special forces teams been found near San Carlos Water the whole landing plan could have been in jeopardy. But the pilot was studying his map too closely to notice the still form of the sergeant below him in what from the air was obviously an OP. The team were not seen. Nor were they seen on other occasions, for each morning before dawn they renewed the turfs of camouflage, in case its faded appearance might leave half a dozen patches of wilted grass on an otherwise fresh piece of upland moor. The fresh hessian may at times have been flown to them; but however the turfs were acquired, the team was nicknamed the 'Interflora Squad' by their comrades back aboard ship.

One major problem was that the sergeant, in his 'secret weapons of long johns and a Marks & Spencer polo-necked jersey', could not radio his reports to *Hermes*. In part this was because he did not have anything more sophisticated than a battlefield radio; it was also because the Argentines were equipped with ultra-modern radio direction finding equipment that might have located the transmission. A factor that would prove particularly difficult for special forces was the complete radio silence that the Royal Navy enforced to avoid being located by D/F or similar electronic devices. All radios and radar equipment were switched off for long periods, with the result that had messages been sent from Ajax Bay there would often have been no acknowledgement. The only way the intelligence gathered by SBS teams could be brought out was by bringing out the team for debriefing. Above Ajax Bay, however, the OP was so successful that the team remained ashore for sixteen days, a long time to live on chemically heated soup and cold rations (although they do not seem to think it so), unless – as one might reasonably expect from the Navy's dedicated helicopter pilots – dry clothes, the occasional hot meal in containers as well as fresh hessian strips, were flown in a couple of times. Reports collected by helicopter had to be occasional rather than regular, for too-frequent visits would have aroused Argentine suspicions. Yet the few reports that were brought out must have reassured the brigadier, as he smoked his ever-billowing pipe, that his proposed landings in San Carlos Water would not meet serious opposition. The OP was no doubt left in because the Argentines might move in unexpected reinforcements, as they did later at Goose Green.

Other SBS and SAS teams were landed during this first week in May. One can imagine the loneliness of, say, four men on Smylies Rocks in the northwest of the Camp (as the islanders called their country outback): here there were no tracks or even the sheep fences accurately drawn elsewhere on the islands' maps. The team typically had three nights to cover 10 km, hiding by day under camouflage nets or among rock outcrops. The steady downpour of rain kept everything miserably wet. Alternatively, a gale could be blowing, driving the rain before it, killing the sound of an accidental rock fall, but making any observation difficult at

night with vision down to less than 100 m. Oh for a nice
clear night when the patrol might see across Race Point, the
broad headland that forms the northern shore of San Carlos
Water. A piece of sweeping moorland with rock outcrops
like Dartmoor, it boasts weather twice as wet and windy as
the British training ground. On a clear still night, even
before moonrise, a team had to move cautiously: a single
falling stone can sound like an avalanche to the man who
dislodged it, and who knows the risk that it may strike some
wary chord in the subconscious of a dozing sentry.

The teams on the island would work for three nights out
from their landing point, and in the next two would move
towards the rendezvous with a Sea King or Wessex.
Although the precise landing or hovering point might be
hard to identify from the air, the helicopter pilot knew at
least that the team on the ground would have made sure no
unwelcome reception was in the area. Conversely the team
on the ground knew that they were making for a friendly
aircraft, as they had transponders identifying friend from
foe, which a team could activate at some 500 m.

Thus far the Argentines, if they suspected anything, had
nothing to confirm their suspicions. On Wednesday 12
May, nine days before the planned landings (D-9 in
military jargon) SBS teams were landed to recce San Carlos
Settlement more closely than could be done from across the
water at Ajax Bay, and to check Port San Carlos. This so-
called port is no more than a dozen brightly coloured
houses and buildings on the north shore of an arm of San
Carlos Water, but the SBS team had apparently found signs
of an Argentine garrison. The port, 6 km north of the
Settlement, is about the same distance from Fanning Head
where the Argentines had established a defended OP (details that were not confirmed that second week in May).
What was known was the strength of Argentine ground-
attack aircraft on Pebble Island airstrip. These seven IA-58
Pucara aircraft armed with rockets, quick-firing 20-mm
cannon and 7.62-mm machine guns were only thirty minutes' or less flying time from San Carlos. Four Aermacchi

fighters and a small freight aircraft were also on this strip in the southeast corner of the island.

On the night of Thursday 13 May, eight men of 'D' Squadron, SAS, paddled their canoes from West Falkland to recce a landing site and set up a radio beacon towards the westward end of Pebble Island. Then, on Friday night, 45 men of the SAS and a naval gunfire observer approached this beacon in three helicopters. Moving from the LZ towards the airstrip took longer than expected, but in thirty minutes they overwhelmed the 120 Argentines of the garrison and destroyed their aircraft, fuel dumps and ammunition stores, before coming out – all at the cost of two minor casualties. Any garrison soldier who has the slightest knowledge of British special forces operations over the years should know that Friday night to early Monday morning are a favourite time for such raids, since the British expect, as we have seen, that the more casual routines of a weekend disrupt many garrison units, with men off duty if not exactly having a night on the town. During the raid, HMS *Glamorgan* gave fire-support from her 4.5-inch (114-mm) guns. Such naval gunfire support was to play an important part in later actions, for this airburst shell fired from the ships is in a different league to that of the Commando batteries' 105-mm light gun. One ship's '4.5' bursts can fling half a tonne of deadly fragments each minute on to the heads of the men in defence works, keeping these heads down and preventing anyone moving about the defences. Virtually all this fire was put down at night, something that ships almost never did in the Second World War: forty years ago, it could not be controlled accurately enough to avoid hitting friendly troops, while inshore in daylight there was always the risk of air attacks. Near the Falklands coast was the added risk from land-based Exocet missiles. Nevertheless, naval support gunfire observation officers ashore as they had been in South Georgia, were to bring down a bombardment at times as little as 100 m ahead of the commandos and paras.

On the following Monday, the SBS teams came out, the Ajax Bay 'Interflora' team *apparently* being replaced by another four men. Another SBS team with an NGS team were landed that night on Sussex Mountain. This ridge, running east-west across the southern approaches to San Carlos Water, formed a natural barrier against any attempt by the Argentines to move north the 700 men of the Darwin garrison. The SBS team protecting the forward observation officer for the gunners, could also patrol and observe the sweep of flat if rough pasture stretching down to Camila Creek. No Argentines appeared from the south, although in the mist and fog of Thursday (D-1) the observers cannot have seen much.

Meanwhile, on the eve of the San Carlos D-day, two SBS teams with a Royal Artillery observation officer and his radio operator were nosing into an inlet on West Falkland, 8 km from the 900 men defending Fox Bay. These had been softened up by Harrier aircraft, but had set up beach defences around the Settlement. They kept a low profile, however, for no patrols greeted the SBS's inflatable as it came inshore to the west. This craft had a GPMG in the bow and perhaps a couple of grenade launchers to cover any enforced withdrawal. Maps of the Falkland Islands show a liberal spread around many coasts of that tough seaweed, kelp; and before the inflatable could beach she jammed her outboard's propeller in a mass of the weed, forcing the crew to paddle the remaining distance to land. Despite difficulties in radio contact with HMS *Plymouth*, some sixty rounds were called up from the frigate's two 4.5-inch guns. The ship's captain needed several hours of darkness to be clear of the islands by dawn, 0700 hours local time, so he was due to pick up the teams and sail at 0200. Daylight approached, and with it a falling tide as he waited offshore while the inflatable was paddled laboriously from the shore as the team struggled to make their RV on time.

That same D-day eve, SAS troops were put ashore on Lafonia to engage the defenders of Darwin at long range with GPMGs and other weapons, keeping the 700 men of this garrison too occupied to worry about what might be happening several days' march away to the north. There a helicopter was scanning Fanning Head and San Carlos Water with a thermal imager – which confirmed that there were troops in defensive positions.

About this time the much publicized but still mysterious flight of a Sea King HC.4 to Chile was causing a deal of speculation. That this troop-carrying helicopter was lost is most unlikely; that it flew from a Royal Fleet Auxiliary cruising along the westward extremity of the TEZ is possible. From wherever it flew, its teams of SAS and/or SBS can only have had one purpose: to monitor and report on the flights of Argentine aircraft taking off from their bases at Rio Gallegos, Comodoro Rivadavia and Rio Grande on the 740-km flight for 'Las Islas Malvinas' as the Argentines call the Falklands. There is a pretty notion in some unsubstantiated newspaper reports that these raiders screwed up – or, less colloquially, unscrewed – Argentine Exocet missiles and bombs, much in the way the Norwegian resistance in 1944 had replaced the cordite type of explosive in the charges of German 88-mm anti-aircraft rounds. (These doctored rounds, after being reintroduced into ammunition dumps, were later loaded in the rush of continuous firing for air barrage defence, but as they were filled with plastic explosive then blew up in the gun, killing its crew. It was a clever piece of sabotage because the Germans attributed these 'accidents' to faulty ammunition.) It seems likely that some Exocet missiles, judging by the pictures of their targets, failed to explode, but that the unspent fuel of their rocket motors burnt fiercely enough to start damaging fires. No doubt we will find, when the facts can be told, that the Exocets' malfunction was due less to British guile than to technical difficulties with such complex weapons. What might be an intelligent guess, if it was not unthinkable that Chile might risk being dragged into the conflict, was that SAS teams on the Chilean borders could monitor with suitable radar these air bases, which lie on a flat coastal strip. Such warnings would certainly have enabled the maximum number from the twenty Sea Harriers with the Battle Group carriers to be airborne in combat air patrols in the vital hours of the landing and establishment of the beachhead.

The first moves in the San Carlos landing came that Thursday night as the weather cleared. The SBS teams, which had been withdrawn from their OPs above San Carlos Settlement and Port San Carlos, had returned on Wednesday night equipped with landing lights ready to set up on the beaches the following night. But, as the helicopter of the Port San Carlos team came in, the Argentine OP on Fanning Head had been spotted: to avoid raising any alarm on D-1, the helicopter did not land the team. Instead, on the following night, as the Assault Group of ships were steaming along the north coast of East Falkland, SBS teams were inserted as soon after dark as possible. The hours of darkness available for them to fulfil their tasks would be few. They landed on the high ground above Port San Carlos, ground they had patrolled on their earlier recces of the island. This enabled them to cover the 10 km or so to the Argentine positions relatively quickly. With them was a naval gunfire support officer, who would control *Antrim*'s fire on to these defences. The intention was to make this appear as just a raid. When the small force was 600 m from their target, a Spanish-speaking Royal Marine captain and a marine went forward to put two loud-hailers (bull horns) within a couple of football-pitch lengths of the enemy trenches.

4.5-inch shells were bursting over the Argentines by this time, bright yellow flashes with a penetrating 'crack!' Yet there was no response to Captain Rod Bell's suggestions of surrender. The young lieutenant commanding these ten Argentines would not give up and firing resumed, the SBS teams using their personal weapons to supplement the heavier fire from *Antrim*. At some point in the next few minutes the Argentine officer was killed and three of his men wounded. The rest surrendered, with the exception of one man who escaped over the hill: but the SBS had no time to look for him. They had to be down on the beach setting up landing lights – 10 km away.

At such moments there is a pay-off for all the hours of hard running along the shingle beach of Eastney or over the mountains near Arbroath. They came back eastward along the aptly named Race Point, and down through the dozen or so buildings and sheep sheds of Port San Carlos. Had there been time to search these, they would have discovered the best part of a company of slumbering Argentines, who came into action themselves when they awoke to the situation. As two light helicopters of Commando Brigade's Air Squadron flew in at about 0815 that morning, both were shot down. They had come in independently as the only armed helicopters that could escort Sea Kings landing survey parties at the proposed Rapier sites. (Flying Gazelle AH.1s was like taking a jeep into battle as David Stirling's men did in the Western Desert, even when these carried GPMGs on pintle mountings and 68-mm Matra SNEB rockets, intended to lay smoke rather than use explosive warheads. The light helicopter proved too vulnerable to fly in well-defended areas, but would be used to evacuate wounded and carry ammunition to forward units, when the larger Sea King or Wessex helicopter would have made too large and less manoeuvrable a target.) The paras coming ashore had a fire-fight with these Argentines, who retreated towards Goose Green.

Argentine air attacks directed at the warships on San Carlos Water began almost as soon as the commandos and paratroops were ashore. The bravery with which these sorties were pressed home may have surprised some observers, for it contrasted vividly with the defensive attitude of the Argentine troops on the ground. But the apparent ease with which SBS and SAS teams were permitted to move about the islands was remarkable. They, like the Royal Marine teams from the Mountain and Arctic Warfare Cadre, who also made deep penetration recces, are highly trained and most skilful troops. The Argentine Army rank and file were conscripts, led by career officers and NCOs of their regular Army, who in every service of any nation tend to look down on men doing short periods of national service. These national servicemen also had that Latin machismo that makes a man disdain such 'womanly' work as cooking and washing clothes; even during their service in the Argentine, their womenfolk were usually in the local town so that the men were not used to looking after themselves. On Fanning Head they had butchered sheep for a meat ration, but elsewhere some were nearly starving because the ample rations in Port Stanley were not properly distributed. In the coming battles, some units would fight with a tenacity to match their air force pilots' courage; others – many – were no more able to keep their rifles clean and free from rust than cook themselves a meal.

Once the beachhead was established there were pressures from London to move with all speed against Port Stanley, but Brigadier Thompson was not to be rushed. Since air superiority could not be achieved, ships had to stay well to the east of the islands and helicopters could not fly outside the Rapier umbrella. Much of the brigadier's reserves of ammunition, fuel and combat supplies had to be put ashore at Ajax Bay. Several of the Pucara and Aermacchi aircraft were flying sorties from the Goose Green airstrip, so before any major advance could be made these would have to be taken out and the airfield installations destroyed.

Harrier aircraft had made a number of sorties against the airstrip, but over two weeks before the landing one was shot down and the pilot killed by anti-aircraft fire at Goose Green. Two others had been lost in a collision in fog. The fleet's dependence on the remaining seventeen combat aircraft was great, for they faced over 130 Argentine high-performance attack aircraft, not counting Pucaras and high-level bombers – odds greater than 6:1. Anything the ground forces might do to reduce these odds would, in the long run, be a help. Goose Green was not, however, worth seizing on tactical grounds as the 700 Argentines there could be easily contained by a small force holding the high ground north of the isthmus.

SAS recce teams had made several patrols on Lafonia and they estimated the garrison to be 700, a 5:7 ratio against 2 Para Battalion, who were due to raid the airstrip on the night of Monday/Tuesday (D+2/3). The 'clag' (low cloud) prevented any 105-mm guns being flown south to support the raid, although one company had moved forward and had to be recalled when the raid was cancelled. Political pressures led to the raid being re-mounted as a battalion offensive intended to seize Darwin and Goose Green in order to provide the British with a clear success in liberating a large area – Lafonia – from Argentine domination. The fact that these hectares had little military significance did not matter in the diplomatic battles at the United Nations. 2 Para therefore launched a battalion attack down the isthmus, skirmishing forward by companies in the early morning of Friday 28 May. The odds turned out to be 3:1 against the paras, who made up for what they lacked in numbers by aggressive tactics and their skill at arms. Their commanding officer, Lieutenant-Colonel 'H' Jones, was killed leading his men, and was subsequently awarded the Victoria Cross for his great bravery, which had inspired his men in the remarkable victory.

But, while the world's and the Argentine staff's attention was concentrated on Goose Green, no inkling was given of other unpublicized moves from the beachhead. Even more attention had been drawn to the southern coastline where the Argentines expected the British landing, by at least one SBS deception. In this a damaged inflatable was left floating somewhere off Bluff Cove, its rubberized fabric skin ripped, the floorboards a jumble as if some recce team had been forced to abandon it. Later it was shown on Argentine television with a piece of its transom crudely marked 'HMS *Hermes*'. The Argentine commentator and no doubt their military made much of this indication of SBS activity which had come unstuck near Port Stanley. For those who knew of the deceptions played by Royal Marine swimmer-canoeists of De-

tachment 385 in the Indian Ocean and South China Sea
nearly forty years earlier the ploy had some familiar
touches.

Less obvious was the arrival in Salvador Water of Royal
Marine raiding craft. They would insert SBS teams along
the coasts of this wide stretch of water, one arm of which,
Estancia Creek, reaches down to the lower slopes of Mount
Kent, some 20 km northwest of Port Stanley. This
mountain, the key to any defence of the hills northwest of
Stanley, is 450 m high, standing at the northern end of the
first of three chains of hills and dominating Mount Challenger to the south. Mount Longdon, Two Sisters and Harriet,
in a north-south chain to the east, are overlooked from
Kent. Nearer to Stanley is an arc of lower hills, Wireless
Ridge, Tumbledown and Mount William. The Commando
Brigade intended to seize these mountains, but in the great
'yomp' from the beachhead would need recce teams to scout
the line of the commandos' and paras' march to make sure
they did not fall into any Argentine ambush; a defence more
likely to be an ambush of crushing artillery fire than men
with rifles and machine guns.

SBS and SAS teams would provide these scouts coming
in from the sea or by helicopter far ahead of the advancing
British columns. By Thursday (D+5) teams from
helicopters had made sure that the entrance to Salvador
Water, only 1500 m wide at one point, was clear of enemy
surveillance posts, or that these could be suitably jammed
long enough for several Rigid Raiding craft to move
through the entrance to Centre Island with its covering of
reeds and tussock grass. Beyond it lay the channel to
Salvador Water, a maze of narrow inlets and bays spreading out some 3 km back northwest of the entrance and 5 km
to the southeast, with a dreary coastline of mud banks and
tufted tussocks, which at some points topped low bluffs,
where earth cliffs provided the deep shadows in which to
hide a Rigid Raider. This high-speed blunt-bowed craft,
usually powered by a 140-hp Johnson outboard, can skim
across calm waters at 30 knots, its coxswain driving it at

speeds that bounce the eight men in its low-sided hull across even a moderate sea. On Salvador Water, however, the craft would be used in a quieter manner.

Raiding craft were used for their convenience in these waters and because helicopters were scarce. On D-day alone, seven Sea King HC.4s had lifted 'close on 1,000,000 lb of equipment and stores and 520 troops' to quote the commanding officer of 846 Naval Air Squadron; yet there were only eleven helicopters available. On D-2, one had struck an albatross or similar large bird and had been lost with an RN officer, 19 senior NCOs and men of the SAS and a marine corporal. (Many of these men had taken part in the raid on Pebble Island and were to have been in diversion raids on the eve of D-day; despite the loss, the SAS continued to provide many patrols, for as is the way of that fine regiment, where a team of four would normally patrol they got by with a couple of men.) The helicopter pilots, flying with courage and panache, could not create more flying hours than their machines could be airborne in 24 hours. There were therefore some impatient customers. Like a man waiting for a cab in the rain on a London or New York street who finds every cab taken, commandos and paras waited for stores to be moved by helicopter.

One great advantage for recce teams landed by helicopter is that they start out on their patrol at least in dry clothing. Landing from the sea can be less comfortable. When one Rigid Raider attempted to relieve an SAS team on West Falkland, for example, the weather was too rough for the craft to beach, although attempts were made on four successive nights. In the end, four marine Mountain Leaders were inserted by helicopter and the SAS team brought out.

Other operations on West Falkland after D-day included a landing by an SBS team and a naval gunfire support team near Port Howard. They went ashore prepared for a stay of five days, during which time ships at night would bombard the port's garrison of more than 780 Argentines. This settlement is protected from the sea by the headland of Bold

Point, making observed fire all the more important, with
the teams on the slopes of Mount Maria (680 m) above the
cluster of houses forming the settlement. The gunfire on this
garrison and elsewhere on West Falkland deterred the
Argentines from raiding the British beachhead across the
Sound. There, 40 Commando were actively patrolling
throughout the campaign, for what the SBS might do could
also be attempted by Argentine marines. Only one such
operation has been reported: a lieutenant-commander
(Argentine marines use naval rather than army ranks) was
caught by one of '40's' patrols. He had probably made his
way up from Goose Green and set up an OP overlooking San
Carlos Water, where he could direct aircraft against the
ships in a similar way to the Forward Air Controllers with
the Commando Brigade. They would go with forward
troops or behind the Argentine defences, looking for suitable targets against which to direct Harrier GR.3s in
ground attacks, giving map grid reference points for
machine-gun posts and camouflaged gun sites that were
invisible from the air. By mid-June, however, more modern
and technical methods were being used to mark targets by
laser beams.

On the shores of Salvador Water SBS patrols moved at
night, much as they did before D-day and often in appalling
weather, before the time of the raiding craft's arrival in the
early hours of Wednesday 26 May. The raiding craft increased the range of patrols by moving slowly, their engines' low rumble easily mistaken for the moaning of the
wind as they probed into Teal Inlet. The settlement here is
small; seven yellow or white timber houses and several
other buildings on flat grassland, with a sheep shed by the
small jetty from which landing a track led to the houses.
From the map, the site seemed ideal for the stores and
ammunition dumps of a Forward Brigade Maintenance
Area. But was the ground firm enough to carry ammunition
stacked two pallets high? Was the LZ adequate for
helicopters to put down? Could the Eager Beaver fork-lift
trucks run over the ground without turning it into a

quagmire? The teams took samples of the earth to find it was generally firm going with shale over clay running up from the beach to the grassland 5 m above sea level. Their findings were reported to the Brigade Intelligence Staff via *Hermes* and later *Fearless*, or at least through the Special Forces Command cell with the Battle Group, which moved ashore on about 31 May with General Moore's Headquarters of Land Forces Falkland Islands.

Other SBS teams had by this date recced the hamlet of Douglas northwest of Teal, on flat open meadow land which has little cover, and they had checked the hills to the west for Argentine patrols. How far they and other special forces had contacts among the civilians is not known, but swimmer-canoeists have in the past passed themselves off as local shepherds and no doubt did so in the Falklands. As these teams watched for enemy patrols to the north, 45 Commando made their great 'yomp' across the trackless waste of the Cerro Montevideo and northeast to New House, 22 km of knee-twisting rock runs, bogs and ankle-snapping clumps of sedge grass, not to mention streams, hills and darkness through which each man carried 54-kg loads or more, mostly of ammunition. Only fifteen of the 500 commandos were forced to fall out through injury, and many of these later rejoined the unit (a revealing sidelight on the toughness of the marines from whom the SBS are recruited). On the night of Friday 28 May, they put out sentries, the remainder sleeping off their exhaustion. Next day, without their packs they 'yomped' a further 11 km to Douglas, before moving on to Teal on the Monday.

There had been no artillery ambush, not even enemy patrols, although these were active among the hills to the south of 45 Commando's route. Here four-man teams of the Royal Marines' Mountain and Arctic Warfare Cadre had been scouting a ring of high hills since D-day, watching for any movement from Stanley westward across the mountains to Teal or Douglas. On the Monday, Argentine commandos were observed landing from helicopters and moving to Top Malo House. This summer home of the shepherds who bring their flocks to the uplands in the mild weather of October to December must have appeared a comfortable place to lay up in the snows and wet of late May as the southern winter had set in. Yet the house had no commanding field of view beyond nearby paddocks and would prove a death trap. The marines, on the other hand, lying beneath 'cam' nets among hillside rocks, may have been desperately chilled after three days in the hills, but were in the stronger position. Their OP overlooking the house was a site which they had taken up by chance, when a corporal was injured in a fall as they were working their way over rough ground during several night recces of the Mount Kent area. Now they requested a Harrier strike on the house, but, as one had already been lost and two damaged beyond repair by anti-aircraft fire when attacking other ground forces, nineteen MLs were flown in by helicopter an hour after dawn. Atmospherics prevented – as they did on several nights – the new arrivals from making radio contact with their OP to the north of the house; but, coming out of the helicopter in ten seconds flat, the MLs nevertheless moved forward quickly.

One group with 66-mm rockets, grenades and rifles were to provide covering fire as the assault teams moved close to the house. As these followed a sheep fence to keep them on line for the house hidden beyond a hillock, the covering team doubled out to the right to come out of cover a few hundred metres from the house. A sentry at one upper window saw them and gave the alarm, but the marines pressed home the attack with anti-tank rockets which set it ablaze within seconds. Reserves of ammunition on the ground floor 'cooked off' and the building peeled open in a ball of flame. Even so, the assault teams were met by steady fire that wounded three of them as they advanced towards the front door, from which several Argentines were firing while others leapt from windows to withdraw down a small valley. One marine sergeant, against orders, made a dash into the open, drawing Argentine fire long enough for his 'oppos' to find the direction of the enemy, before he fell hit in the left shoulder. His move gave the marines the momentary sighting that was all they needed to follow their quarry; and all seventeen Argentines were killed or captured after what had been forty minutes of sharp action.

That same Monday the men of 42 Commando were consolidating their positions on Mount Kent after an advance company and mortars had flown there on Sunday night, landing in the midst of a skirmish between SAS troopers and an Argentine patrol. With '42' established on this commanding height and Mount Challenger nearby, with '45' ready to establish a patrol base on Kent's western slopes, both Commandos would patrol forward to recce their next objectives: Two Sisters and Mount Harriet. What opposition they might encounter from long-range artillery, from air strikes (all OPs reporting by radio when possible the approach of hostile aircraft) or even a counterattack, would now require special forces patrols closer to Port Stanley. Again the naval gunfire officers would be among the first teams ashore with the SBS. Inflatables and Klepper canoes brought into the creeks north of Mount Kent could be hauled overland the few kilometres which divided these water highways, probably enabling SBS teams to cross to Long Island where Port Louis Water runs into Berkeley Sound with its shores no more than 10 km from Stanley in the next major bay to the south.

One further point which must be grasped is the distances which they covered among these tidal creeks and waterways. A boat making, say, 5 knots to avoid undue noise and any white wake pushed out at speed, took a full night to move men or stores from Teal Inlet to Estancia Creek where combat stores were off-loaded for 45 Commando's patrols. This link could be made by a Chinook HC.1 in an hour, but 'Bravo November' was the sole survivor of four of these large helicopters shipped out on *Atlantic Conveyor*, the container ship with a roll-on roll-off stern ramp, lost with much else besides when hit by an Exocet. 'Bravo November' nevertheless gave a good account of the logistic value of such a 'lift', carrying 81 troops on one occasion. More prosaically, a Rigid Raider could land eight or nine men, depending mainly on the weight of ammunition and combat stores they each carried, although the one hidden on the rat-infested Centre Island at the entrance to Salvador Water, carried a more striking load. Hidden with her under a topping – the top halves – of metre-high reeds cut away to make a hide were light anti-tank weapons, ready should any Argentine fast patrol boats attempt to pass through Salvador Channel until this coastline was secured.

By the time this defence was no longer necessary, SBS teams had established what appears to have been almost a forward base in Volunteer Lagoon. There, just north of Berkeley Sound, was a cache of stores, not as large a centre for raiding as the SB Squadron's advanced base of 1944 in the Dodecanese had been, but a good deal nearer the enemy. The base was resupplied by the Navy's Lynx helicopters; an unusual role for this offensive weapon system with a primary role of ASW. In a Lynx you know when you are about to be hit by a homing missile, for there is an electronic box of tricks to warn you; the pilot may also take better evasive action, for the Lynx travels faster and is more manoeuvrable than a 'flying truck'. Despite all this technical ingenuity, some old-fashioned precautions were probably taken, the helicopter flying in as if her crew were only spotting the fall of shot from ships firing over the lagoon and Berkeley Sound: any anti-aircraft sentry watching it dip for a few seconds over the SBS 'base' would imagine the crew were just taking a breather under the lee of Rugged Hill. Patrols from the base in the first four days of June had searched the northern shore of Berkeley Sound and had found no permanent defences. What land-based Exocets the Argentines were using must therefore be sited – or at least towed on their trailers to sites, as subsequently became apparent – on the few kilometres of road immediately outside Stanley.

The possibilities of sabotaging the airfield installations at Port Stanley must have been in the minds of the special forces staff, but if teams tried to do this they had no more success than the RAF in closing the runway. Argentine transport aircraft were flying into Pebble Island and laying up there for some thirty minutes until their fighters drew the attention of the British CAP, before the freighter could fly the last 90 km to Stanley. Another target that escaped the attention of special forces was the battery of three 155-mm guns hidden among the houses of Stanley, as they shelled the men of 3 Commando Brigade and 5 Infantry Brigade in the mountains. The reasons for this are not clear, but presumably the British special forces were not to be risked in what might have been extremely hazardous operations.

The area to be patrolled by SBS and SAS teams was now becoming much smaller than 'the area of Wales' over which they first had to make their reconnaissances. The chance of an accidental clash between friendly teams was thus almost inevitable. While all teams carried a Union Jack for immediate recognition in case of any ambiguities on a meeting, the opportunity to display such a universally recognized British symbol depended on clear visibility. One clash appears to have taken place in the first week of June, judging by the casualty lists. The mishap, in the confusion of early morning mists and half light, with wireless communications bedevilled by atmospherics, could happen in the crack of a single round.

Such accidents happened even in the electronic age when the special forces team had some remarkable aids, although perhaps too few of the cunning devices which would have made recognition easier between friend and foe. One piece of equipment which they did use was the laser target marker. Reports suggest that this somewhat bulky and delicate equipment needs conditions more akin to the laboratories in which it was designed than the jagged crags from which it might have had to be used in the Falklands. Here also the signallers who blithely carry their radios with aerials erect on exercises, were more circumspect on patrols in Argentine areas when a waving rod aerial on a skyline might be spotted by enemy patrols or the transmissions D/F-ed by enemy eavesdroppers. The messages transmitted were no doubt in code using the one-time-pad ciphers, with the sender and receiver each having a matching sheet of codes used only for a single transmission, the sheets being torn off the respective pads for a fresh cipher when the next set of messages are sent.

Moving on to the main battleground in the mountains, the British planned to advance on a broad front, taking Mount Longdon (3 Para), Two Sisters (45 Commando) and Mount Harriet (42 Commando) on the night of Friday/ Saturday 11/12 June. The attack had been delayed after the tragic loss of many Welsh Guardsmen aboard the LSL *Sir Galahad* the previous Tuesday. At this time SBS and SAS teams were 'conducting saturation patrolling on West Falkland' blocking any possibility of the 2000 Argentines on this island taking part in the coming battle. Other teams were making sketches of the countryside around Stanley.

The weather had continued its cold, wet and gale-ridden worst throughout the previous ten days, except for an occasional fine day when detailed observations over long distances were possible in the clear South Atlantic air. One such fine day occurred in the week before the attack on Stanley when an SAS team on Beagle Ridge enjoyed a clear view 7 km south across flat pastures and sea inlets to Stanley. The type of sketch drawn from such telescope observations gave a profile of the hills, the visible gun pits and strongpoints built by the Argentines on the reverse slopes of Sapper Hill (135 m) and across Stanley Common. As the Argentines had now realized that the British marines and paras had crossed what to 'Argies' was impassable country, they tightened their perimeter around Stanley. Any move that might draw their front-line troops away from the west would ease the odds for the attackers. Such a move is a long-established tactic for amphibious special forces, a sharp rap at the back door, bringing a force to defend it out of all proportion to the numbers needed for the attack. As far as the enemy commander knows, this may be more than a raid, especially if the landing party are backed up by appropriate audible and electronic deceptions. In the Second World War such noises included the screams of

Japanese women mingled with the jabbering of monkeys, played loudly on speakers in motor launches; more subtle 'shrieks' are used in the electronic battles of the 1980s, while the raiders carry through a traditional British pastime of small-scale amphibious attacks mounted by marines since the seventeenth century.

Two stern-net trawlers serving as minesweepers may not be the ideal carriers for such operations, but they sufficed to launch Rigid Raiders off the southern shore of Berkeley Sound on the Tuesday (?) night. The raiders planned to lay up next day among the kelp beaches of Kidney Cove, screened by Kidney Island from any passing Argentine patrol boat. A tangle of kelp, as we have seen, can be disastrous for powered craft, but the marine coxswains handled their boats with a delicate touch on this occasion, reversing out of trouble and avoiding those flashing phosphorescent trails that bedevil such operations in warmer seas. The landfall on Kidney Island proved unsuitable and the party lay up instead a couple of kilometres to the northwest on Cochon Island. The next night they were moving towards the entrance to Stanley Harbour, an anchorage in the days of whaling, when they saw a hospital ship coming to anchor on their route. The raid was therefore deferred until the next night. The skill of these SBS, SAS and their Raiding Squadron coxswains in remaining undetected for another day says much not only for their skill but also for the professional way in which they continued to prepare their hides. For they did not become careless after five weeks of escaping detection in a great variety of terrain, from the crags of Race Point to the mud flats of Salvador Water, and now on the approaches to Stanley with its garrison of over 8000 troops.

On the Thursday night they set out again for their target, the oil storage tanks across the western arm of the Harbour entrance. The craft had crept along the far shore of the outer bay before heading south for their landing point. There they were to put the raiders ashore and wait while the marines and troopers climbed a small cliff on to the low

Cortley Ridge, from where grenades fired from rifle cup-dischargers would set alight the oil tanks south of the Ridge. But as they crossed towards this landing, the hospital ship put on its floodlights, illuminating the raiding craft whose coxswains now opened up their throttles. They came ashore despite machine-gun fire and the raiding teams went up the Ridge. The operation had now to be completed in double-quick time, for with surprise lost the raiders were caught in Argentine mortar fire. The craft left just before the mortar-men found their range, but took casualties from machine-gun fire. By a bold move, the leading craft headed for the hospital ship and had passed her before the 105-mm shells began falling with great spouts of water among the craft. This shelling followed them to the northern beach where they scrambled ashore and marched clear of the thickening barrage, carrying their wounded. They made the few kilometres to a rendezvous with helicopters and the wounded were 'casevacced'. The oil tanks had not been set alight, but the raid must have drawn more Argentine forces into the defences to the north and east of Stanley.

After the successful Brigade attack in the mountains on the Friday/Saturday night, and the advances of Sunday, negotiations for a cease-fire had begun. Four British ships also came inshore, as it proved for the last time, to anchor in Berkeley Sound, but they did not bombard the defences.

The report of the secretary of state for defence to the British parliament said of the special forces that: 'In most demand-ing circumstances . . . [they] were thoroughly tested in the skills and tactics which they would employ in any future war in the NATO area.' Their response had justified his confidence in their selection and training, combining in 'a single patrol of intelligence-gathering skills and the capacity to mount highly destructive raids', but experience in the islands had, the secretary continued, provided useful lessons about 'improvements in equipment' – improve-ments the SBS had been seeking despite the financial constraints on all service requirements. Their personal heroism was recognized in the award of an OBE, an MBE, an MM to the sergeant leading the 'Interflora' team, another MM and twelve Mentions in Despatches. The SBS, as the Royal Navy's special force, had lived up to their Royal Marine traditions and the Squadron's own reputation since it became a purely Royal Marine unit in 1946.

12 The Inside Story

There is more to being a marine swimmer-canoeist than being able to free-fall or to dive unseen to place limpet-mines on an enemy bridge or the hull of one of his destroyers. Even more than being able to operate far behind the enemy front line and report on his forces from close quarters without being seen. Essential as all these skills are, they are only a means to an end which has parallels with the semi-clandestine and clandestine forces that the Allies had built up by 1944. These forces arrived too late on the scene to play a decisive role, as the main Allied armies were rolling forward on all fronts, in some cases without any help from clandestine teams. But had these forces been available even in small numbers much earlier, say in Europe in 1940 or in Malaya in December 1941, then the Allies would have reaped the benefit of such operations by highly trained operators: men who are confident in their own ability, bold enough to assume other identities, and with the grim determination to keep their secrets when caught by some mischance. It is a rough, tough game, one in which the operator cannot expect the niceties of the Geneva Convention to hold sway.

Should the perceived threat from the Soviet Union ever materialize into direct confrontation, then the SBS operators will be among the very few men of the special forces who stand between the British forces and instant defeat. A few handfuls of marines and other special forces could not stop their enemy's advance, but if the history of the SBS demonstrates anything it is that they will do much to slow the momentum of any attack, giving the regular forces that essential time to 'get their act together'. And should an attack be made then that air station disrupted will not be at Gosport nor the OP at Warrenpoint – they will be as far to the East as necessary.

The men of whom this history has been written will recognize where the picture has been clouded so that they may remain invisible. Others can draw their own conclusions but in the private world of secret services on which the British rely more perhaps than many realize in peacetime, only an occasional glimpse can be given to reassure us that we are in safe hands. Much has been written in recent years of the confusions of interest and occasional betrayal among those engaged in secret work, but the SBS – in so far as their strategic role brings them in contact with such agencies – show a remarkable clarity of motive in loyalty to the British government. A dependability which has served several prime ministers, one suspects, when there were possibly doubts over the dependability of the conventional spy to produce the right information or cut some Gordian knot.

So what manner of men are these SCs? Their story has shown something of their wartime activities and peacetime training, but only one has so far put on record some thoughts on his philosophy and interests. Yet his comments, before he was tragically killed, seem close in general tenor to those of the marine swimmers in the Squadron since 1946. Captain Antony L. Easterbrook, RM, was not on an operational assignment when he met his death in 1960, but was giving a public display of the death-slide in Madison Square Garden, New York. A tall lean man of thirty-one, belied by his youthful features, Easterbrook was at the time in charge of 30 commandos who nightly put on a display which ended with himself somersaulting out of a cage 25 m up in the Garden's roof, 'to rip down a 200-foot-long rope . . . attired as our man from Havana in a black suit and bowler hat'. As he came down one-handed, he waved an umbrella with his free hand in a friendly gesture to the spectators, although travelling a good deal faster than walking pace. 'I wouldn't care to estimate how fast I and the other marines come down', Easterbrook told a reporter. 'We're all slightly mad, but we do enjoy it. It's what we do in our training.' He could have added that he had also trained as a PTI and a swimmer-canoeist. Yet his greatest loves were opera and ballet. His mother had been a singer with the Covent Garden opera company. His father was a solicitor who had served with the Royal Air Force in both World Wars. Tony had left school at eighteen to join the Royal Marines and under one of its study schemes he went straight from the Corps to Cambridge University where he read French and Russian.

On his return to service in the Corps, he served mainly with the SBS in Malta, Cyprus and the UK, taking part in several exercises in Sardinia and Tripoli. He had his share of mishaps in his younger days: once when trying to break an assault course record, he attempted to jump 4 m across a ravine, missed the far edge and fell, breaking a leg; he broke a shoulder on a night parachute drop when he did not hear his instructor's shouted directions from the ground and belly-flopped into it. Why had Easterbrook chosen this sort of life? 'There are certain things you are prepared to forgo for a certain kind of life' was his reply. 'I wanted excitement, varied work and comradeship, and by nature I think I am adventurous. I have always been disobedient. The marines would satisfy the first and cure the second.' One example of how he had learnt this self-discipline was when at the age of twenty-eight he took up the piano, which he explained as 'an absorbing determination to do one particular thing, as one sometimes gets in life'.

Many other swimmer-canoeists have equally broad interests as thinking men while at the same time having a bubbling sense of fun. As lieutenants the younger officers have the opportunity with a Section of independent command. 'I really mean independent,' a senior officer has written, 'being given a training directive and told to get on with training the Section. He can more or less go where he pleases, organize exercises with submarines, do some parachuting [weather and wind permitting] or go to the lake for some underwater swimming – he's boss and can generally do what he likes to improve the efficiency of the Section.' There is also better pay, although this alone is never a valid reason for undertaking any special duties in the forces: in the late 1950s an SBS lieutenant could add up to 10 per cent to his basic pay through gaining allowances as a parachutist, for diving (even more for diving supervisors) and when embarked in a submarine.

Some indication of the way swimmer-canoeists adjust to civilian jobs can be seen in the trades of two who have retired. 'Gillie' Howe, DCM, MM, BEM, MSM, has his own gun-making business, and deals in both modern and antique firearms. Major Stuart Syrad, OBE, MC, has set up Springdale Services Ltd, which trains men for the protection of personnel and installations in the offshore oil industry. Others who have retired have found that contacts during their time in the service lead them to set up their own businesses.

Conversations between canoeists are, according to one report, concerned more with 'shop' than any other subject – even girls. Although not being privy to their shop talk in 1983, one can certainly observe that they are as red-blooded males as any other marines, even warmer-blooded perhaps after all the cold underwater swimming. Certainly, they are excellent company, especially when they tell their tales of sport diving in out-of-the-way places. As in the New Hebrides, 800 km west of Fiji, where a couple of years ago several marine divers went out with the New Zealand family running 'Nautilus Diving', to see the spectacular and beautiful reefs off Port Villa. In one dive to a sunken Sandringham flying-boat – it had hit a canoe on take-off thirty years earlier – they went down 30 m of line to the tail of this large aircraft. 'Its wings stretched out beyond the limits of visibility in the gloom of the harbour waters', the huge fuselage nose down was explored 'with appropriate respect for the depth, as the nose lies at 40 m'. On other dives a short way out of the harbour, the water was gin-clear to this depth. Here, the divers swam along walls of living coral which in places plunged to depths where the water appeared indigo blue. 'In no time an unsuspecting diver could be at 50 m without realizing the fact.' He had to make a special effort to watch his depth and air consumption, while taking in the exotic scenes of gorgonians (sea fantails) sprouting between corals of many kinds. The lion fish, sea cucumbers and other abundant varieties of fish life could be photographed with the camera lens set at infinity; a novel freedom for the diving photographer who had previously operated in water no clearer than that found off the Cornish coast, where visibility is about 4 m. Diving in Plymouth Sound would never be the same again for these marines.

Another summer, in the SB Squadron's exercise 'Green Dragon' off Gibraltar, the diving had a more serious purpose in making exits and re-entries from and to the submarine *Otis*. In this part of four weeks' training the SCs worked with the Submarine Parachute Assistance Group (SPAG) of naval divers, who are expert in giving advice and the practical assistance needed to recover the crew of a submarine trapped on the bottom. They came from the submarine training base HMS *Dolphin* while other parachutists later joined the exercise who came from commando bases. The parties included Royal Artillery commando gunners of 148 (Meiktila) Forward Observation Battery and an Explosive Ordnance Disposal (EOD) team from the Royal Ordnance Corps. Their 'chutes of man-made fibre had a seven-metre steerable canopy with non-corrosive fittings, enabling a 'chute to be used time and again for successive jumps into the sea. And what water drops these were for, as one SC laconically recalled, 'It is really quite something to jump into an open ocean' (in order to RV with a submarine) 'to find [yourself] in an area where sharks have been seen.' On other days, two-man Klepper canoe teams practised firing GPMGs from their craft, each 'No. 2 paddling like mad to overcome the effect of the recoil' in trying to keep his canoe lined up on the target. If this machine gun did not destroy it, then the 66-mm rockets which they also fired from canoes almost certainly would, even with practice heads. But even after many direct hits the old harbour launch at which they were firing refused to sink and had finally to be rolled over by the escort tug *Cyclone*. The following January to April many of these canoeists were training in the much colder waters of north Norway.

These sharp contrasts of diving among coral reefs, firing machine guns from a 'canvas' canoe weighing little over 30 kg and free diving beneath Arctic ice, are taken in their stride by the Special Boat Squadron. Indeed, their training, operational skills and manner of life constitute – as we have seen – one of the most adventurous callings in military service. Very few people have knowingly met any of these specialists, who have always shunned the limelight and will continue to do so, as it is their invisibility which makes them such dangerous foes of any who would challenge the British people's right to freedom.

List of Abbreviations

AIB: Australian Intelligence Bureaux

APD: Auxiliary Personnel Destroyer

ARA: *Armada Republica Argentina*

ASW: Anti-Submarine Warfare

ATTURM: Amphibious Trials and Training Unit Royal Marines

AVRE: Assault Vehicle Royal Engineers

AXE: Amphibious Experimental Establishment

BAOR: British Army of the Rhine

Buffs: Royal East Kent Regiment

CAP: Combat/Cover Air Patrols

Commando: Commando unit

commando: commando marine, sailor or soldier

CO: Commanding Officer

COBBS: Combined Operations Beach and Boat Section

COPP: Combined Operations Assault Pilotage Party

COXE: Combined Operations Experimental Establishment

CXD: Coordinator of Experiments and Developments

D/F: Direction Finding (in radio location)

DLF: Dhofar Liberation Front

DLG: Destroyer Leader (of) Group

DSEA: Davis Submerged Escape Apparatus

DXSR: Directorate of Experiments and Staff Requirements

DZ: Dropping Zone

EAM: *Ethnikon Apeleftherotikon Metopon*

EDES: *Ethnikon Dimokraticos Ellenikos*

ELAS: *Ethnikon Apeleftherotikos Stratos*

ETA: Estimated Time of Arrival

EW: Electronic Warfare

FAC: Forward Air Controller

FOLEM: Flag Officer the Levant and Eastern Mediterranean

FLOSY: Front for the Liberation of South Yemen

FRA: Federation Regular Army

GPMG: General Purpose
Machine Gun

HAS: Helicopter
Anti Submarine
HC: Helicopter Commando
HDML: Harbour Defence
Motor Launch
HE: High Explosive
helo: helicopter
HO: Hostilities Only
HU: Helicopter Utility

IBT: Indonesian Border
Terrorist
IC: Intermediate Carrier
IRA: Irish Republican Army
IS: Internal Security
ISTDC: Inter-Service Training
and Development Centre

JCLO: Junior Civil Liaison
Officer

KKO: *Korps Kommando Operasi*

LCA: Landing Craft, Assault
LCI(L): Landing Craft,
Infantry (Large)
LCM: Landing Craft,
Mechanized
LCN: Landing Craft,
Navigation
LCP(Sy): Landing Craft,
Personnel (Survey)
LCT: Landing Craft, Tank
LCU: Landing Craft, Utility
LMG: Light Machine Gun
LPD: Landing Platform Dock
LRDG: Long Range Desert
Group
LSI: Landing Ship, Infantry

LST: Landing Ship, Tank
LTMR: Laser Target Marker
and Rangefinder
LZ: Landing Zone

MFU: Mobile Flotation Unit
MGB: Motor Gun Boat
ML: Motor Launch
ML: Mountain Leader
MOD: Ministry of Defence
MPAJA: Malayan People's
Anti-Japanese Army
MRF: Military
Reconnaissance Force
MRLA: Malayan Races
Liberation Army
MSC: Motor Submersible
Canoe

NAS: Naval Air Station
NATO: North Atlantic Treaty
Organization
NGFO: Naval Gunfire
Forward Observer
NGS: Naval Gunfire Support
NGSO: Naval Gunfire Support
Officer
NLF: National Liberation
Front

OP: Observation Point
'oppo': opposite number
(friend)
OSS: Office of Strategic
Services

PE: Plastic Explosive
PFLOAG: Popular Front for
the Liberation of Oman and
Arabian Gulf
PIAT: Projector Infantry
Anti-Tank

PNG: Passive Night Goggles

RAE: Royal Aircraft Establishment

RFA: Royal Fleet Auxiliary

RFC: Royal Flying Corps

RG: infra-red signalling equipment

RM: Royal Marine or Marines

RMLI: Royal Marine Light Infantry

RMBPD: Royal Marine Boom Patrol Detachment

RMR: Royal Marine Reserve or Royal Malaya Regiment

RPKAD: *Resemen Para Kommando Angaton Darat*

rpm: rounds per minute

R/T: Radio Telephone

RUC: Royal Ulster Constabulary

RV: Rendezvous

SAF: Sultan's Armed Forces

SAS: Special Air Service

SBA: Sick Berth Attendant

SBS: Special Boat Section/ Squadron

SC1, SC2, SC3: Swimmer-Canoeist 1 (highest qualification), 2 (intermediate) and 3

SCUBA: Self-Contained Underwater Breathing Apparatus

SEAC: Southeast Asia Command

SIV: Swimmer Insertion Vehicle

SLR: Self-Loading Rifle

SMG: Sub-machine Gun

SOE: Special Operations Executive

SOG: Small Operations Group

SPAG: Submarine, Parachute Assistance Group

SQ: Specialist Qualification

SRF: Special Raiding Force(s)

SRU: Sea Reconnaissance Unit

SSRF: Small Scale Raiding Force

Tac(HQ): Tactical (Headquarters)

TEZ: Total Exclusion Zone

TNKU: *Tentara Nasional Kalimantan Utara*

UDT: Underwater Demolition Team

USMC: United States Marine Corps

Related Organizations and the Special Boat Squadron

Inter-Service Training and Development Committee (ISTDC) Formed in 1936 at Fort Cumberland near Eastney, Hampshire, the committee's purpose was to make studies by representatives of all three services into the problems of amphibious landings, supplying forces in the field by air and similar logistics problems. Royal Marines, including future swimmer-canoeists, did experimental work for ISTDC.

Directorate of Experiments and Staff Requirements (DXSR) and its successors The Directorate took over the work of ISTDC, the senior staff being augmented by the scientists Professors J. D. Bernal and S. Zuckerman, and N. G. Pyke. This staff, formed as the Directorate on 13 April 1942, was headed by the former Coordinator of Experiments and Developments (CXD). In August 1942 the Directorate became that of Experiments and Scientific Research (DXSR) which in May 1943 became the Directorate of Experiments and Operations Research (DXOR). Sections of RMBPD worked with the Directorate's Experimental Establishment at Westward Ho, Devon, as did teams from COPPs and other amphibious recce units. After the Second World War the work of the Combined Operations Experimental Establishment (COXE) in Devon passed to the Amphibious Experimental Establishment (AXE) which, by the 1980s, became the Amphibious Trials and Training Unit Royal Marines (ATTURM) at Instow, Devon.

SB Section of 8 Commando This Section was formed in the late summer of 1940 with about 20 canoeists trained by Captain (later Major) R. Courtney, RE, who took 15 of them to the Middle East with 'Layforce' in February 1941. There as 1 SBS these canoeists received reinforcements to raise their number to some 48 all ranks. They operated mainly from submarines after Courtney, with Admiral Maund's approval, transferred the Section from 'Layforce's' Commando to the 1st Submarine Flotilla in April 1941. The Section was then absorbed into Lord Jellicoe's SB Squadron at the end of the year. Plans in 1940 to have a Troop of canoeist Sections with each Commando were not fulfilled (see 101 Troop details below).

SAS Canoe Sections A detachment of the SAS was trained at Kabrit, Egypt, in the spring of 1941. These Sections formed the core of Lord Jellicoe's Special Boat Squadron.

SB Section in Middle East A number of volunteers were trained as canoeists for this Section at Kabrit in the spring of 1941. They were later absorbed into Lord Jellicoe's Squadron after operations in the eastern Mediterranean loosely coordinated with those of 'Z' Section working from Gibraltar.

SB Section (of 1942) In February 1942 a meeting at Combined Operations HQ set up an SB Section 'similar to that operating in the Middle East'. A number of canoeists were recalled from the Middle East and Major Roger Courtney who had already returned to the UK was to command them. They were to carry out operations from coastal craft and not 'on spec' from submarines as was the practice in 1 SBS. Their War Establishment totalled 47. This 2 SBS completed several recces of the French coast before being sent to join SOG as 'A' Group (7 officers), 'B' Group (4 officers and 32 other ranks), 'C' Group (16 other ranks) and 'Z' Group (7 officers and 6 other ranks, probably from the Middle East). Their administration was carried out by SOG.

101 Troop The first independent unit of canoeists, it was formed from volunteers serving in 6 Cdo in November 1941. The Troop undertook from its base in Dover several recce raids against the French coast and one anti-shipping raid in December 1941.

Small Scale Raiding Force (SSRF) This unit was administered by the staff of the Chief of Combined Operations for work on behalf of SOE in landing agents, as well as raiding the occupied Channel coast. These 60 all ranks had been training as 5 Detachment of the Raiding School before being renamed the SSRF early in 1942. The Force was disbanded after major losses in raids during the autumn, several of its surviving personnel joining the SAS with some in the SAS canoe sections.

Combined Operations Assault Pilotage Parties (COPPs) The first of these Parties was formed in September 1942 from naval navigator and Royal Engineer officers training for the reconnaissance of the North African beaches in preparation for the 'Torch' landings of November. By June 1944 there were 57 all ranks in the HQ and Training Cadre at their base in the clubhouse and buildings of Hayling Island Sailing Club, Hampshire, and ten operational parties each with an establishment of twelve officers, although Nos. 7–9 were each one man below strength. The operations of each Party included:

No. 1 made beach surveys for Normandy landings in the early months of 1944; provided crews for X-craft which were marker boats in beach navigation of invasion fleets in the Seine Bay, 6 June 1944; surveyed Mediterranean beaches for Allied invasion of southern France in August 1944; and in 1945 under command of SOG carried out several operations including the clearing of a gap in beach obstacles at Myebon, in the Arakan, for commando landings on 12 January 1945. In August 1945 they were in Madrao and returned to the UK to be reorganized when HOs were demobilized in 1946.

No.2 operated LCN for Normandy surveys in January 1944; and in 1944–5 worked on beach surveys in the Aegean and Adriatic. Disbanded in 1946.

No. 3 made recces in February 1943 of landing points on 24 km of Sicily's beaches from Sciacco to the River Belice, three of the Party being lost, probably drowned during recces. No. 3 joined SOG in July 1944 to make recces in the Arakan and landed on Phuket Island in March 1945 when the landing team were all killed or captured; after the replacements for casualties arrived from the UK, other members of the Party surveyed the Morib beaches west of Singapore in July; and returned to UK for reorganization.

No. 4 made recces on the northwest Sicilian beaches when two were captured in recces on 26 February and 9 March 1943; in the summer of 1944, while attached to SOG, they made recces in the Arakan before returning to UK.

No. 5 made successful surveys of southeastern beaches of Sicily in June 1943, finding batteries tunnelled into cliffs which had not been visible in air reconnaissance; on 9 July (D-1 of Allied invasion of Sicily) laid three navigation beacon buoys off landing beaches and their canoes were launched from submarines despite a storm, just before H-hour in the early dark hours of 10 July to provide leading navigation lights, while other COPPists in MLs guided in the assault waves to the navigation beacons; at end July, No. 5 surveyed beaches in the Gulf of Gioia on the west coast of the toe of Italy (beaches not used for the later invasion); began several days of recces off Salerno beaches on 30 August radioing reports in code to approaching Allied invasion forces; transferred at sea to MLs to guide in Salerno assault waves; returned to UK and at 24 hours' notice in the third week of March made a survey of Rhine river banks near Wesel; reached India in August 1945 but returned to UK as hostilities had ceased in southeast Asia.

No. 6 surveyed Sicilian beaches with 'No. 5' in June 1943 and provided men for MLs to guide in assault forces on 10 July; on 6 June 1944 guided in AVRE in van of Normandy landings; disbanded in 1945.

No. 7 made recces of Akyab Island, Burma, beaches in October 1943, being the first COPP to arrive in the Far East; made deception recce off Sumatra in March 1944 before returning to UK; in 1945 made several recces of river crossings in northwest Europe, including the Elbe in March; were returned to SEAC in August 1945 and then disbanded.

No. 8 made recces of Akyab and a northern Sumatra beach early in 1944 before returning to UK; some teams from this COPP participated in northwest Europe river recces; disbanded on reorganization in summer of 1945.

No. 9 provided navigators for X-craft on 6 June 1944 before joining SOG in the Far East in 1945; disbanded on their return to UK.

No. 10 operated in the Mediterranean from 1 June to 30 November 1944 carrying out 31 operations including surveys of the beaches at Anzio, Italy, the Adriatic islands and beaches near Salonika; in the summer of 1945 had reached India before war ended and they returned to UK.

'S' COPP was formed in 1945 on reorganization of Parties as Senior COPP Officer's Party and transferred to SCOBBS in 1946.

'A' COPP was a Party of the second senior officer on reorganization in 1945; disbanded in 1946.

'M' COPP were maintenance teams for operational COPPs in 1945 on reorganization; disbanded 1946.

'E' COPP was the third operational Party on reorganization in 1945 and was comprised of sappers; disbanded in 1946.

(Note: the type of beach reconnaissance carried out by COPPs is a principal role of the SBS in the 1980s.)

Naval Beach Reconnaissance Parties (Middle East) Formed at Kabrit, Egypt, in the winter of 1942–3 by the Combined Operations Training Centre; from there two Parties joined Nos. 3 and 4 COPPs in Malta for recces of Sicilian beaches in February–March 1943; four men were lost in the raids and these Beach Recce Parties were then disbanded.

SB Squadron (Middle East) Formed initially in the summer of 1941 with three Sections of men trained at Kabrit, as part of Colonel David Stirling's SAS, these Sections under Lord Jellicoe raided Crete in June 1942. After the Middle East SBS and 1 SBS had suffered substantial losses in raids, they were absorbed into 'D' Squadron of the SAS in the autumn of 1942 along with all SAS canoeists. In the spring of 1943 the three SB Sections were reorganized as three Squadrons, retaining the initial letters of the surnames of the first Section commanders as 'L', 'M' and 'S' Squadrons, totalling 180 all ranks. In the early summer of 1944 a detachment of RMBPD also came under Jellicoe's command, these marines exchanging their blue berets for SAS sand (buff) berets. The marines returned to the UK. Later the Squadron (Middle East) came under the command of 2 Commando Brigade for operations on Lake Comacchio in April 1945, after which the Squadron returned to the UK for remustering with SAS regiments preparing to go to the Far East, but these canoeists were not sent there and the SAS units were disbanded in 1946 not to be reformed until 1950, although a Territorial unit 21 SAS was formed in 1947.

Raiding Forces Middle East The Force was formed with an HQ effective from 26 October 1943 under the War Establishment, VI/1092/2. Under its command at different times were: the Greek Sacred Squadron (royalist officers taking their unit name from the 'Squadron' killed to a man at Thebes resisting the Spartans in 370BC); OSS operational groups totalling 200 all ranks; the Corsican Bataillon de Choc, comprising 500 all ranks; a Demolition Squad of 75 engineers; Jellicoe's SB Squadron of 180 all ranks; teams totalling 240 men from the LRDG; twenty 'Kalpak' guides and saboteurs; and men of RMBPD for training as coast-watchers. These forces were disbanded in the winter of 1945.

1st Special Raiding Squadron This SAS formation, commanded by Major 'Paddy' Mayne with 15 officers and 238 other ranks, operated in the eastern Mediterranean and Italy. It returned to the UK in 1943 whereupon it was remustered in SAS units for operations in northwest Europe.

Combined Operations Scout Units In June 1944 40 all ranks of these RN units – each with an officer, a petty officer and 6 qualified radio operators and 2 radio mechanics – were trained to create diversions by playing recordings of battle noises over loud hailers. In 1945, after training in MLs, they were in the Far East but not used operationally before being disbanded in 1945–6. Some of their diversion roles have been taken over by the SBS since 1946.

Royal Marine Boom Patrol Detachment Formed in July 1942 with a major commanding, a lieutenant as second in command and a small administrative section (one senior NCO and three marines) the Detachment initially had two Sections each of fifteen men commanded by a second lieutenant. The Canoe Section took part in the raid on Bordeaux in December 1942. The Explosive Boat Section was never used operationally although it stood ready for action in the winter of 1944–5. By this date the Detachment had been divided into a Motorized Submersible Canoe Section (MSC), a Canoe Section, which had been with Jellicoe's Squadron in the Middle East, and an Explosive Boat Section, a total of 75 all ranks. In 1946, after the demobilization of HO ranks, the reduced Detachment was at Appledore, Devon, but in the autumn of 1947 moved back to Eastney, Hampshire, to become part of the Small Raids Wing of the RM Amphibious School. The Special Boat Squadron Royal Marines is a direct descendant of RMBPD.

Sea Reconnaissance Unit (SRU) Formed in December 1942, the Unit was the creation of Lieutenant-Commander Bruce Wright, SC, RCN, who had been working since January 1941 on the concept of long-distance swimmers using paddle-boards. He spent some time with RMBPD in 1943 before recruiting strong swimmers from all three services for SCUBA (Self-Contained Underwater Breathing Apparatus) Sections with an establishment of ten men in each (although No. 4 Section was one man under strength in June 1944) and an HQ of eight all ranks. The Sections joined SOG late in 1944 and made a number of recces of crossings of the Irrawaddy in February 1945 for the Fourteenth Army. Afterwards they moved to the An Pass area of the Arakan coast, working with COPPs to clear mined barriers that the retreating Japanese had left across chaungs. The Unit was disbanded by early 1946, at least one of its marine swimmers joining SCOBBS.

HMS Rodent In September 1943 an RN captain was appointed 'Captain Special Boat Unit' to command COPPs, new SBS formed in 1943, the SRU, Naval Boom Commandos (naval LCOCU teams), Camouflage 'B' the forerunners of Combined Operations Scout Units, 30 Commando of RN engineers collecting intelligence from enemy shore headquarters as soon as these were overrun or at times before the Allied advance reached them. The captain's HQ was near Liss, Hampshire and known as HMS *Rodent* until his command was disbanded in the winter of 1945–6. The captain of *Rodent* was irreverently known as 'King Rat'.

Small Operations Group (SOG) Formed by SEAC in June 1944 to control small-scale amphibious raids in this theatre, the Group was commanded by a Royal Marine colonel. Marines provided the administration for the units under command which, early in 1945, reached the Group's maximum strength of: four COPPs (Parties being relieved in rotation from the UK), Groups 'A', 'B' and 'C' of the SBS, Detachment 385, and the SRU. The Group headquarters was disbanded in the autumn of 1945.

'X' Group Formed in Australia in September 1944 as a unit of the AIB for anti-shipping raids, the Group then went to Singapore for Operation 'Rimau' (Malay for 'Tiger') in which 32 swimmers were killed or captured between 28 September and the end of October.

RM Detachment 385 Formed from Royal Marine volunteers in April–May 1944, the Detachment became operational in January 1945 under command of SOG. Its three Troops, each of 31 men, were organized in teams to suit the type of operation being carried out, including deception raids, reconnaissance and landing clandestine forces in sixteen operations, some involving more than one raiding party. The Detachment returned to Britain and re-mustered as SCOBBS.

Z Group 10 canoeists from 2 SBS who did 18 operations in the Mediterranean (1943–4). Five later served with SOE in SEAC and the other with Australian forces.

School of Combined Operations Beach and Boat Section (SCOBBS) This unit was formed at the School of Combined Operations at Instow, north Devon, in the summer of 1946 from men of SRU, '385' and COPPs who had not been demobilized. In October 1947 these swimmer-canoeists were transferred to the Amphibious School at Eastney, Hampshire (see COBBS), where they continued to demonstrate beach survey techniques. They were absorbed with RMBPD into the Small Raids Wing.

Combined Operations Beach and Boat Section (COBBS) When SCOBBS moved to Eastney in 1947, they unofficially dropped the 'S' in their title before being absorbed into the Small Raids Wing.

Amphibious School, Royal Marines (ASRM) Formed at Eastney in October 1947, the School had the following wings: the Landing Craft Wing of 461 and 416 LC Flotillas from Rothesay, Scotland, training coxswains and other landing craft crewmen; the Beach Wing – a cadre of the Royal Naval Beach Control Party for controlling the landing of men and stores into a beachhead, the men in this RNBCP included trained landing craft crews and underwater swimmers; Landing Craft Obstruction Clearance Unit (LCOCU) – a cadre of underwater swimmers to clear beach obstacles; Landing Craft Recovery Unit (LCRU) – equipped with bulldozers and cranes to bring damaged landing craft ashore after these had been patched and pumped free of water; Small Raids Wing – see below. On 1 December 1954 the School moved to Poole in Dorset where much later it became Royal Marines, Poole, with a Landing Craft Company, a Technical Training Company and other units.

Small Raids Wing/Small Boat Wing This Wing of the Amphibious School was formed in October 1947 with COBBS and RMBPD. Also for a time known as the SB Unit. By 1950 it had an SB Cadre for training swimmer-canoeists and No. 1 SB Section (see below). This Wing became the SB Company.

Special Boat Company (SBC) and Special Boat Squadron (SBS) The SB headquarters and the Training Cadre with the SB Sections formerly in the Special Boat Wing became the SB Unit in 1957 and the SB Company by August 1958. In 1975 the

Company was renamed SB Squadron as the abbreviation SBS then could cover both SB Squadron and SB Sections.

No. 1 SB Section This Section was formed at Eastney in 1951 and remained one of the operational Sections of the SBS in Europe throughout the next three decades.

No. 2 SB Section This Section went to Germany as the RM Demolition Unit in February 1950 with twelve swimmer-canoeists and some landing craft ratings to join the Rhine Flotilla, RN. During 1950 the Unit was renamed No. 2 SB Section with two officers (one commanding the Section and the other to advise the army commander – at Divisional, Army or higher level – on the swimmers' capabilities). The three teams in the Section, each of two 2-man canoes, were administered through an SNCO who was not necessarily an SC but acted as the Section's quartermaster, with a corporal as the second man in the OC's canoe, making the Section's total establishment of seventeen all ranks. The Section served in Germany until 1958, when it returned to the UK as the Demonstration Section of the Joint Services Amphibious Warfare Centre (JSAWC). The Section sailed for Singapore in March 1960, and saw service in Malaya and Borneo before returning to the UK in the late 1960s.

No. 3 SB Section This Section was formed in 1950 from men of the SBS Company for service with the Rhine Squadron and returned to the UK in 1958.

Nos. 4 and 5 SB Sections (R) These Sections have been provided by teams of reservists from various RMR Centres since the early 1950s. They may be mobilized even though the rest of the RMR are not called to join the regular forces. Swimmer-canoeist reservists trained with the Amphibious School, Eastney, in the summer of 1951 and reservists have continued such training to the present day.

No. 6 Section Formed by 3 Commando Brigade in Malta in 1952, this Section moved with the Brigade to the Far East in 1961 and returned with the Brigade to the UK in 1971.

Equipment

Boats and Canoes

Rob Roy This canoe of the 1930s was the first decked touring canoe introduced in Europe. Designed by John McGregor, it had a large open oval cockpit, was clinker-built and heavy with a length of about 5 m.

Folbot (Cockle Mk I) This was a two-man collapsible sports canoe, made by the Folbot Company (which went out of business early in 1940 owing to sheer lack of orders). Major Roger Courtney's canoeists in 1940 used this type of craft, without any buoyancy aids. The canoe consisted of a wooden frame within a rubberized canvas cover. Although collapsible, it was normally kept assembled, all the joints (metal tube-joints, like tent poles) bound up by black, heavy electrical insulation tape to avoid accidental disconnection. It was 15.2 m long, and the rudder, as in all Cockle canoes, had lines running forward to whichever paddler was steering. One possible drawback was that the canoe was too lightly constructed to drag across mud flats when loaded.

Cockle Mk I** This was a development from the Mk I as modified by COPP to get a more stable canoe by having two inflated tubes, one on either side of the gunwale. Its heavy three-ply waterproofed canvas skin, camouflaged in khaki-buff, was reinforced at points likely to chafe, and there was a cockpit cover 'split' down the centre to allow two canoeists easy access and then clipped along the centreline by bulldog-type clips to prevent water slopping into the cockpit. The cover also incorporated two annular skirts of stiffened canvas rising 12.5 cm above the cover around the waist of each paddler. Improved stability was achieved by the insertion of two removable tubes 3 m long, 10 cm in diameter, which could be inflated by mouth in canvas envelopes, 'two inches [5 cm] below the top and outboard of the port and starboard gunwales'. These countered any tendency to list. Additional flotation bags, triangular in section, were inserted fore and aft; these could be inflated by the paddlers by means of 1.75-m-long mouth tubes. Dimensions were 5.2 m × 74 cm × 46 cm, and the canoe weighed 51 kg. A conversion kit was developed in order to add an extra section and seat to make this a three-man canoe. Yet another development of the Folbot enabled the midships frame to hinge off-centre, bringing the beam down to 46 cm, which made it possible to pass the assembled canoe through a submarine's torpedo hatch; once on the outer casing of the submarine, the canoe frame was fixed at right-angles to the keel to bring the beam up to 71 cm.

Cockle Mk I *** This canoe, built at Twickenham, Middlesex, was a development of the Mk I**, being slightly lighter and fitted with a rudder.

Cockle Mk II and Mk II** Designed to stand up to being dragged over beaches, the Mk II was a craft with plywood deck and hull bottom, but with canvas sides (similar in concept to the Goatley boat). The struts normally holding the deck up could be hinged forward to collapse the canoe to a compact depth of 15 cm. These Mark II canoes were used on the 'Frankton' raid. The type continued in service many years before being replaced by the Klepper canoe.

Cockle Mk III** (later renamed Mussel I) This was used where Mk II collapsible canoes would be unsuitable, for example when launched from a Country Craft. It would be developed as a powered canoe. The Mk III** hull was of 3-mm moulded plywood (birch, as used in aircraft construction), covered with roped fabric and lined with heavy rubberized stockingette 'to ensure water-tightness even if [the] wooden hull is fractured'. Two fabric-covered wooden outriggers on light alloy arms could be extended outwards to 16 cm from the hull as a means of increasing stability. The canoe hull was in three watertight sections, the bow and stern being filled with table-tennis balls for buoyancy. A camouflaged lateen sail and yard, rudder, perspex window in the cockpit cover above the compass, lockers and breakwaters at bow and stern were all standard fittings. The overall length was 5.5 m, beam 75 cm, depth 41 cm.

(In June 1942, official attempts were made to distinguish the different types of canoes by altering the nomenclature. Mk III became 'Mussel I', Mk IV 'Mussel II' and Mk V 'Tadpole I'. The new names did not 'stick' however: generally, canoe types continued to be referred to as 'Cockles', and even in 1943 combined operations publications referred to Marks of canoe without any identifying names.)

Cockle Mk VI This canoe was powered by a 4-hp two-stroke engine situated between the two canoeists. A wooden engine cover replaced part of the central canvas canopy and this had a wire-stiffened skirt to protect the engine from spray. The small propeller was driven by an underwater gear unit, which could be retracted when beaching. In the event of engine failure or running out of fuel, the engine could be jettisoned, in which case a large stopper plate was provided to prevent drag created by the engine retracting gear tunnel. There were two silencers, one water-cooled and integral to the engine, the other connected by hand when particularly silent running was essential. The engine's main tank carried only 3.4 litres of fuel, made up in the ratio of 4.5 litres of automobile petrol to 333 millilitres of oil, but four supplementary tanks carried a further 29 litres which could be syphoned by filler hoses. This gave a maximum range of 110 km at full throttle, a speed in calm water of 7 knots, and 145 km at half throttle. The canoe was supplied with a sail as for the Mk III**, but would carry only half that canoe's load in addition to two men. Visually the Mk VI was distinguished by the increased sheer and flare to the bow.

Cockle Mk VIII A development of the Mk VI, this motorized canoe could carry two men and 364 kg of stores and equipment, or four men and 182 kg. Its engine, similar to that in the Mk VI, gave it a range of 113 km at 6¼ knots, or 113 km at 5 knots. Dimensions were 6.1 m × 70 cm × 41 cm. It was one of a series of RMBPD developments to increase the distances covered by canoes infiltrating an enemy beach area. Refuelling from the spare tanks required the engine to be switched off, and it often proved difficult to restart, even when hot.

Motor Submersible Canoe (MSC, or 'Sleeping Beauty') The history, so far as is known, of this extraordinary craft is described on pages 149–51. Early prototypes had outriggers, which could be retracted close to the hull by arms operated through tubes. The operational version, without these outriggers, was powered by a ½-hp heavy-duty vehicle electric starter motor. Some air and other pressure tanks fitted in these craft had been salvaged from enemy aircraft. A developed version in the late 1940s had bow hydroplanes, but these probably proved an encumbrance when the MSC was submerged alongside the target.

Alloy canoe This Mk VII canoe of 1944 built in three sections, with the bow and stern for watertight storage, had outriggers, mast, sail and gun mounting when required. Weight 50 kg, length 4 m.

Klepper Introduced in the 1950s and still used in the 1980s, this German two-man collapsible sports canoe proved lighter than Cockle II and more stable in the tidal mangroves of southeast Asia. The longitudinal stringers are of the 'elastic hardwood Mountain Ash', and the cross-members are of nine-ply Finnish Birch, with snap-lock fittings. The deck covering is long-staple cotton woven with hemp (self-drying and self-sealing) and the hull skin is of a material similar in make-up to that of an industrial conveyor belt: rubber inside and outside, with a core of polyester cord. The skin fits loosely over the frame until 'airsponsons' running under each gunwale are inflated. Dimensions are 5.2 m × 89 cm × 61 cm, and in its sports version the canoe packs away into a bag 69 ×58 × 20 cm.

Dories The designs of prototype dories and other small boats by the yacht builders Camper & Nicholsons were developed in 1941 with Major Gus March-Phillips of the SSRF, resulting in the 18-footer (see below) and other developments. This yard also worked with Major Hasler on the MSC. Many of the dories and canoes of these designs continued to be used into the late 1950s.

18-foot Dory (CN1) This was built to carry eight men, including the coxswain and driver (engineer). It had a maximum speed of 5.7 knots over 161 km on a full petrol tank of 55 litres for the 10-hp Austin engine, fitted with Burgess silencers. The all-up weight was 645.5 kg, length 5.5 m, beam 1.8 m, total depth 1.2 m. The kapok fender added 5 cm to the overall length and 18 cm to the beam.

20-foot Dory (SN6) This wooden hull was carvel-built with double-diagonal construction. Powered by a two-cylinder 8-hp Stuart Turner, the SN6 could make 6 knots. Its length overall was 6.1 m, beam 1.6 m, approximate weight 305 kg, capacity (by one report) 1930 kg (eight to ten men), and length of oars 3 m.

22-foot Dory (CN3) This was built like CN1 as a multiple hard-chine boat but with high bow and stern to give a surf-riding ability.

It carried a load of 2032 kg and had a length of 6.6 m, beam 1.8 m, depth amidships 82.5 cm. The coxswain used a long steering oar.

Collapsible boats *The Goatley Boat* This wooden-bottomed boat with collapsible canvas sides was described by 6 Commando as 'very manoeuvrable due to its oblong shape which makes it possible to go in either direction'.* It could be carried across country after being assembled by two men in 1½ minutes, was a reasonable seaboat and 'the best folding boat 6 Commando have been issued with'.* Normally paddled by ten men, it measured 5.4 m by 76 cm by 2.7 m and weighed 152.4 kg. Mr Goatley's original designs of October 1940 were lost in Combined Operations HQ files but by January 1941 trials were under way and the boat accepted for use by Royal Engineer Field Coys as well as commandos for waterborne operations in sheltered waters.

Punts were 5.8 m long and weighed 305 kg. They could carry eleven men, but were 'slow and unmanageable in cross-winds'.*

Assault Boat Mk II With a metal bottom, wooden frame and canvas sides, this was 3.5 m long and weighed 102 kg. Its sturdy construction enabled it to stand up 'to rough usage'* and it could carry seven men.

Assault Boat Mk III This heavy (406-kg) boat was 7.2 m long and could take fourteen men, but it proved 'a bad boat in wind, and more suitable as a pontoon than for commando operations'.*

Inflatables *Infantry Recce Boat* 'Black rubber skin inflated by hand pump, carried 6 men, two of whom paddled but for speed all 6 might do so. 'Good for river crossings . . . [although] not manoeuvrable in a wind, silent and easy to conceal' in the opinion of 6 Commando*. Inflated to length 2.6 m, beam 1.1 m, depth 38 cm, and weight 28 kg, but folded when deflated into canvas bag 1.1 m by 56 cm by 23 cm.

7-man (US Intruder) The craft had heavy rubberized skin to give a raised and pointed bow, with reinforced patches to prevent chafing. The floorboards and general construction were stoutly made with the main hull inflated by CO_2, with 'stiffeners' inflated by hand pumps as was the 'floor' of the skin. It could be fitted with a 5-hp outboard which in 1942–3 was prone to cut-out when caught by a following sea. Length 3 m, beam 1.5 m, weight *c.* 115 kg. Its

*From a report by 6 Commando to the Commodore, Combined Operations (sic) on 24 February 1942.

speed over long distances was 2 knots when paddled, but experienced crews achieved 3.5 knots over short distances.

Y-type This was a Combined Operations team design to provide a light-weight six-man inflatable, weighing a little less than one-fifth the weight of an Intruder, at 31 kg, yet carrying nearly half the load at 544 kg. The three-ply proofed fabric skin had a hinged slatted floorboard which folded along its length (2.1 m). It was inflated by CO_2 to 2.5 m by 1.5 m by 38 cm. Although light in construction, the skin had rubbing patches to prevent paddles chafing the buoyancy chambers. The YA-type was inflated by hand pump and the YS-type by air from Mark III CO_2 bottles. All Y-types folded into canvas bags.

Two-man recce boat of rubberized canvas. The specifications were 2 m by 38 cm when inflated.

Gemini This is the current standard-use inflatable, and can be powered by either an 18-hp or 40-hp outboard motor. There are three sizes: a twelve-man boat 5.2 m long, a ten-man boat 3.8 m long and an eight-man version 1.6 m long.

Midget submarines *Welman* This one-man submersible was steered by a joystick. It was designed by ISRB to carry 255 kg of explosive as an external charge in the form of an extremely large limpet with heavy magnets. The endurance on a 2½-hp electric motor was ten hours at 2.5 knots, and twenty hours at 1.7 knots. When the craft was submerged at the normal depth of 22.9 m (maximum 90 m), the pilot could steer by gyro instruments pre-set on his target before he dived. Specifications were: length 6.2 m, height 1.8 m, beam at saddle 1.1 m and surface displacement 2086 kg.

X-craft This Vickers-designed midget submarine was used to place two 2-ton explosive charges under enemy ships. They were equipped with a gyro compass, oxygen supply, CO_2 absorption equipment, 2.7-m day periscope, short fix night periscope, directional hydrophones, radio-telephones, Chernikeef log, and an automatic steering device. A few of these craft were modified to carry COPP reconnaissance parties, and the equipment to release the explosive charges was replaced by extra navigation aids. The craft's 42-hp main engine, powered by 112 battery cells, gave 4 knots at 1800 rpm for a surface range of 2993 km. The endurance of the five-man crew was seven to ten days. X-craft could be safely dived to 91 m, but in its COPP role operated near the surface in daylight. It could be towed at 10½ knots by a submerged T-class and other submarines, reducing the endurance of the T-class by 5½ per cent. Specifications were: surface displacement 27,433 kg, submerged displacement 30,177 kg, overall length 15.8 m, beam 1.8 m. A modified and updated type of X-craft was used in the 1980s.

Miscellaneous craft *'Country' craft* This converted naval cutter could carry two canoes and was designed in 1943–4 also to carry two MSCs. Colonel Hasler decided to opt for the intermediate carrier principle because submarines and destroyers could not be risked inshore for some operations once the German use of radar became widespread and efficient. (Coastal forces craft were considered too noisy.) By the 1980s Rigid Raider craft could perform a similar role as intermediate carriers.

LCN(avigation) The first design of these special craft of 11 m was an adaptation of the LCP(L) – an assault-type landing craft – with a superstructure added to cover a wireless room and a control position. The LCN's equipment included WS radar on a short mast, Loran or Decca navigation aids, which gave the craft's precise position in relation to the radio beacons used in these systems, echo sounder and a reel of 14 km of surveyor's wire for 'taut wire' measurements of distances run. Its speed was about 9 knots, range 200 km. In 1945–6 a purpose-built LCN hull was designed with a motorboat bow but otherwise equipment was similar to that in the first mark. These were mothballed or scrapped in the late 1940s.

Mobile Flotation Unit This submersible could carry two MSCs and as an intermediate carrier take them inshore. The canoes were carried on the flat midships length of this steel boat, which had a slightly raised forecastle and motorboat-flared bow. Aft was a cockpit in which the canoeists stood or sat until they required to launch their craft; at the stern was a watertight engine compartment, the craft being steered by a tiller. On approaching the launching point, the canoeists prepared to flood the MFU's buoyancy tanks below the midships canoe deck, securing both the engine and forecastle compartments and setting a time mechanism. The MFU then sank, floating off the two canoes with their crews; it would automatically surface at the pre-set time, which could be between three hours and seven days of submerging. The craft's equipment automatically 'blowing' the buoyancy tanks, the canoeists could RV with their MFU on the surface, open up the forecastle compartment for rations, changes of clothing etc., and then return on the surface to their parent ship or base. The MFU was approximately 10 m long with a 2-m beam (narrow for two canoes) with a range of 100 km, but varying according to weather conditions. On occasions the MFU would tow canoes. (No record has been traced of MFUs being used operationally.)

CLOTHING AND ACCESSORIES

Gloves With roughened surface to increase diver's grip, the rubber glove – sizes 8, 9 and 10 – had considerable fullness over the back of the hand and the palm to fit over a Radiant Heat Sachet, artificial silk under gloves and special woollen mittens. The gloves had cuffs which sealed around the wrist to make them waterproof.

Rope soles These prevented feet slipping on wet decks and were mounted on a piece of fabric which could be fixed by a rubber (?) solution to the soles of swim suits or waders. Note: the manual of stores reads, 'Quote two sizes larger than normal foot measurement when ordering.'

Net overboot It was made of rotproof cord in 'a 1-inch squared mesh with draw string', which was tied at the heel and then back towards the toe to be woven through the mesh at the instep to secure the net in order to prevent the boot slipping on moss-covered rocks, etc.

Canoe paddler's suit This had leather patches at the knees, providing protection against rain, spray and cold winds, but it was not waterproof. Its inflatable stole and kapok belt kept the wearer afloat although this was 'not intended as a swim suit'. Weight complete 3.6 kg (not including contents of four large pockets).

Surface swimmer's waterproofed suit Made of rubberized Grenfell fabric, black stretch rubber neck with folds sealed firmly by small metal clips, the suit fabric was closed by a 'fly' (zip) from neck to groin and closed by means of buttons. A urination valve was fitted in the crutch. Buoyancy provided by kapok lining and mouth-inflated rubber stole. The suits were made to measure and weighed about 6.3 kg.

Shallow water diver's suit This forerunner of the modern 'dry' suit was made of rubberized fabric and was tight fitting at the cuffs, hood and ankles. The swimmer adjusted his buoyancy to float high or low in the water by releasing trapped air momentarily through raising the edge of the hood at the cheek.

Shallow water COPP diving suit The rubberized fabric of this suit had waterproof tight-fitting cuffs, ankles and hood. Entered through a vertical slit over a loose-fitting rubber apron made watertight by clamps before being stowed under a zip. The swimmer adjusted his buoyancy to float lower in the water by momentarily lifting the face mesh at either cheek to release trapped air. His life jacket was inflated by mouth, its tube passing through a waterproofed point in the left chest of the suit.

Surface swimmer's tropical suit This comprised light-weight jacket and trousers intended to protect the swimmer against abrasions from rocks or fish stings. Leather patches gave added protection at elbows and knees. The jacket had an inflatable stole and kapok buoyancy. The weight of the suit was 2.3 kg.

Thigh waders Made of the same material apparently as the tropical suit, the lacing down the lower portion of the shin gave tight effect and formed a boot. Straps fixed to the heels buckled over each instep to prevent suction (in mud, for example) pulling off the waders.

Swim shoes A pair of these was worn by swimmer-canoeists to prevent their swim fins chafing and to protect the feet when ashore. The integrated plimsoll-type sole on a calf-length sock ensured that the shoe stayed in place.

Abseiling strap This was intended to protect the groin of a man sliding down a rope. The light-weight curved metal plates of the strap were riveted on to strong webbing, which was then fixed to the man's body by leather fittings.

Beach gradient reel and stake This metal fishing reel with a 13-cm drum carried 135 m of fishing line with a breaking strain of 54.5 kg. The device was gradated by split lead pellets for 'reading' the line in the dark. The reel had a strong manually operated brake. The landboard end of the line was held by a ring in a 27-cm brass stake. The reel could be fitted to a 44-cm rod with a ring at its top through which the line passed to a fishrod type of fitting for reel on the butt.

Swim fins Naval issue Mark II, described in one Combined Operations manual as 'shaped like a frog's foot . . . increases power and endurance of the swimmer by 100 per cent'.

Sleeping bag covers Two types of waterproofed covers were available to fit over a 1.4-kg or a 1.8-kg sleeping bag. Each cover weighed over 1.4 kg.

Parachute type knife This general purpose and killing knife was similar to the type issued to parachute troops. It had a 15-cm handle retaining a 10-cm heavy blade which was released by a trigger operated by pushing forward with the thumb. The blade remained open until the trigger was reset with the thumb. Opposite the trigger side of the handle was a strong pick.

Rubber cosh This was a solid rubber shaft with flexible steel cable core, to which a 5-cm solid rubber ball was attached. Only 25 cm long, the cosh could fit easily into a swimmer's pocket. Its similarity to the passenger straps found on London Underground trains is obvious and a quantity of such straps, although longer than the special item, were issued to commandos for use as coshes.

Fluorescent map case The specially treated case illuminated a map when an ultra-violet torch was used. Reports suggest it was not effective.

Safety floats These white blocks of balsa wood with orange buoyancy line marked with bands of luminous paint were attached to divers under training to enable their 'attendants to follow the swimmer's movements under water'.

Various Waterproof covers were specially made for matches, wristwatches, compasses, pocket watches and there were several sizes of general purpose waterproof bags. Brandy flasks made to fit a swimmer's suit pocket had a 124-g capacity. The standard army issue 155-g flask was known as 'Flask, Royal Marine Office', the RMO being the staff now designated the Department of the Commandant General, RM. The earth auger for taking soil samples weighed 311 g, was 57 cm long with the gauge notched at 8-cm intervals. Each sample core taken with this auger was placed in a sample bag or waterproofed 'battery' cases before being stowed in one of the twelve pouches on a bandolier designed to take the battery cases.

Type 6 mine detector The amplifier of this standard design of metal detector had been made ultra sensitive, the shoe and earphones waterproofed. The pole to which the shoe was attached divided into three or four 30-cm sections. The Type 6 could therefore be used when the operator was 'in the prone position', lying on the ground to sweep for mines using only two sections of the pole.

Bongle The type used on 6 June 1944 had a mechanical hammer manually cranked by a handle above the casing and a metal rod of predetermined length to give sound waves of recognized pitch on Asdic at ranges up to 19 km. A simpler version used after the Second World War was a 1.3-cm tube 10 cm long sealed at both ends with a ball-bearing inside to emit sound underwater for a swimmer's position to be picked up on Asdic.

Unofficial badge This is generally portrayed in the 1980s as a frog surmounted by a pair of uniform parachute wings (blue wings and silver 'chute) with crossed paddles behind the animal, their blades extended either side of a scroll (paddles, frog's chest and scroll in pale gold) with 'SBS' in dark green on the scroll to match the deep green of the frog. The frog has broad gold lips. The first such badge was designed in 1946 for a Christmas card, by Captain S. Hurst, RM, with a smaller frog and incorporating a symbolic silver 'explosion' to represent PE exploding below the frog in place of the present-day scroll; this frog also had swim fins, but varieties of the badge were used, for example in the 1950s, as a blazer badge.

Index

THE LIFE AND DEATH OF ST KILDA

Tom Steel

On 29 August 1930, the remaining 36 inhabitants of this bleak bu
spectacular island group off the western coast of Scotland too
ship for the mainland. Until the evacuation St Kilda was the mos
remote inhabited part of the United Kingdom, and indeed one c
the most remote points of the British Empire; its inhabitants ha
more in common with the people of Tristan da Cunha than the
ever had with their fellow Scots in Glasgow or Edinburgh. Th
St Kildans had preserved a unique and unchanging way of life fo
centuries; untroubled by the fluctuations of events on th
mainland, their tightly knit community had become a virtua
republic in its own right. But increasing contact with – and late
reliance on – the mainland in the nineteenth and twentiet
centuries gradually eroded their independence until evacuatio
became inevitable.

What their lives had been like for century after century, wh
they left, and what happened to them afterwards is the subject c
Tom Steel's fascinating book. It is the story of a way of life unlik
any other, told here in words and pictures, and of how the impac
of civilization finally led to its death.

'. . . first-rate recreation of a vanished way of life'
The Scotsman

'. . . compulsive reading'
The Guardian

WILD WALES

ITS PEOPLE, LANGUAGE AND SCENERY

George Borrow

Wild Wales is a classic travel book, one that ranks with the work of Defoe or Cobbett. George Borrow immortalized the 'land of old renown and wonder, the land of Arthur and Merlin', the wild mountains, the green valleys, the tiny villages, the kindly, hospitable but mysterious people. Compiled by a great artist who understood and respected his subject, it describes landscapes and industrial works, mansions and cottages. Welsh heroes and poets have their high places, and even the people to be met with on the highway are rendered with astonishing vigour, for Borrow knew how to elevate a commonplace conversation and how to give it pathos and a new significance.

All Borrow's art, his insight, keenness of observation and feeling for human destiny, were used to give his readers an affectionate interpretation of the Welsh and their history. His own character and interests gave shape, as well as humour and directness, to a wholly delightful book. More than a hundred years after its first publication, *Wild Wales* remains the best book about Wales ever written.

Fontana Paperbacks: Non-fiction

Fontana is a leading paperback publisher of non-fiction, both popular and academic. Below are some recent titles.

- ☐ WHAT DO WOMEN WANT? Luise Eichenbaum and Susie Orbach £1.75
- ☐ AVALONIAN QUEST Geoffrey Ashe £2.50
- ☐ WAR AND SOCIETY IN EUROPE, 1870–1970 Brian Bond £3.50
- ☐ MARRIAGE Maureen Green £2.75
- ☐ AMERICA AND THE AMERICANS Edmund Fawcett and Tony Thomas £2.95
- ☐ FRANCE, 1815–1914: THE BOURGEOIS CENTURY Roger Magraw £4.95
- ☐ RULES OF THE GAME Nicholas Mosley £2.50
- ☐ THIS IS THE SAS Tony Geraghty £4.95
- ☐ THE IMPENDING GLEAM Glen Baxter £2.95
- ☐ A BOOK OF AIR JOURNEYS Ludovic Kennedy (ed.) £3.95
- ☐ TRUE LOVE Posy Simmonds £2.95
- ☐ THE SUPPER BOOK Elizabeth Kent £2.95
- ☐ THE FONTANA BIOGRAPHICAL COMPANION TO MODERN THOUGHT Alan Bullock and R. B. Woodings (eds.) £6.95
- ☐ LIVING WITH LOSS Liz McNeill Taylor £1.75
- ☐ RASPUTIN Alex de Jonge £2.95
- ☐ THE PRIVATE EYE STORY Patrick Marnham £4.95
- ☐ BARTHES: SELECTED WRITINGS Susan Sontag (ed.) £4.95
- ☐ A POCKET POPPER David Miller (ed.) £4.95
- ☐ THE WRITINGS OF GANDHI Ronald Duncan (ed.) £2.50

You can buy Fontana paperbacks at your local bookshop or newsagent. Or you can order them from Fontana Paperbacks, Cash Sales Department, Box 29, Douglas, Isle of Man. Please send a cheque, postal or money order (not currency) worth the purchase price plus 15p per book for postage (maximum postage required is £3).

NAME (Block letters) _____

ADDRESS _____

_____